Basic

electronics

for tomorrow's world

Len Jones

KT-557-845

CAMBRIDGE UNIVERSITY PRESS

Published by the Press Syndicate of the University of Cambridge
The Pitt Building, Trumpington Street, Cambridge CB2 1RP
40 West 20th Street, New York, NY 10011-4211, USA
10 Stamford Road, Oakleigh, Melbourne 3166, Australia

© Cambridge University Press 1993

First published 1993

Printed in Great Britain by Ebenezer Baylis & Son Ltd, The Trinity
Press, Worcester and London

A catalogue record for this book is available from the British Library

ISBN 0 521 40917 9 paperback

Cover photograph by Graham Portlock

Contents

Preface   This book is for all students and staff who are interested in electronics. It is designed to cover the age range from 14 upwards and to cover courses such as GCSE, AS Level, BTEC (First), BTEC (Nat), CPVE and City and Guilds (726). It is designed for use predominantly as an electronics text but it could also be used in the design and technology and information technology areas of the curriculum.

The material can be used for students of mixed ability. All exercises and projects are designed so that students can work through them at their own pace, with little need for extensive blackboard work from the teacher.

The book can be used for reference, as a source of written and practical exercises and as a source of project work. The whole emphasis is on practical activities and teachers should find this an excellent support to their teaching.

Practical work can be carried out using the prototype board. However, all project work is designed for construction either on copper stripboard or on printed circuit board. Information on the use of prototype board, stripboard and printed circuit board is included in the text.

Chapter 6 offers extensive exercises on some of the chief components found in electronics and is designed to be used independently of the rest of the text if so desired by the users. Chapter 9 covers project work and students who have a reasonable experience of electronics and who are eager to start circuit construction may go directly to this chapter.

I would like to thank my wife for all her help, advice and support and the rest of my family for their understanding and encouragement during the writing of this book.

1 Safety and mains electricity

1.1 Electric shock

Care must be taken when working with electricity, in order to reduce the risk of electric shock. An electric shock is when an electric current passes through the body; what happens to the body depends on the size of the current. One milliamp is the largest safe current. Two to five milliamps feels very unpleasant to most people. A current of ten milliamps causes muscular spasms which make it difficult to move. One hundred milliamps passing through the heart will kill within a second. Currents larger than this will kill instantly. The size of the current depends on the voltage and also the resistance of the body. The resistance decreases if the body is wet.

How to avoid electric shock

The following procedure should be adopted when working with electricity to minimise the risk of an electric shock.
1 Always use low voltages (less than 50 V).
2 Use currents less than five milliamps.
3 Hands should always be dry.
4 Work area should be kept dry and clean.
5 Both hands should never be touching the equipment at the same time.

Treating electric shock

1 Switch off the supply. If this is not possible then pull the victim away using an insulator such as a piece of dry wood, a piece of rope or clothing. Do not use your hands.
2 Send for help. Preferably this should be someone qualified in First Aid.
3 Check the heart and breathing. If there is no sign of breathing or heartbeat then apply artificial respiration and if you are properly trained apply chest compression if this is considered necessary.
4 Burns should be treated immediately with cold water and then covered with a clean, dry cotton cloth until help arrives.
5 The person may be in a state of shock and therefore it is important that the person remain either sitting or lying down and be kept warm. An unconscious person should be placed on their side and not be given food or drink as there is a risk of choking.
6 Fill in an accident report form. If you are not in a position to do this then a report should be given to someone who is in a position to fill in the form.

1.2 Electrical safety precautions

1 Mains plugs must be correctly fitted and the cable securely held by the cord grip.

2 Plugs must have the correct fuse fitted and circuits going to the consumer unit must be protected by fuses of the right value.

3 Fuses, single-pole switches and all types of circuit breakers must be fitted to the 'live' wire of mains equipment.

4 Holes through which flexes enter an appliance must have a rubber grommet (rubber washer) to protect the outer insulation of the flex from unnecessary wear. In addition the flex should be held by the strain relief cable clamp fitted inside the appliance.

5 There is a legal requirement for all electricity supplies to be earthed. This is done at the electricity substations and IEE (Institute of Electrical Engineers) members also ensure that this is done at the consumer unit in the home.

6 Special care should be taken when working with capacitors as these can store a large charge for a long time after the supply has been disconnected. Capacitors should be discharged by shorting the terminals with an insulated conductor.

1.3 General safety precautions

Hand tools

All tools must be used in a safe manner, in particular sharp tools such as knives or screwdrivers. These should be held in such a way as to minimise the chances of cuts to the user if they slip from the work. The snipping of wires with side-cutters can lead to bits of wire entering the eye and therefore goggles should be worn for such work.

Power tools

These tools must be electrically safe and should be inspected regularly for cable wear and loose connections. They should never be used without a guard or some form of protection fitted and adjustments to these tools should only be made once they have been disconnected from the supply.

Soldering irons

Soldering irons should always be kept covered to prevent accidents leading to burning of the skin or of the flex of the soldering iron. The work being soldered or desoldered should be securely gripped and the work should take place on a heat-proof mat. Excess solder should be wiped off using a wet cloth or sponge and should not be flicked off. Care should also be taken to avoid breathing in the fumes of the flux.

Protective clothing

Whether or not this is worn depends on the regulations and on the work taking place in the workshop. Long hair should be tied back and if hair preparation is used the hair should also be covered whenever working close to a naked flame.

General workshop discipline

All persons working in a workshop must behave in a mature, responsible way. No one should work alone in a workshop unless help can be summoned easily.

Questions

1 What electrical property of the body changes when it is wet and how does this affect electrical safety?
2 What is considered to be a fatal current and what factor(s) determine the amount of current flowing through the body?
3 Give a number of ways to minimise the risk of an electric shock.
4 Describe how you would deal with a person being electrocuted.
5 What safety precautions should be taken when soldering?

1.4 The mains supply

The mains supply presents the biggest hazard when servicing electronic equipment. In the UK this is a 240 V 50 Hz supply. Three connections are made at the domestic supply. These are labelled live (L), neutral (N) and earth (E). The live connection can pass a current to either of the other two. The normal return path is via the neutral. However, if there is a fault then the earth provides an emergency path for current flow. Connection to the supply is made with a 13 A three-pin plug.

The three-pin plug

This plug is designed so that it raises the shutters in the socket when correctly inserted. The terminals and their connections are shown in figure 1.4.1.

L is the **live** terminal, which provides the 240 V supply.
N is the **neutral** terminal, which carries the current back to the supply.
E is the **earth** terminal, which is connected to a plate buried in the earth.

The wires to the terminals are brown for live, blue for neutral and yellow and green for the earth.

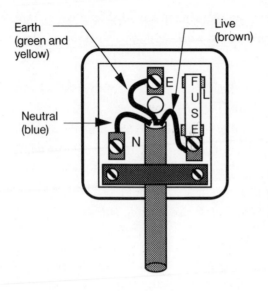

Figure 1.4.1 The three-pin plug

Always check that the plug is correctly wired, i.e.:

1 all connections are tight, with no loose strands of wire;

2 the individual wires are cut to such a length that if the cable is pulled out of the plug then the live will come free before the earth or the neutral;

3 the cable is firmly clamped without damage to the insulation; and

4 a fuse of the correct rating for the appliance is fitted. Two fuses are in common use, 3 A (red) and 13 A (brown).

Mains circuits Electricity enters the home by an underground cable containing a live and a neutral wire. The cable comes from a substation where the neutral is earthed by connection to a metal plate buried in the ground.

There are two types of circuits found in the home: the lighting circuit and the ring main circuit. Both of these circuits are connected in parallel to the mains supply (between the live and the neutral) and therefore they are supplied by the 240 V a.c. supply. These circuits are connected to the mains cable entering the home by a box called a consumer unit, which contains a double-pole isolation switch to disconnect the circuits from the mains supply and fuses to protect the circuits from excessive currents.

The ring main circuit has three wires running in three complete rings around the house. The sockets are connected to the live, neutral and the earth. The live wire is connected to the fuse bar of the consumer unit, the neutral to the neutral of the consumer unit and the earth is connected via the consumer unit to a metal pipe running into the ground. Sockets are rated as 13 A and are protected by a 13 A fuse. A house can have a number of ring mains.

1.5 Circuit protection

Each circuit going to the consumer unit is protected by a fuse, a miniature circuit breaker (MCB) or an earth leakage circuit breaker (ELCB). Lighting circuits are protected by a 5 A fuse, immersion heaters by a 15 A fuse, heaters by a 20 A fuse, the ring mains by a 30 A fuse and cookers by a 45 A fuse.

Miniature circuit breakers and earth leakage circuit breakers can be fitted in the consumer unit instead of fuses. These are more expensive but can be reset and automatically cut off the supply to an overloaded circuit in less than one hundredth of a second. Both MCBs and ELCBs are available in various current ratings.

Earth leakage circuit breakers can interfere with the earth connection and more modern arrangements make use of a residual current circuit breaker (RCCB).

Operation of ELCB and RCCB

These both operate on very small currents. In the ELCB shown in figure 1.5.1 the current passes to earth through the coil of an electromagnet when the casing of the equipment becomes live. The resulting magnetic field pulls on the rod, opening the switch and thereby breaking the circuit.

The RCCB as shown in figure 1.5.2 operates slightly differently in that the electromagnet has two windings, both of which connect the live and the neutral of the supply to the live and the neutral of the socket. In normal use the current flowing in these should be equal and opposite and the electromagnet is not magnetised. If there is a fault there is a leakage of current from the live to earth. This extra current (called the **residual current**) operates the electromagnet, causing it to pull on the rod and thereby opening the switch and breaking the circuit.

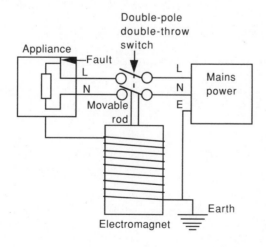

Figure 1.5.1 Earth leakage circuit breaker (ELCB)

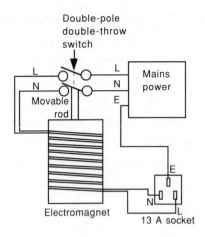

Figure 1.5.2 Residual current circuit breaker (RCCB)

Fuses
A fuse is a short piece of wire which is designed to melt when the current passing through it exceeds the rated value. Fuses are always placed in the live wire of a circuit. All 13 A plugs carry a fuse. This is of the cartridge type and is usually of one of two ratings:

3 A (colour-coded red) for appliances with power up to 720 W; and

13 A (colour-coded brown) for those between 720 W and 3 kW.

Ratings
All domestic electrical equipment is rated, specifying the maximum current, voltage or power required for safe operation of the appliance.

Working out fuse values
The simplest way of doing this is to look at the power rating of the appliance. If it is 720 W or below then a 3 A fuse should be used, or a 13 A fuse if the power rating is over 720 W.

If more specific fuse values are required then it is important to know the current flowing through the appliance. This can be calculated from the power and the voltage ratings in the following way.

$$\text{power} = \text{current} \times \text{voltage} \quad \text{or} \quad \text{current} = \frac{\text{power}}{\text{voltage}}$$

Therefore, a 2 kW kettle operating off the 240 V supply would require a current given by

$$\text{current} = \frac{2000}{240} = 8.3 \text{ A}$$

Therefore, the current is equal to 8.3 A and you should use either a 10 A fuse or a 13 A fuse.

1.6 Paying for electricity

The electricity company charges for the number of kilowatt-hours (kWh) you use. The **kilowatt-hour** is the amount of energy used by a one-kilowatt appliance in one hour and is called a **unit** of electricity, for which you are charged so many pence per unit.

The total number of units used is calculated by taking the power of the appliance in kilowatts (if it is in watts then divide by 1000), and multiplying by the number of hours that the appliance is on for (if this is in minutes then change it to hours by dividing by 60). To find the cost take the number of units and multiply by the cost per unit.

Example A two-kilowatt kettle which is used for two hours per week uses 4 (2×2) units of electricity. If the charge per unit is 5p, then the total cost for the week is 20p ($4 \times 5p$).

Questions
1 What is the frequency and voltage of the mains?
2 Describe the function of the live, neutral and earth connections to the mains supply.
3 Draw and label a properly wired three-pin 13 A plug.
4 Work out the fuse required for a two-kilowatt electric kettle.
5 What are the names and functions of the two main types of domestic circuits and how are these circuits connected to the mains supply in the house?
6 Write down the meaning of MCB, RCCB and ELCB. Explain the function of each of these devices and state the differences between them.
7 An electric iron is rated at 2 kW 240 V a.c. Explain the meaning of these terms.
8 How much would it cost to operate a 100 W electric light continuously for one week assuming that the cost of one unit is 10p?

2 Terms and concepts

2.1 Charge, current and voltage

The electric charge   Tiny pieces of matter can sometimes attract or repel each other. Matter that behaves in this way is said to possess **electric charge**.

The fact that attraction and repulsion occur indicates that there are two types of charge. These are associated with the basic structure of matter and are called **positive** and **negative** to correspond to the positive nucleus of the atom and the negative electrons orbiting the nucleus.

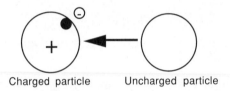

Charged particle   Uncharged particle

Figure 2.1.1   Charged matter

Most material contains equal numbers of each kind of charge and is said to be **neutral**. If there is an excess of one kind of charge over another then the material is said to be **charged**, either positively as shown in figure 2.1.2 or negatively as in figure 2.1.3.

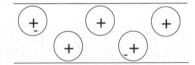

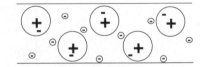

Figure 2.1.2
Positively charged material

Figure 2.1.3
Negatively charged material

Unlike charge attracts whilst like charge repels. The amount of charge is measured in **coulombs**, the coulomb being the **unit of charge**. The symbol used to represent the amount of charge is Q; for the coulomb the symbol is C.

The electric current An electric current is the movement of all the charges in a conductor in the same direction. In metallic conductors there are many free electrons moving in a random direction. However, when a battery is connected, an electric field is set up which provides energy to free more electrons and produces an electric force to accelerate the free electrons so that they all move in the same direction. An electric current is defined as the amount of charge passing each point in a circuit each second or

current = amount of charge/time

The unit of current is the **ampere** represented by the letter A. The ampere is the flow of one coulomb past each point of a circuit each second. Smaller units are the **milliampere** (mA), one thousandth of an ampere, and the **microampere** (μA), one millionth of an ampere. The symbol for current is I and therefore

current (I) = amount of charge (Q) / time (t)

and likewise

amount of charge (Q) = current $(I) \times$ time (t)

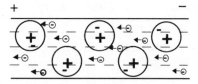

Figure 2.1.4   Current flow in conductor

Although it is now recognised that the flow of current is due to the flow of electrons or negative charge from negative to positive, by convention the direction of a current is taken as that in which a positive charge would move, i.e. from positive to negative.

The volt As an electric current is a movement of charge it follows that the charge must possess energy and therefore is able to do work. This energy comes from the battery connected across the conductor and is called the **electromotive force** (e.m.f.). The e.m.f. is the energy given to each coulomb of charge flowing through the battery. It is measured in **volts**, the volt being the unit of e.m.f., defined as one joule of energy carried by each coulomb of charge through the battery. As an example, a 1.5 V cell would give each coulomb 1.5 J of energy; a 6 V battery would give each coulomb 6 J of energy and a 12 V battery would give each coulomb 12 J of energy. This is easily seen by the amount of energy converted to heat and light in identical lamps.

Energy is required for a current to pass through the wires of a circuit and through the various components making up the circuit. This means that the current will be carrying less energy after passing through a component (e.g. a light bulb) than before entering. The voltage is a measure of the energy carried by each coulomb of charge and therefore the voltage on one side of the light bulb should be higher than on the other side. The voltage is referred to as a potential and this difference is called a potential difference. The **p.d.** or **potential difference** is the difference in voltage which exists across *all* components in a circuit when there is a current flowing and it is a measure of the energy needed to drive charge through the components. Potential difference is also measured in volts and the symbol for the voltage is *V*.

Questions

1 How do we know that electric charge exists?

2 What unit is charge measured in and what is the symbol used for it?

3 What is a current and what part does a battery play in the flow of a current?

4 If current = charge/time, write down the expression for the amount of charge, and work out the amount of charge produced when a current of 0.5 A flows for 20 seconds.

5 Express (a) 0.02 A in milliamps and in microamps and (b) 2000 µA in terms of milliamps and amps.

6 What is the direction of a conventional current?

7 Distinguish between e.m.f. and p.d.

8 The volt = joule/coulomb. What does this mean? How much energy is produced when a 9 V battery drives a current of 5 A for 2 minutes?

9 Where would you find a potential difference and why?

10 The p.d. across a component is 5 V. How much energy is needed to drive 0.5 A of current through this component in 20 seconds?

2.2 Conductors, insulators and semiconductors

Conductors

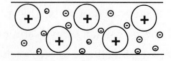

Figure 2.2.1   A conductor

Conductors are materials which allow a current to flow easily. They have many electrons which are free to move. Some conductors are better than others. The atoms of the common metals have a large number of electrons orbiting at various distances from the nucleus. The electrostatic force responsible for keeping the electrons in orbit decreases with distance from the nucleus. This together with the screening effect of the inner electrons means that the outer electrons are easily removed, which results in metals being good conductors. The best conductor is gold followed by silver and then copper. However, some non-metals such as carbon are also good conductors. Conductors may be classified as either **ohmic** or **non-ohmic**. Ohmic conductors obey Ohm's Law and are usually metals, whilst non-ohmic conductors do not obey Ohm's Law.

Insulators

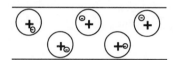

Figure 2.2.2   An insulator

Insulators do not allow a current to flow easily and should be considered as very poor conductors. The electrons within insulators are very tightly bonded to the atoms and a lot of energy is needed to free them. This energy is more than can be supplied by batteries or most voltage sources. Common electrical insulators are poly-vinyl chloride (PVC), polythene and rubber. Others include perspex, dry wood, air and ceramics.

Semiconductors

Semiconductors are materials whose electrical properties are between those of good conductors and good insulators. In many cases they behave like conductors when the temperature is high or when there is a lot of light, and as insulators when the temperature is low or when there are low light conditions. Although the charge carriers in semiconductors are bonded to the atoms they are not as tightly bonded as they are in insulators. As a result both heat and light can supply sufficient energy to free charges so that conduction can take place. Examples of semiconductors are germanium, silicon, cadmium sulphide, selenium and gallium arsenide.

Questions

1 What is a conductor?

2 Which are the two best metallic conductors?

3 Why is copper the most commonly used metallic conductor?

4 What makes an insulator different from a conductor?

5 Why are some conductors referred to as ohmic conductors?

6 Why are semiconductors called semiconductors?

7 What determines whether a semiconductor behaves as a conductor or as an insulator?

8 Give a number of examples of semiconductors.

2.3 Alternating current

So far the description of current has involved a flow of charge in one direction only. This is called **direct current** (d.c.) and is the current which is caused to flow when a battery is connected across any device. A d.c. waveform, as shown in figure 2.3.1, must have the same constant direction, even though its value from one second to the next might vary.

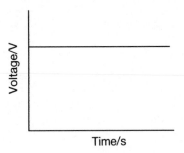

Figure 2.3.1   D.c. waveform

An **alternating current** (a.c.) is one that is continually changing its direction. The simplest a.c. waveform is that of a sine wave, and as can be seen in figure 2.3.2 both the magnitude of the current and its direction changes repeatedly, going from zero to a maximum positive value, falling back to zero again before going to a maximum negative value, and then returning to zero to complete the cycle.

Like d.c., the flow of a.c. is due to the presence of an e.m.f. or p.d. However, in this case it must be an alternating e.m.f. or p.d. For all ohmic conductors, i.e. conductors obeying Ohm's Law, an alternating e.m.f./p.d. causes the flow of an alternating current with waveform similar to that of the e.m.f./p.d., as shown in figure 2.3.3.

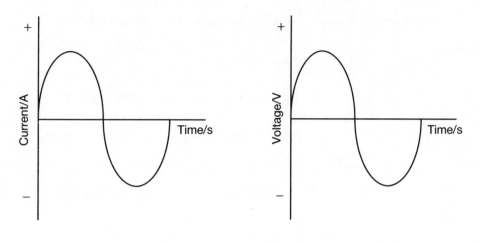

Figure 2.3.2   A.c. waveform   Figure 2.3.3   A.c. voltage waveform

Properties of waveforms   Properties of a waveform associated with all alternating waveforms are the frequency, period and amplitude or peak value.

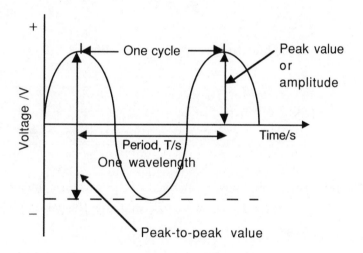

Figure 2.3.4   Properties of a waveform

Frequency   This is the number of cycles of the waveform occurring each second. Frequency is measured in **hertz** (Hz), one hertz being defined as one cycle per second. A thousand cycles per second is called a **kilohertz** (kHz) and a million cycles per second, a **megahertz** (MHz). One thousand megahertz is called a **gigahertz** (GHz).

Frequency ranges   Table 2.3.1 Recognised frequency ranges

Name	Range	Notes
Low frequency (l.f.)	Below 50 Hz	
Audio frequency (a.f.)	20 Hz – 16 kHz	Sounds detectable by the average human ear
Radio frequency	Above 20 kHz	This range is sub-divided into those listed below
Low frequency radio (l.f.)	100 – 300 kHz	
Medium frequency radio (m.f.)	300 kHz – 3 MHz	'long wave' broadcasting
High frequency radio (h.f.)	3 MHz – 30 MHz	long range communication
Very high frequency (VHF)	30 MHz – 300 MHz	FM broadcasting and short range communication
Ultra high frequency (UHF)	300 MHz – 1 GHz	used mainly for television broadcasting
Microwave	Above 1 GHz	'Line of sight' communication, radar and microwave ovens

Period   This is the time for one cycle of the waveform, measured in units of a second (s), millisecond (ms), or microsecond (μs). The period is simply the inverse of the frequency.

$$\text{period} = \frac{1}{\text{frequency}}$$

Amplitude   This is the **peak value** of the waveform. It measures from zero to the maximum positive or to the maximum negative value of the alternating voltage or current. The amplitude is therefore measured in the same unit as the magnitude of the waveform. The **peak-to-peak value** measures from the positive maximum to the negative maximum and is therefore twice the amplitude.

Root-mean-square (r.m.s.)   This is the average for an alternating voltage or current, defined as that steady d.c. which would produce the same heating effect.

For a sine wave (as shown in figure 2.3.2) the r.m.s. value is given by

$$\text{r.m.s. current} = \text{peak current}/\sqrt{2}$$
$$= \text{peak current} \times 0.707$$

Similarly,

$$\text{r.m.s. voltage} = \text{peak voltage}/\sqrt{2}$$
$$= \text{peak voltage} \times 0.707$$

For a square wave the r.m.s. average is simply the peak value

$$\text{r.m.s. current} = \text{peak current} \quad \text{and} \quad \text{r.m.s. voltage} = \text{peak voltage}$$

The mains supply is an alternating voltage of r.m.s. average of 240 V, a peak value of 339 V and a frequency of 50 Hz. Thus the peak value of the mains is approximately 100 V greater than the average value and as a result constitutes a serious safety hazard.

Mark-to-space ratio   Rectangular waveforms have an associated mark-to-space ratio. This is simply the mark-time divided by the space-time, both of which are illustrated in figure 2.3.5. **Mark-time** is the time over which the signal level has a high value. **Space-time** is the time over which the signal level has a low value. A square wave has a mark-to-space ratio of 1. This means that the mark-time is equal to the space-time.

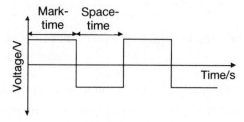

Figure 2.3.5   Square waveform

Questions

1 Explain the difference between a.c. and d.c. Give the name of one a.c. and one d.c. voltage source.

2 Name a number of properties associated with an a.c. waveform and define each of these properties using appropriate units where necessary.

3 Show clearly how to work out the peak value for the mains voltage and explain the implications of this from the point of view of safety.

4 The mains voltage has a frequency of 50 Hz. What is the period of this waveform?

5 What is r.m.s.? What is it used for and how does it differ for a rectangular waveform?

2.4 Resistance

All conductors offer some opposition to the flow of current, some more than others. For d.c. this opposition is called **resistance** and is thought to be due to (a) the vibration of the positive ions making up the bulk of the material and (b) the collision of the free charges with these relatively fixed atomic centres. Obviously, the greater the amplitude of vibration of these centres the greater the number of collisions and the greater the opposition to the flow of current. The amplitude of vibration depends on the amount of energy possessed by the atom and therefore heating the conductor will lead to an increase in its resistance.

Ohm's Law

Resistance is associated with Ohm's Law, which states that the current flowing through a conductor is directly proportional to the voltage applied across it providing all physical conditions (e.g. temperature) remain constant. This can be expressed as

$$\text{current} \propto \text{voltage} \quad \text{or} \quad \frac{\text{voltage}}{\text{current}} = \text{constant}$$

This constant is called the resistance of the conductor and is given the symbol R. The unit of resistance is the **ohm** (Ω); larger units being kΩ, the **kilohm** (= 1000 ohm) and the **megohm** MΩ (= 1 million ohm). In essence then

$$R = \frac{\text{voltage}}{\text{current}} \quad \text{or} \quad R = \frac{V}{I}$$

This equation can be written in two other forms, as $V = IR$ and as $I = V/R$.

The resistance of a conductor is found to be directly proportional to its length and to be inversely proportional to its cross-sectional area. This means that the resistance increases with increasing length, l, of the conductor and decreases with increasing cross-sectional area, A. This can be written as

resistance is proportional to length

and

resistance is proportional to 1/cross-sectional area

or

resistance = constant × (length/cross-sectional area)

The constant is represented by the symbol ρ (rho) and is called the **resistivity**. Therefore

$$R = \rho \frac{l}{A}$$

The resistivity is a measure of the resistance per unit length of the conductor. It is different for each material and as a result materials having the same length and cross-sectional area will have different resistance. Resistivity is measured in ohm metres (Ωm).

The resistance of semiconductors does not increase with temperature. Because an increase in temperature leads to the freeing of more electrons to be involved in conduction, an increase in temperature results in a decrease in the resistance.

Questions

1 State Ohm's Law and from it derive the expression for resistance.
2 What is responsible for the resistance of a conductor?
3 Explain why the resistance of a conductor increases with temperature, whilst that of a semiconductor decreases with temperature.
4 Express the following in ohms:
(a) 2.2 MΩ; (b) 10 kΩ; (c) 470 kΩ; (d) 4.7 MΩ.
5 Express the following in kilohm or megohm:
(a) 1 200 000 Ω; (b) 9600 Ω; (c) 24 000 Ω; (d) 1 000 000 Ω.
6 If a 5 V supply drives a current of 0.1 A through a device, what is the resistance of the device?
7 What is the p.d. across a resistance of 100 Ω when a current of 0.25 A is flowing through it?
8 Explain why conductors of different materials having the same length and cross-sectional area will have different resistances.

2.5 Circuit symbols and codes

Basic electrical units and common multipliers are shown in tables 2.5.1 and 2.5.2 respectively.

Table 2.5.1 Basic electrical units

Physical quantity	Symbol	Unit	Symbol
Time	t	second, minute, hour	s, minute, h
Frequency	f	hertz	Hz
Current	I	ampere	A
Voltage	V	volt	V
Resistance	R	ohm	Ω
Power	P	watt	W
Inductance	L	henry	H
Capacitance	C	farad, microfarad	F, μF

Table 2.5.2 Common multipliers of units

Multiplying factor	Prefix	Symbol
10^9	giga	G
10^6	mega	M
10^3	kilo	k
10^{-3}	milli	m
10^{-6}	micro	μ
10^{-9}	nano	n
10^{-12}	pico	p

Resistors

Resistors use two codes to represent their value and other information. One of these codes consists of a number of coloured bands, the other a series of letters. Colour code resistors can have four or five bands. The first three bands of a four-band resistor give the value of the resistor and the fourth band the tolerance. On a five-band resistor the first four bands give the value and the fifth the tolerance. Additional information on resistor colour code is contained in section 3.5.

Table 2.5.3 Resistor colour code

Colour	Number	Multiplier	Tolerance
Black	0	1	—
Brown	1	10	—
Red	2	10^2	± 2%
Orange	3	10^3	—
Yellow	4	10^4	—
Green	5	10^5	—
Blue	6	10^6	—
Violet	7	10^7	—
Grey	8	10^8	—
White	9	10^9	—
Silver	—	10^{-2}	± 10%
Gold	—	10^{-1}	± 5%

Table 2.5.4 BS 1852 resistor code

Letter	Multiplier	Tolerance
F	—	± 1%
G	10^9	± 2%
J	—	± 5%
K	10^3	± 10%
M	10^6	± 20%
R	1	—

Table 2.5.3 shows the available colours. Letter-coded resistors use the BS 1852 code, as shown in table 2.5.4. Using this code 0.33 Ω is written as R33, 1 Ω is written as 1R0, 3.3 Ω as 3R3, 10 Ω as 10R; 1 kΩ is written as 1K0, 10 kΩ as 10K and 3.3 kΩ as 3K3; 1 MΩ is written as 1M0, 10 MΩ as 10M and 3.3 MΩ as 3M3.

Using the BS 1852 code it is possible to write the code of resistor values in the following way: 0.47 Ω ±10% tolerance is written as R47K, 4.7 Ω ± 5% as 4R7J, 47 kΩ ± 20% as 47KM, 4.7 MΩ ± 2% as 4M7G.

Coding for integrated circuit

Integrated circuits (ICs) fall into two groups: TTL (transistor, transistor logic); and CMOS (complementary metal oxide semiconductor). The most common family of TTL devices is the 7400 series, while the 4000 series are the most common CMOS devices — 4 is the code used to identify these components.

Integrated circuits are identified by a string of letters and numbers which, in addition to coding for the group of the IC, also codes for the manufacture, the sub-family and the type of package of each device. The following are some of the codes used to identify the manufacturer:

DM	National Semiconductor
NS	National Semiconductor
SN	Texas Instruments
M	Motorola
TI	Texas Instruments
NE	New Era Electronics

The following letters are used to identify the sub-family of the ICs:

ALS	advanced low power Schottky
C	CMOS TTL devices
F	fast
H	high speed
HC	high speed CMOS
L	low power
LS	low power Schottky
S	Schottky

CMOS devices may have a suffix:

A	A-series IC
B	a buffered B-series IC
UB	an unbuffered B-series IC

Questions

1 Write down the units for (a) power, (b) current, (c) inductance, (d) capacitance and (e) frequency.

2 What is the name of the following prefixes? (a) 10^9, (b) 10^{-9}, (c) 10^6, (d) 10^{-12} and (e) 10^{-6}.

3 Write down the values of the resistances with the following colour codes: (a) red, red, red, red; (b) brown, black, orange, silver; (c) yellow, purple, yellow, gold; (d) green, blue, brown, silver; (e) brown, green, yellow, silver. (To answer this question you will first have to refer to section 3.5.)

4 Use the BS 1852 code to write out the values of the resistor codes given in question 3.

5 An integrated circuit has the following code on its surface: SN74HC04. What information does this code provides about the IC?

Circuit symbols

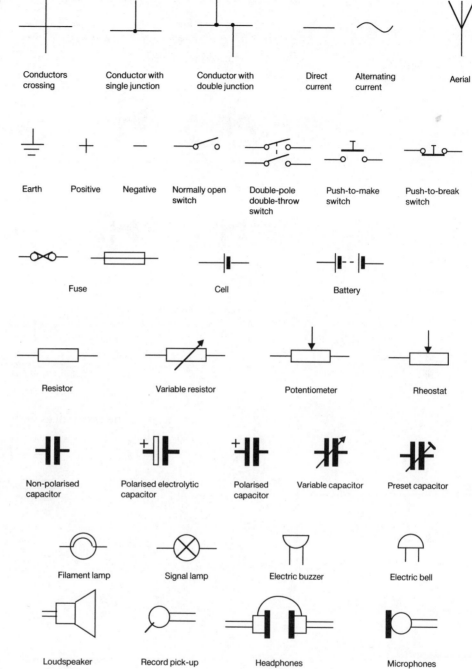

Conductors crossing	Conductor with single junction	Conductor with double junction	Direct current / Alternating current	Aerial

Earth	Positive	Negative	Normally open switch	Double-pole double-throw switch	Push-to-make switch	Push-to-break switch

Fuse	Cell	Battery

Resistor	Variable resistor	Potentiometer	Rheostat

Non-polarised capacitor	Polarised electrolytic capacitor	Polarised capacitor	Variable capacitor	Preset capacitor

Filament lamp	Signal lamp	Electric buzzer	Electric bell

Loudspeaker	Record pick-up	Headphones	Microphones

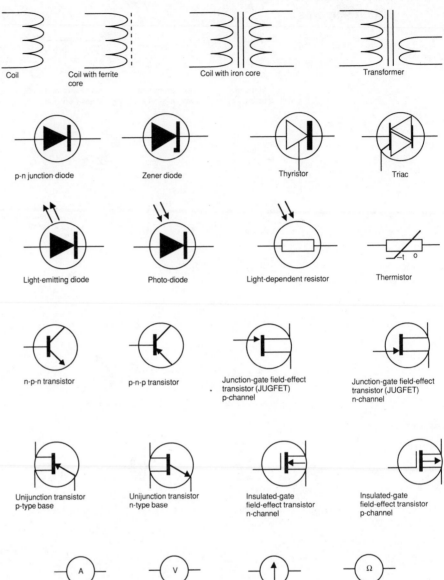

Coil

Coil with ferrite core

Coil with iron core

Transformer

p-n junction diode

Zener diode

Thyristor

Triac

Light-emitting diode

Photo-diode

Light-dependent resistor

Thermistor

n-p-n transistor

p-n-p transistor

Junction-gate field-effect transistor (JUGFET) p-channel

Junction-gate field-effect transistor (JUGFET) n-channel

Unijunction transistor p-type base

Unijunction transistor n-type base

Insulated-gate field-effect transistor n-channel

Insulated-gate field-effect transistor p-channel

Ammeter

Voltmeter

Galvanometer

Ohmmeter

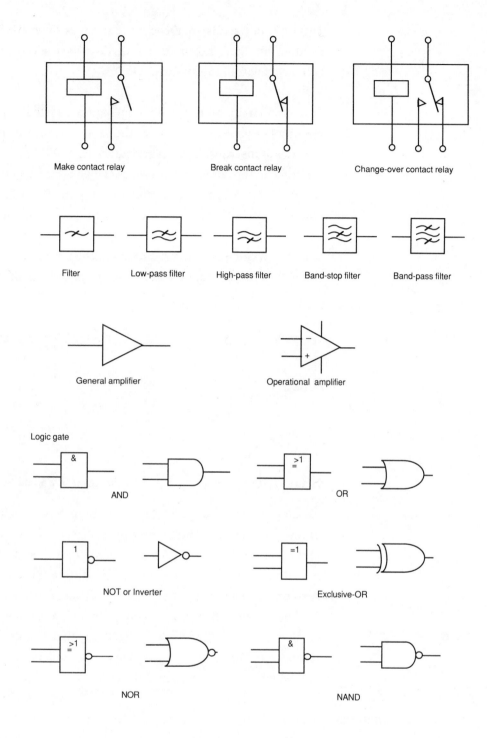

Make contact relay   Break contact relay   Change-over contact relay

Filter   Low-pass filter   High-pass filter   Band-stop filter   Band-pass filter

General amplifier   Operational amplifier

Logic gate

AND   OR

NOT or Inverter   Exclusive-OR

NOR   NAND

2.6 Circuit diagrams

Circuits A circuit consists of a number of components connected together in such a way as to carry out a specific task. A circuit must have a source of electrical power and therefore every circuit must have some form of power unit connected to it. Most electronic circuits make use of very low power and can be operated from small d.c. supplies.

Two types of circuits are recognised: series as shown in figure 2.6.1a and parallel as shown in figure 2.6.1b; the names describe the way in which components are connected within the circuits.

In a series circuit all the components are connected one after the other in the circuit. The power supply drives the same current through all the components in series and because of their resistance they will have a corresponding potential difference. The potential differences when added together will equal that of the supply. A break in a series circuit will stop the flow of current through all the components. If one component is shorting out (allowing more current to flow through the other components than is normal) then the circuit will continue to work; however, due to the reduction in the resistance, the current will have increased and this might lead to damage of the remaining components.

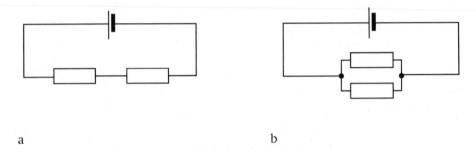

a   b

Figure 2.6.1(a) Simple series circuit; (b) simple parallel circuit

Parallel circuits consist of a number of branches, each branch being connected to the same voltage. The current being driven around the circuit will be flowing in different paths and as each path may have different components they may have different resistances and therefore different current values. The value of current flowing through the various branches must add up to the total current flowing through the whole circuit. If there is a component failure leading to a break in the circuit then it will affect only that branch containing the faulty component. Therefore it is possible to have independent control of the individual branches of a parallel circuit.

Circuit diagrams   In general, circuit diagrams are representations of how the various components making up a circuit are joined together. However, there are some diagrams which show the interrelationship of electronic sub-systems. **Systems** are electronic circuits which are able to carry out specific functions and **sub-systems** are the electronic units making up the whole system. Diagrams showing how systems are joined together are called **block diagrams**. Other types of circuit diagrams show the way components are laid out for connection onto particular types of circuit boards; these types of diagrams are called **layout diagrams**.

When designing an electronic system it is usual to start with a block diagram of the system giving full details of how all sub-units are interlinked. Figure 2.6.2 shows a block diagram for a burglar alarm system.

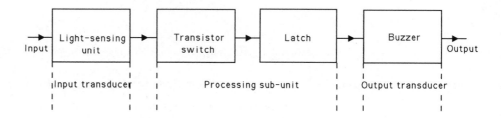

Figure 2.6.2   Block diagram of a burglar alarm

The details of the sub-units are given in a **circuit diagram** in which symbols are used to show the components and their relationship to each other. Various conventions are used to interpret the information contained in the circuits; for example wires are represented by straight lines and frequently sharp angles are used when linking two components with a piece of wire. Because of this many students find it difficult to relate these diagrams to the actual circuit they represent. Figure 2.6.3 is a picture of a circuit showing a battery, two light bulbs and a switch connected together using leads, while figure 2.6.4 shows the corresponding circuit diagram.

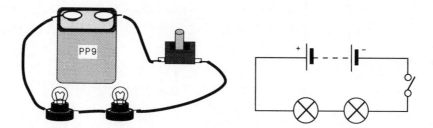

Figure 2.6.3   Simple series circuit

Figure 2.6.4 Circuit diagram of series circuit

After deciding on the method of construction a layout diagram should be produced. The diagram should show the actual connections of components to points on the circuit board. For instance, if a veroboard (or stripboard) construction was chosen then the diagram should show the tracks of the board with the components correctly located. This arrangement is shown in figure 2.6.5 for the simple circuit shown in figure 2.6.4.

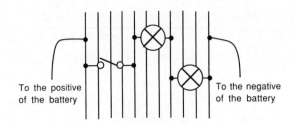

Figure 2.6.5 Layout diagram of series circuit

Questions

1 Use the words provided to fill in the missing words in the passage below: short-circuit, series, conductors, resistance, batteries, components, break, line, branches, parallel.

A circuit consists of a number of _____ connected together by _____ and powered by either a d.c. or an a.c. supply. Small d.c. voltages can be supplied by _____ . The two basic types of circuits are known as _____ and _____ . In a series circuit all the components are connected together in a _____ and have the same current flowing through each, whilst in a parallel circuit the components are arranged in different _____ with the current flowing through each branch being determined by the _____ of the branch. All the components in a series circuit are affected by a _____ , regardless of where it occurs. If the same fault occurs in one of the branches of a parallel circuit, then only the components in that branch will be affected. _____ faults will lead to more current flowing in the circuit and this could lead to damage of certain components.

2 The circuit shown in figure 2.6.6 is that of a simple light switch. Draw (a) a block diagram and (b) the stripboard layout diagram for this circuit.

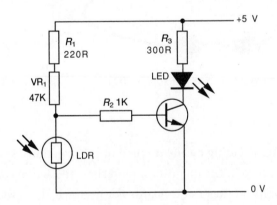

Figure 2.6.6 Simple light switch

3 Tools, materials and components

3.1 Basic tools used in electronics

The following is a list of basic tools used in electronics. Some are more essential than others for the construction of simple projects.

Cutters	Side cutters
	Wire strippers
Pliers	Plain pliers
	Pointed-nose pliers
	Combination pliers
Crimping tools	
Files	Small round file (6 mm)
	Hand file
Screwdrivers	Small instrument set
	Small and large Phillips
Clamps	G-clamps
	Toolmaker's clamp
Hacksaws	Junior hacksaw
Hand drill	
Twist drill bits	Set of drills covering a range of diameters
Spot face cutter	
Rulers	Plastic or steel type
Soldering irons	Small tip, low-wattage (24 W)
	Low-voltage soldering irons
Desoldering tools	Suction desoldering tools

3.2 Wires, cables and flexes

Wires

Wires are used to provide links between different sections of a circuit board or between the board and connectors or terminals on the container housing the board. Below are a few common types of wires.

Tinned copper

This is usually single-stranded with a dimension of 0.6 mm and is represented in catalogues by 1/0.6 mm – the 1 meaning single-stranded and the 0.6 its diameter in millimetres. Tinned copper is usually uninsulated and can be used to link tracks on copper track boards and, although not as common, on printed circuit boards.

Enamelled copper Again this is a single-stranded wire (1/0.6 mm) but coated with a layer of insulating enamel. This layer of enamel is commonly coppery in colour and therefore it is important to remember to scrape off the insulation from the ends of the wire making electrical connections. This wire can be used in all forms of circuit connections but is particularly useful in the winding of coils.

Insulated copper These are single-stranded and multiple-stranded and are coated with **poly-vinyl chloride (PVC)** or **polytetrafluoroethylene (PTFE)** insulations. The most commonly used insulated copper wires are the single-stranded 0.6 mm diameter type used for links on circuit boards and in wiring prototype boards and the multiple-stranded types with diameter of 0.2 mm consisting of 7 strands (7/0.2 mm) or 16 strands (16/0.2 mm). These multiple-stranded wires are used in the connection of 'free standing' components to circuit boards and in making connections where a lot of flexibility is required.

The physical dimensions of wires make them very different from cables and flexes, which on the whole are much thicker and are designed to carry much higher currents. Cable and flex are not interchangeable words. They are both different in construction and perform different functions.

Cables Many cables consist of one or more single-strand conductors, each individually insulated with PVC or rubber. These conductors are fairly thick and are somewhat inflexible.

In domestic electricity the cables are usually out of sight and make up the permanent wiring of the house. They connect the electricity supply from the consumer unit to the sockets and ceiling roses around the house. These types of cables are colour-coded: red for live, black for neutral and green for earth, although it is now common to find a bare uninsulated wire being used as the earth.

Domestic cables can be single-core, twin-core, twin-core and earth, or three-core and earth. In electronics, a cable can be considered as a number of conductors sharing the same outer insulation. A number of different cables are recognised which do not fully conform to the above definition of domestic cables. Amongst these are **screened**, **coaxial**, **telephone** and **ribbon** cables.

Screened cable These come in a number of different sizes and types. They are either single-core or multicore and are able to carry a large number of individual wires. All wires are screened by a wire braid contained within the outer insulation of the cable. They are useful where multiple connections are required to sensitive equipment such as computer interfacing devices.

Coaxial cables   These consist of a single, central, insulated wire which is either single-stranded or multiple-stranded. Outside the inner insulation there is a braided metal screen (which stops interference from unwanted signals) followed by the outer insulation. Coaxial cables are connected using BNC or TNC connectors and are used in radio, television and video applications, as well as for the connection of local area networks (LANs) of computer systems.

Telephone and ribbon cables   Telephone cables may consist of a number of pairs of insulated wires surrounded by an outer insulation, whilst a ribbon cable may consist of many strands of parallel conductors laminated between layers of PVC insulator to make a flat ribbon. Each strand is made from seven strands of 0.2 mm diameter (7/0.2 mm) tinned copper wire.

Ribbon cables are connected using **insulation displacement connectors (IDC)** and are used in situations where many parallel connections are required, such as parallel interfaces on computer systems.

Flexes   Flex is short for flexible, and as the name suggests it is a conductor which can be twisted many times without breaking. A flex consists of a number of insulated conductors each of which is made up of many strands of fine wire – the finer the wires the more flexible and therefore the stronger the flex. Mains flexes are either two-core or three-core. Each core of a two-core flex consists of 16 strands of 0.2 mm diameter wire (16/0.2 mm), whilst for a three-core flex each core consist of 24 strands of 0.2 mm wire (24/0.2 mm) or 40 strands of 0.2 mm wire (40/0.2 mm).

Flexes are used for connecting lamp holders to the ceiling roses within a house or other appliances to the mains sockets.

Flexes must have the international colour code used for PVC insulation covering. By law three-core flexes must have insulation coloured brown for the live wire, blue for the neutral wire and green and yellow for the earth.

Cables and flexes are rated according to the cross-sectional area of the individual conductors. For instance, a 1 sq mm cable is used for domestic lighting and a 2.5 sq mm cable is used for the ring mains.

3.3 Connectors

Modern electronic equipment usually has a range of different connectors, the specific type depending on the use of the equipment. For example, hi-fi equipment will have a number of connectors of which few will be similar to those found on computing equipment. Below are a number of common types of connectors with a brief description of their use.

4-mm banana plugs/ sockets   These are used widely for general-purpose connections. Sockets are found on a wide variety of equipment including many meters, signal generators and oscilloscopes. However, unlike the stackable 4-mm plugs (see below) it is not possible to stack these by using the back of the plug as a socket for another plug.

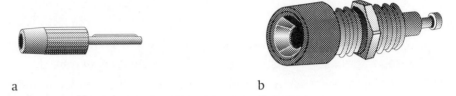

a   b

Figure 3.3.1(a) The 4-mm banana plug and (b) the 4-mm socket

BNC/TNC connectors   These are the connectors for coaxial cables. They are obtained as two types, the bayonet type or the screw type. The sockets are found on many items of equipment in which it is necessary to screen the input cables from electromagnetic interference, e.g. television, video and local area networking (LAN) on computer systems.

Clip-on test probe   This is a special test probe lead which allows connection of a test instrument to any uninsulated point in a circuit.

Crocodile clip   This is a very versatile connector which is designed to fit onto the 4-mm plugs allowing a connection to be made to any uninsulated point on a conductor. Crocodile clips are obtained in a number of different sizes and occasionally with insulation cover.

Dual-in-line (DIL) plugs/ sockets   These are used in applications where multiple, parallel connectors are needed.

DIN plugs/sockets   DIN plugs are obtained in two sizes, standard and mini. They range from three pins to eight pins and are used with multicore cables on equipment such as computers and hi-fi.

Figure 3.3.2 The DIN plug

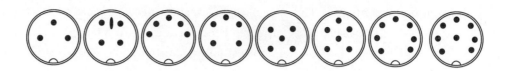

Figure 3.3.3 Different types of pin arrangements of DIN connectors

'D' type plugs/sockets These are obtained in standard form consisting of 9, 15, 25, 37 and 50 pins and are used with multicore screened cables for connecting computer equipment.

Insulation displacement connectors (IDC) Unlike the other connectors, IDC plugs do not require soldering. They are designed for ribbon cables and a vice (or a special vice-like tool) is needed to fit the plug onto the cable. They are obtained in standard form consisting of 10, 14, 16, 20, 26, 34, 40 and 50 ways. The design of the connectors allows for polarisation of the cables and the plugs to the sockets.

Jack plugs/sockets These consist of a single, fairly large pin having two or three distinct and insulated regions, as shown in figure 3.3.4. Therefore they are used with two-core or three-core cables, such as a signal line and earth or two signal lines and earth. A common application is on hi-fi equipment.

Figure 3.3.4 Jack plug

Mains plugs/sockets All mains connectors are designed for use with the a.c. mains supply. The most common mains connector is the 13 A three-pin plug. However, on appliances with a detachable mains lead there are a number of different sockets and plugs available. Of these the two-core lead used for cassette players and calculators is the most familiar. Other types are shown in figure 3.3.5

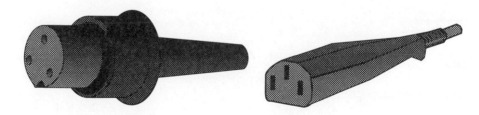

Figure 3.3.5 Mains connectors

Phono connectors These are used for speaker connections. They consist of a single centre pin, as shown in figure 3.3.6, which is used to carry the signal, and an outer connector, which is the ground.

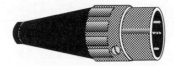

Figure 3.3.6 The speaker plug

Stackable 4-mm plug/ socket These are used in many of the same applications as suggested for the 4-mm banana plug above. However, because of the way they are designed it is possible to have multiple connections to the same point by making use of the socket at the back of the plug.

Figure 3.3.7 The 4-mm stackable plug

Tag strips Tag strips are circuit board mounted connectors which allow for multiple soldered connections using either multicore cables or many individual wires. Components can be connected directly to these connectors and therefore on a small scale they can be used for circuit construction.

Terminal blocks These are commonly obtained in blocks of twelve individually insulated connectors. Each connector has two screws, one for holding the incoming wire and the other for the outgoing as shown in figure 3.3.8. The insulation can be polythene, nylon or PVC. The whole block can be sub-divided into single or multiple units which make these blocks very versatile connectors for certain applications.

Figure 3.3.8 Terminal blocks

3.4   Circuit boards

Prototype boards

S-Dec An S-Dec is a plastic box having seventy holes arranged in two blocks on its surface, as shown in figure 3.4.1. The holes are numbered in groups of five in seven parallel rows and are connected together below by metal strips. The strips are used to join all the holes in a particular row together and therefore if a piece of bare, single-stranded wire is placed in hole number 3 it will also be connected to holes 1, 2, 4 and 5. There is no connection between rows or between the two separate blocks and therefore wire links are used to extend rows if more holes are required than are available. Components are mounted by connecting across rows, i.e. the terminal on one side of a component is placed vertically into a hole on one row and the terminal on the other side of the component is placed into a hole on another row; the rows need not be side by side. There is a control panel which may be positioned in slots provided on the side of the box and which provides three large holes for the positioning of components which are too large to be mounted directly. The S-Dec can accept wires up to 1 mm in diameter.

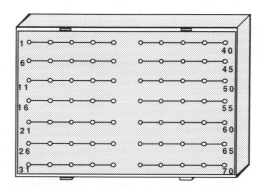

Figure 3.4.1 The S-Dec

Although the S-Dec is an excellent device for constructing prototypes of simple electronics circuits it has a number of disadvantages, the principle one being the spacing between holes in a row and between rows. Both the holes and the rows are spaced about 1 cm apart and as a result components having short terminal leads or too many terminals cannot be used without modification. In the case of a transistor the legs can be lengthened with tinned copper wire joined with plastic sleeves. For integrated circuits extensive modifications would be necessary if these are to be used successfully. Other disadvantages are the conceptual difficulty of many students in translating a circuit diagram to a set of holes and rows and then the problem of tracking down faults when they do occur. Misuse of the boards can result in damaged metal strips, which then lead to faulty circuits, or wire connectors can have tiny fractures, sometimes below the insulation, which can also lead to circuit failure.

Professional prototype board

This type of prototype board, shown in figure 3.4.2, contains 47 rows of five interconnected holes on each side of a central channel and either one or two of 40 interconnected holes grouped in blocks of fives running at the top and bottom of the board for use as the positive and negative supply rails. Like the S-Dec, these boards have control panels for mounting connectors and components which are too large to be directly linked to the board. Components are mounted

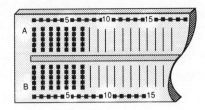

Figure 3.4.2 Prototype board

by pushing one lead vertically into a hole in one row and pushing the lead of the other terminal into the hole of another row. The holes and rows are close enough to allow all components to be connected directly; integrated circuits are connected so that each row of pins sits on either side of the central channel. Suitable connecting wire for this type of board is the single-stranded 0.6 mm diameter (1/0.6 mm) insulated tinned copper, with about 10 mm of insulation stripped off the end.

Professional prototype boards allow all types of circuits to be constructed on a temporary basis suitable for experimental work. However, there are drawbacks associated with this particular board since, unless properly planned, the closeness of the holes allows for a high density of component, which requires high levels of concentration and dexterity on the part of the students. In addition, because of the proximity of the components the possibility of them touching and shorting against each other is very likely.

The principal advantage of the prototype board is that circuits can be easily assembled, without the use of solder, and disassembled so that all the components can be reused.

Matrix board This is a resin sheet having holes drilled in either a 0.1 in or a 0.15 in matrix on the board. Press fit terminal pins are needed to mount the components and the pins are interlinked using insulated or bare tinned copper wires. The components must be soldered to the pins and although not essential the wires used for interlinks are also soldered. The 0.1 in matrix allows the mounting of ICs and overall quite complicated circuits can be built up on this board. The main disadvantage of this board is the amount of work needed to set up a circuit. It needs a clear understanding of the positioning of the pins, all the interconnections have to be made with the wire connectors and then all the components have to be soldered. In addition the components cannot easily be reused. The advantages are that it is cheaper than the copper stripboard described below, it is conceptually easy for students to translate a printed circuit diagram onto this board for construction, and it is easy to check for faults.

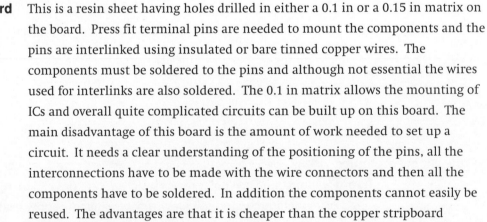

Copper stripboard In every way this is the same as the matrix board above except that it has copper tracks running along the length of one side. The tracks are used to link together rows of holes. Components are mounted by passing their terminals through the holes on the non-copper side of the board and then soldering them to the copper tracks underneath. They are mounted across rows as in the prototype board. No terminal pins are needed nor the extensive amount of wire interlinks as the tracks serve both these functions. ICs can be mounted using the 0.1 in matrix. However, it is important to break the tracks linking the two rows of legs. Copper stripboard provides one of the easiest ways of constructing permanent circuits. However, like the prototype boards, it is conceptually difficult for students to translate a circuit diagram onto it for construction. The quality of the soldering is also important when using this board, since poor soldering may result in cross-connections between the tracks and therefore increasing the possibility of shorting. It can also lead to dry solder joints resulting in a range of electrical problems. Finally, overheating the copper strips can lead to them breaking, which results in open-circuit faults.

Printed circuit boards These are commonly referred to as p.c.b.s and require a higher level of practical skill if they are to be used properly. A p.c.b. is designed for a particular circuit. The layout diagram is either drawn with an etch-resist pen or photographed onto a special type of light-sensitive board. This is either synthetic resin bonded paper (SRBP) or epoxy glass, both of which are clad on one or both sides with copper. Special etch-resist transfers are also available to transcribe the layout diagram onto the board. Once the diagram is in place the board is then etched with some form of etch solution. This is usually ferric chloride solution and it is used to remove all the copper not covered with etch-resist ink or transfer. The resulting copper tracks are then cleaned and holes drilled at appropriate places to allow the components to be inserted. Components are mounted on the side opposite to the tracks and the leads are soldered onto the tracks. The design of the p.c.b. should minimise the requirement for wire connectors and these are kept for connecting large components to the relevant points on the board and in bringing the power supply to the positive and negative rails on the p.c.b. Wire used for this purpose is perhaps the multi-stranded (7/0.2 mm) type. Printed circuit boards are the most advanced way of constructing circuits. Its main advantage is that it contains only those tracks which are relevant to the circuit. This makes it easy to check the circuit for faults. In addition the components can be well spaced, which minimises the risk of short-circuiting as a result of poor soldering and other circuit problems which arise as a consequence of high-density packing of components. A big disadvantage of this type of circuit is that the accuracy depends on firstly the accuracy of the original diagram and then the accuracy in transcribing this diagram to the board. Any errors in this process will lead to an incorrect p.c.b. and as this cannot be corrected the faulty board will have to be thrown away and a new one prepared. The method is also time-consuming, and involves a high level of both concentration and design skill on the part of the student. On the whole students will need a lot of help and support before they become fully competent in this method.

3.5 Passive components

These are components which cannot increase the strength of a signal, i.e. they cannot by themselves produce a gain in signal strength. Passive components are not capable of producing waveforms by themselves nor when connected with other passive components. Examples of passive components are resistors, capacitors, diodes, transformers and inductors.

Resistors

The symbol for a fixed-value resistor is shown in figure 3.5.1.

Figure 3.5.1   Resistor symbol

Resistors are used to reduce or limit the amount of current flowing in a circuit. They oppose the flow of current. This opposition is called resistance and it is measured in ohms (Ω). Larger units of resistance are the kilohm (kΩ) and the megohm (MΩ), where 1 kΩ = 1000 Ω and 1 MΩ = 1000 kΩ = 1 000 000 Ω.

A small resistor offers little resistance to the flow of current, whilst a larger resistor offers a larger resistance and thereby causes a smaller current to flow. All conductors have resistance which is given by Ohm's Law which states

$$\text{resistance of a conductor in ohms} = \frac{\text{voltage across the resistor in volts}}{\text{current through the resistor in amps}}$$

Using letters this can be written as

$$R = \frac{V}{I} \quad \text{or} \quad V = I \times R$$

where V = p.d., I = current and R = resistance.

Resistor colour code

The value of the resistance is given on the resistor in the form of a code consisting of four or five coloured bands, three or four giving the size of the resistance and the fourth or fifth the tolerance. The tolerance is the percentage by which the resistance may be higher or lower than the coded value. For example, 1 kΩ resistor with a 10% tolerance may have a value as high as 1100 Ω or as low as 900 Ω, and as shown in figure 3.5.2 would have a silver band to represent the tolerance level.

The colour code used for the value of the resistance is as shown in figure 3.5.2 interpreting the coloured bands as follows:

Black = 0	Brown = 1	Red = 2	Orange = 3	Yellow = 4
Green = 5	Blue = 6	Violet = 7	Grey = 8	White = 9

The number of zeros is the same as the multiplier in the sense that 10^1 equals one zero, 10^2 equals two zeros and 10^3 equals three zeros, etc. This should be added to the two digits given by the previous two bands to give the full value of the resistor.

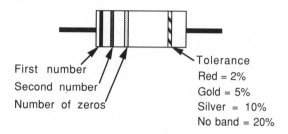

First number
Second number
Number of zeros
Tolerance
Red = 2%
Gold = 5%
Silver = 10%
No band = 20%

Figure 3.5.2   Resistor colour code

The BS 1852 code This system is used to mark the value of resistors on circuit diagrams. BS stands for British Standard. Using this code the letter R is used for ohms, therefore 10R = 10 Ω; 8R2 = 8.2 Ω; 1R0 = 1.0 Ω. K is used for kilohms and 10K = 10 kΩ; 8K2 = 8.2 kΩ, 680K = 680 kΩ. M is used for megohm, therefore 10M = 10 MΩ; 1M2 = 1.2 MΩ.

The tolerance codes are: F = ± 1%; G = ± 2%; J = ± 5%; K= ± 10%; M = ± 20%.

Preferred resistor values Only certain values of resistors are manufactured, called preferred values. These are contained in two series called the **E12** and **E24** series, where the E12 has a 10% tolerance and the E24 has 5%.

In the E12 series 12 resistor values make up the range from 10 to 100, 100 to 1000, 1000 to 10 000 etc.

10	12	15	18	22	27	33	39	47	56	68	82
100	120	150	180	220	270	330	390	470	560	680	820
1K	1K2	1K5	1K8	2K2	2K7	3K3	3K9	4K7	5K6	6K8	8K2

The E24 series, in which there are 24 resistor values from 10 to 100, comprises all the E12 series plus the following:

11	13	16	20	24	30	36	43	51	62	75	91
110	130	60	200	240	300	360	430	510	620	750	910
1K1	1K3	1K6	2K	2K4	3K	3K6	4K3	5K1	6K2	7K5	9K1

Power of a resistor All resistors have a power rating which is the rate at which heat energy can be given out without the resistor overheating. The power rating is given in watts, where one watt is one joule of energy per second. In general the larger the physical size of the resistor the larger the power rating and in electronics the 0.125 W, 0.25 W and the 0.5 W are the most commonly used types.

The energy released every second in a resistor is given by

$$W = I^2 \times R \quad \text{or} \quad W = V^2/R$$

where W is the energy per second in watts, I is the current through the resistor in amperes, V is the voltage across the resistor in volts and R is the resistance in ohms.

In addition, power is given by the formula

$$\text{power in watts} = \frac{\text{energy in joules}}{\text{time in seconds}}$$

Types of fixed-value resistors There are a number of different types of resistors, each having different maximum values, different tolerances, power ratings and stabilities. (**Stability** is the ability to maintain the same value over time and over a range of temperatures.) The various different types are **carbon composite, carbon/metal film** and **wire-wound**; see figure 3.5.3.

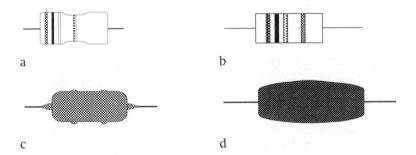

a   b

c   d

Figure 3.5.3 (a) Carbon composite, (b) carbon/metal film, (c) wire-wound ceramic, (d) wire-wound vitreous.

Carbon composite resistors consist of a ceramic tube containing a mixture of carbon and clay. They have a tolerance of ± 10%, a power rating of 0.125 W to 1.0 W, a resistance range from 10 Ω to 2 MΩ and are usually of poor stability. They are used for general-purpose work.

Carbon/metal film resistors are made from a thin carbon or metal film on the outside of a ceramic rod. The carbon film type have a tolerance of ± 5%, a power rating of 0.25 W to 1.0 W, and a resistance range from 10 Ω to 1 MΩ (10 MΩ can be obtained with 10% tolerance). The stability is usually better than carbon composite and they are used for general-purpose work. Metal film resistors have a tolerance of ± 2%, a power rating of 0.125 W to 0.5 W, a resistance range from 10 Ω to 1 MΩ and have very high stability. They are usually used for very accurate work.

Wire-wound resistors are manufactured by winding resistance wire onto an insulating tube and coating with silicone, epoxy resin or some form of vitreous medium. They have a tolerance of ± 5%, a power rating of 2.5 W, and a resistance range from 10 Ω to 10 kΩ (for silicone the maximum resistance range is 270 Ω). These have very high stability and are used for low-value, accurate work.

Variable resistors   These are resistors whose resistance changes with the position of a movable contact. They are commonly made from a circular track of resistance material (such as carbon) and a slider which moves over the track. They are referred to as **rotary variable resistors** or **potentiometers**. The resistance is taken from one end of the track to the slider and the maximum value is indicated on the case, either in letters or by using the colour code. Some variable resistors will have additional markings such as 'LIN' or 'LOG'. LIN means linear, which means that the resistance is proportional to the slider position along the track. LOG means logarithmic; in this case the log of the resistance is proportional to the position of the slide contact.

Rotary potentiometers are obtained with power ratings ranging from 0.25 W to 5 W and are available either singly or in tandem (ganged). The two basic types of rotary potentiometer are the **preset**, which has a screwdriver slot for adjustment, and the **standard**, which has a fairly long shaft and is commonly used in volume control (see figure 3.5.4).

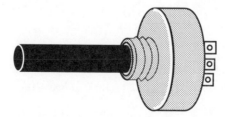

Figure 3.5.4   Rotary variable resistor or potentiometer

Slide potentiometers have a straight resistance track with a slide control. These are obtained in both the log and the linear forms and are used as slide controls on equipment.

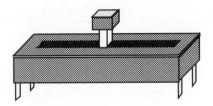

Figure 3.5.5 Slide potentiometer

Questions

1 (a) What is a resistor? (b) Draw the symbol for (i) a fixed resistor and (ii) a variable resistor.

2 What is the relationship between the Ω, kΩ and MΩ?

3 State Ohm's Law (a) in your own words and (b) in equation form using the correct symbols.

4 Work out the values of these resistors:

(a) brown, green, brown, silver; (b) yellow, purple, orange, gold;

(c) white, brown, brown, silver; (d) red, red, red, red, red.

5 Using the tolerance band on the resistors shown in question 4 calculate the maximum and the minimum values of each.

6 Write out the resistor values of question 4 using the BS 1852 code.

7 Write out in full the values of the following:

(a) 390RM; (b) 9K2J; (c) 68KG; (d) 2K2F.

8 Which of the following resistor values occur in the E24 series: 10 kΩ, 130R, 1.8 kΩ, 240R, 27 kΩ, 360 kΩ, 62R, 56 kΩ?

9 Define electrical power. What is it measured in? What is the maximum energy dissipated from a 0.5 W resistor which passes a current for 2 minutes?

10 What type of resistor would you choose to carry out very precise, accurate work?

Other types of resistors

Light-dependent resistor (LDR) This is a resistor, shown in figure 3.5.6, whose resistance changes with the intensity of light falling on it. The **ORP12** is a very popular LDR and its resistance varies from around 10 MΩ in the dark to less than 1 kΩ in bright daylight.

LDRs are used in electronic circuits as transducers which change light energy into electrical energy. Hence they are also referred to as **photoconductive** cells or **photocell**s.

They are made from semiconductor materials such as cadmium sulphide in which the energy from the incident light causes the release of more charge carriers and this in turn leads to a decrease in the resistance of the material.

Figure 3.5 6 Light-dependent resistor

LDRs are an essential component in any light-sensing circuit and are used in automatic light switches and burglar alarms. However, due to their fairly slow response to light (about 100 ms) they are not used in situations which involve rapidly changing light levels. Then, other devices such as photodetectors or phototransistors are used instead.

Thermistor This is a resistor whose resistance changes with the temperature of its surroundings. It comes in a number of different shapes and forms of which the most common are as shown in figure 3.5.7.

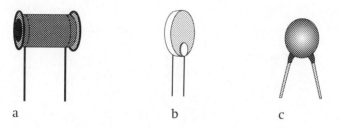

a   b   c

Figure 3.5.7 Types of thermistors: (a) rod; (b) disc ; (c) bead

Thermistors are used in electronic circuits as transducers which change heat energy to electrical energy. There are two basic types of thermistors. These are known as **negative temperature coefficient** (n.t.c.) and **positive temperature coefficient** (p.t.c.).

The n.t.c. thermistors are the most common; their resistance decreases as the temperature increases and this leads to an increase in current in any temperature-sensitive circuit. The resistance of p.t.c. thermistors increases as the temperature increases. In fact, some are designed so that there is a significant increase in the resistance at a specific, predetermined temperature.

Thermistors are made from semiconductor materials such as nickel oxide, manganese oxide or cobalt oxide and are all able to release more charge carriers as the amount of heat energy is increased.

Because of the change in the resistance with temperature the thermistors can be used to automatically control the flow of current in circuits which are temperature sensitive. In addition, they are used as heat sensors in fire-alarms and temperature sender units in car engines.

Questions

1 What is a light-dependent resistor?
2 What is the resistance of the ORP12 when it is (a) in the light and (b) in the dark?
3 What is the LDR made from and how does light cause a change in its resistance?
4 Why is the LDR a transducer?
5 Give a number of uses for the LDR.
6 What is a thermistor?
7 Why are thermistors known as transducers?
8 What do n.t.c. and p.t.c. stand for and how do they differ?
9 What are thermistors made from and what is responsible for the change in resistance with temperature?
10 Give a number of uses for thermistors in electronic circuits.

Capacitors Figure 3.5.8 shows the symbols for capacitors.

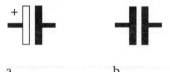

a   b

Figure 3.5.8 (a) Electrolytic capacitor; (b) non-electrolytic capacitor

A capacitor stores electric charge. Basically it consists of two metal plates separated by an insulator called the **dielectric**. When connected to a battery the capacitor charges up until the p.d. between its terminals is the same as the e.m.f. of the battery. If the battery is removed, the charge may take a long time to leak away unless a conductor is connected across the terminals.

The **capacitance** of a capacitor is its charge-storing ability, and is measured in **farads** (F). The capacitance depends on the area of the plates (being large if the area is large) and the distance between the plates (being large if the distance is small) and the type of dielectric used. In general for a charge Q and p.d. V

$$C = Q/V$$

i.e.

capacitance = charge divided by voltage

Smaller, more convenient, units are the **microfarad**, µF (= 1/1 000 000 F), the **nanofarad**, nF (= 1/1 000 000 000 F) and the **picofarad**, pF (= 1/1 000 000 000 000 F).

When choosing a capacitor it is important to consider the value, tolerance, **working voltage** and **leakage current**.

Value   This is either marked on the capacitor or is colour-coded (see figure 3.5.9). The code is the same as that for resistors except that there is a fifth band which stands for the working voltage of the capacitor.

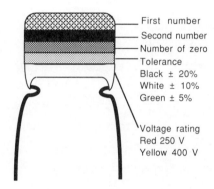

Figure 3.5.9 Capacitor colour code

Tolerance   The fourth band in the colour code indicates how much more or less the actual capacitance may be than that stated on the capacitor.

Working voltage   The fifth band specifies the maximum voltage (d.c. or peak a.c.) that the capacitor can withstand before the insulation (dielectric) breaks down.

Leakage current   Ideally this should be zero, but no capacitor is perfect and there is always a small leakage current.

Capacitors are either **polarised (electrolytic)** or **non-polarised (non-electrolytic)**. Polarised capacitors have both a positive and a negative terminal and therefore must be connected the right way round in a circuit. Non-polarised capacitors can be connected either way round.

Capacitors and a.c.   Capacitors block d.c. and allow a.c. to pass. The amount of a.c. allowed to pass depends on the opposition of the capacitor to the a.c. This opposition is called the **capacitative reactance** and is given the symbol X_c. It is given by the formula

$$X_c = \frac{1}{2\pi f C}$$

where f is the frequency of the a.c. and C is the capacitance of the capacitor. Reactance is measured in ohms. Note that X_c depends on both f and C and decreases if either f or C increases.

Energy stored in a capacitor

A charged capacitor stores energy. The amount of energy stored is given by the following equations:

$$E = QV/2; \quad E = CV^2/2; \quad E = Q^2/2C$$

where E is the energy in joules. This energy is released as electrical energy when the capacitor discharges.

Charging and discharging of a capacitor

The charging and discharging of a capacitor can be slowed down by placing a resistor in series with it. By looking at the current and the voltage associated with the capacitor it can be seen that both of these change exponentially with time. Thus, in the charging process, it can be shown that the current has its maximum value at the start and slowly decreases to zero as the capacitor is charged, whilst the voltage across the capacitor starts at zero and slowly rises to that of the supply voltage when the capacitor is fully charged. This is illustrated in figure 3.5.10.

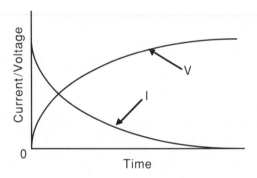

Figure 3.5.10 Voltage/current against time as the capacitor charges

Time constant of a capacitor–resistor (CR) series circuit

The time for charging and discharging of a capacitor can be increased by placing a resistor in series with the capacitor. The larger the value of the resistance the longer the charge/discharge time. The time constant is a measure of this time, represented by the symbol T and given by the formula

$$T = \text{capacitance} \times \text{resistance} \quad \text{or} \quad T = CR$$

Types of capacitor

Non-electrolytic or non-polarised capacitors are usually less than 1 μF and are obtained in a number of different forms (as shown in figure 3.5.11) depending on the type of dielectric used.

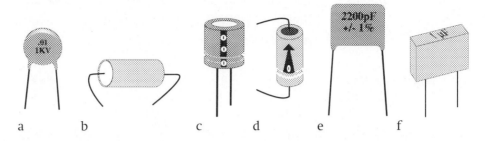

Figure 3.5.11 Main types of capacitor: (a) ceramic; (b) polypropylene; (c) aluminium radial; (d) aluminium axial; (e) silver mica; (f) plastic epoxy cased

Ceramic capacitors are disk-shaped and have values up to 0.1 μF. Some ceramic types are tubular and have values from 1 to 500 pF.

Paper capacitors cover the range 0.001 μF to 1.0 μF. They are obtained either as the tubular type or the encapsulated type. They are constructed from two rolls of tinfoil separated by a tissue paper insulator. The whole is rolled into a tight cylinder.

Mica capacitors are often used for small capacitance values of 50 pF to 500 pF. They give good stability, high accuracy and good high-frequency performance. They are expensive and generally used as trimmers (small variable capacitors).

There are a number of different **plastic insulation type capacitors**. Polystyrene is used to make accurate capacitors; polycarbonate is used to make capacitors having high stability; polyester types are cheap but not very stable and polypropylene is used in capacitors required for high-voltage work.

Electrolytic capacitors are of two types: the aluminium type and the tantalum bead type.

Aluminium types consist of two aluminium plates separated by an electrolyte of borax, phosphate or carbonate. A d.c. current leads to the formation of a thin layer of aluminium oxide which serves as the dielectric. Because of the very thin dielectric, the capacitance of this capacitor is very large, usually from 1 μF to above 2200 μF.

The **tantalum bead type** is similar to the aluminium type but for the fact that tantalum electrodes are used instead. These capacitors have very large values of C for a very small physical size. They are very stable and have a much smaller leakage current than the aluminium capacitors.

Uses of capacitors   Capacitors are used for storing charge or electrical energy, for separating a.c. from d.c. (it blocks d.c. whilst allowing a.c. to pass), and for smoothing in power supply circuits and in time-delay circuits.

Questions

1 Describe the construction of the capacitor. What is the name given to the insulation material inside the capacitor?

2 What is the capacitance of a capacitor and what is it measured in?

3 What are µF, nF and pF and how are they related?

4 What factors should be considered when choosing a capacitor?

5 What is the difference between a non-electrolytic and an electrolytic capacitor? Draw the circuit symbols for both of these.

6 Write down the formula for the energy stored in a capacitor and use the appropriate formula to calculate the energy stored in a 1000 µF at its working voltage of 50 V.

7 Explain the changes to the current flowing to a capacitor and the voltage across it as it charges up.

8 What is the time constant of a capacitor–resistor series circuit? What is it a measure of?

9 Why is it possible for electrolytic capacitors to have such large capacitance values?

10 Give a number of uses for the capacitor.

11 Explain the term 'capacitative reactance'. How does this reactance depend on frequency?

12 Calculate the reactance of (a) a 100 µF and (b) a 1000 µF capacitor to a 100 Hz signal and use this information to explain why large-value capacitors are used in the smoothing of d.c. in power supplies.

The diode   Figure 3.5.12 shows the symbol for the diode.

a   b

Figure 3.5.12 (a) Diode symbol; (b) one type of diode

The diode is a semiconductor device which allows a current to flow through it in one direction only. Diodes are made from germanium or silicon and are commonly referred to as **junction diodes** due to the fact that they are made so that one half of the material has a predominance of positive charge carriers, whilst the other half has a predominance of negative charge carriers. The junction between these two regions is called a **p-n junction** (see figure 3.5.13). The connection to the p-side of the diode is called the **anode** and the connection to the n-side, the **cathode**. In most diodes the cathode end is identified by a black band as shown in figure 3.5.12b.

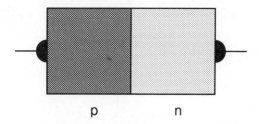

Figure 3.5.13   p-n junction

A diode which is connected with its anode positive and its cathode negative is said to be **forward-biased**. If connected so that its anode is negative and its cathode is positive then the diode is said to be **reverse-biased**. A diode conducts when it is forward-biased, i.e. when the anode is positive and the cathode is negative, as shown in the diode characteristic in figure 3.5.14a. The direction of current flow is in the same direction as the arrow on the symbol. It is essential that the diode is connected the correct way round in a circuit if it is to work as desired.

A small voltage is needed to push a current through a diode in the forward direction. This is called the **forward voltage** (V_f), the **junction potential** or the **turn-on voltage**. Silicon diodes need a forward voltage of about 0.7 V, whilst a germanium diode needs a forward voltage of 0.15 V.

A diode will be damaged if too large a current is allowed to pass through it. Therefore, it is important to note the **maximum forward current** (I_f) which can pass through the diode.

A diode which is reverse-biased will not pass a significant current. However, if the reversed voltage is made too large the diode breaks down and a large current will then flow in the reverse direction. This current is independent of the applied voltage. The maximum reverse voltage is called the **peak inverse voltage** (PIV).

Table 3.5.1 shows typical values of I_f, V_f and PIV for three different diodes.

Table 3.5.1 Basic diode information

Diode type	I_f	PIV	V_f
1N4001 silicon	1 A	50 V	0.7 V
1N4002 silicon	1 A	100 V	0.7 V
OA90 germanium	24 mA	30 V	0.15 V

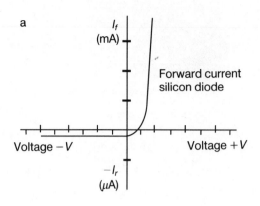

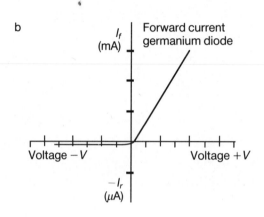

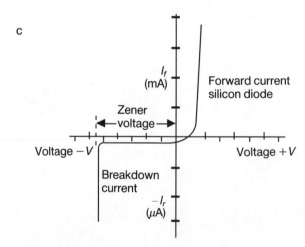

Figure 3.5.14 a, b and c Diode characteristics

Diodes which are used for one-way conduction are called **rectifier diodes** or **signal diodes**. They are indicated by the symbol shown in figure 3.5.12a. Other types of diodes are the light-emitting diode and the Zener diode, both of which are discussed below.

Light-emitting diode (LED)

Figure 3.5.15 LED symbol

Light-emitting diodes (LEDs) give off light when a current passes through them in the forward direction. An LED is a transducer which is used to change electrical energy into light energy and is made from the semiconductor gallium arsenide phosphide. The LED must be connected in a circuit the correct way round if it is to work; its anode must be positive and its cathode must be negative. The anode is usually the longer of the two terminals. See figure 3.5.16.

When forward-biased (anode positive and cathode negative) it conducts and emits red, yellow or green light depending on its composition. No light emission occurs if the LED is reverse-biased (anode negative and cathode positive).

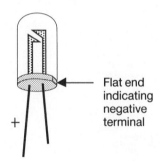

Flat end indicating negative terminal

+

Figure 3.5.16 The light-emitting diode

The LED must have an external resistor connected in series to limit the forward current, which may have a maximum value of 30 mA (0.03 A) and a typical value of 10 mA (0.01 A). This forward current causes a 2 V drop across the LED. The value of the series resistor to use can be calculated from the expression

$$\text{Series resistance} = \frac{\text{supply voltage} - 2.0\ V}{0.01\ A}$$

For example, on a 5 V supply, $R = 3.0/0.01\ \Omega = 300\ \Omega$.

LEDs are used as indicator lamps and in seven-segment displays. They are small, reliable, having long life and high operating speed. They also use far less current than a filament lamp.

The seven-segment display This consists of seven LED segments arranged as a figure eight (see figure 3.5.17) so that the digits 0 to 9 can be displayed when different segments are lit.

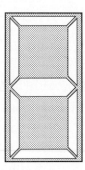

Figure 3.5.17 The seven-segment display

As for ordinary LEDs each of the segments has an anode and a cathode, and must be protected by a current-limiting resistor calculated as shown above. In one type of seven-segment display called the **common anode** all the anodes are joined together and in the other type called the **common cathode** all seven cathodes are joined together.

The seven-segment display is usually driven by a **binary coded decimal (BCD) to seven-segment decoder/driver**, which for the common anode type is the 74LS47 (TTL); the 74LS48 is used for the common cathode display.

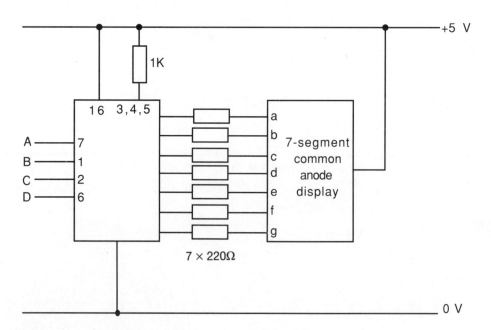

Figure 3.5.18 Seven-segment display and decoder

54

The Zener diode

Figure 3.5.19 Symbol for the Zener diode

Zener diodes are used for voltage regulation and make use of the breakdown property of diodes when reverse-biased. The diode is designed to break down when the reverse voltage reaches a particular value. Breakdown occurs when the reverse current suddenly changes from a very small value to a very large value which is independent of the voltage. The voltage at which this happens is called the **Zener** or **reference voltage** (V_z). The current flowing is sufficiently large to cause damage to the diode and a series resistor is required to limit this current. The resistor must also cope with the power requirement of the diode and must pass the maximum current, consistent with the diode power rating. Whatever the current flowing through this resistor, the voltage across the diode remains constant. It is this property which makes the Zener diode ideal for voltage regulation. Zener diodes can have power ratings from 400 mW up to 20 W and a range of voltages from 2.4 V up to 75 V.

Questions

1 What is the function of a diode?

2 What kind of material are diodes made from? Give two examples of this material.

3 Why are diodes called junction diodes?

4 Draw the symbol for the diode and identify its positive and negative terminals.

5 Draw a diode connected to a battery so that it is (a) forward-biased and (b) reverse-biased.

6 What is the junction potential of a diode and what is its value for (a) a silicon diode and (b) a germanium diode?

7 What is I_f and what is its value for (a) a silicon diode and (b) a germanium diode?

8 Describe what happens to a diode as the reverse voltage is increased.

9 Draw the symbols for, and identify the terminals of, (a) a Zener diode and (b) a light-emitting diode.

10 Give the main uses for (a) the Zener diode and (b) the light-emitting diode.

Transformers   Figure 3.5.20 shows the symbol for the transformer.

Figure 3.5.20 Transformer symbol

A transformer is used to change the value of an alternating p.d. It can either increase the value of the p.d., in which case it is called a **step-up transformer** or it can decrease the value of the p.d. and is called a **step-down transformer**. Some transformers are not used to step-up or step-down the voltage but are used for **impedance matching**. Impedance is the total opposition to alternating current and it is important to ensure that the output impedance of an amplifier matches the input impedance of the load being fed.

Transformers consist of a pair of coils or windings, one for the input called the **primary** and the other for the output, the **secondary**. They lie side by side or one on top of the other on a common laminated (consisting of layers) soft iron core. An alternating voltage connected to the primary causes an alternating current which produces an alternating magnetic field. This field links with the second coil through the soft iron core and induces an e.m.f. in it. This e.m.f. is 180° out of phase with the input and oscillates at the same frequency. If a load is connected then an induced alternating current will flow through it.

In circuit calculations, transformers are assumed to be 100% efficient (many are almost so) and therefore it is possible to show that secondary p.d. is proportional to the number of turns in the secondary winding and the primary p.d. is proportional to the number of turns in the primary winding. This can be expressed in equation form as follows :

$$\frac{\text{primary voltage}}{\text{secondary voltage}} = \frac{\text{number of turns on the primary}}{\text{number of turns on the secondary}}$$

Using symbols this can be written as

$$\frac{V_p}{V_s} = \frac{N_p}{N_s}$$

where V_p, V_s, N_p, N_s are the primary voltage, the secondary voltage, the primary number of turns and the secondary number of turns respectively. This expression is called the **turns ratio** and it states that the ratio of the voltages is equal to the ratio of the number of turns.

A second formula, derived from the assumption of 100% efficiency which implies input power is equal to output power, is

primary voltage $\times$ primary current = secondary voltage $\times$ secondary current

or

$$V_p \times I_p = V_s \times I_s$$

where I_p and I_s are the primary and secondary currents respectively. The power rating of transformers is given in terms of volt-ampere (VA).

Inductors   Figure 3.5.21 is the symbol for an inductor.

Figure 3.5.21 Inductor symbol

An inductor is simply a coil of wire with a core of iron or some other magnetic material. It has a property called an **inductance**, which is given the symbol L and which is measured in **henry** (H), or more commonly the **millihenry** (mH) and the **microhenry** (μH). The henry is defined as that inductance which produces an e.m.f. of 1 V when the current changes at a rate of 1 A per second.

An inductor has no effect on d.c. but opposes any changes in current. Therefore it offers opposition to a.c. and the higher the frequency of the a.c. the greater the opposition. The inductor works on the principle that a change in current in the coil produces a change in the magnetic field surrounding the coil. This changing magnetic field induces an e.m.f. which acts in such a direction as to oppose the change in the current through the coil. The opposition to a.c. is called the **reactance**, measured in ohms and given the symbol X_L, with

$$X_L = 2\pi fL$$

where f is the frequency of the a.c. and L is the inductance. Note that X_L depends on both f and L, increasing if either of these two quantities increases.

An inductor stores energy in its magnetic field, this energy being given by the formula

$$W = \frac{LI^2}{2}$$

where W is the energy in joules and I is the current in amps.

Uses   There are three basic types of inductors: air-cored, iron-cored and iron dust or ferrite types. Each of these have different applications. The **air-cored** types have small inductances to the order of a few millihenry and are used for radio frequency work (above 1 MHz). They are used in radio tuning circuits and as inductors in filter circuits. **Iron-cored** types have a laminated soft iron core on which the coil is wound. They have much larger inductances of the order of a few henry and are used for low-frequency applications, generally below 100 kHz. One specific use is as a 'choke' in power supply smoothing units. **Ferrite-cored** or **iron dust** types operate at frequencies between 100 kHz and 100 MHz and are used in radio tuning applications.

Questions

1 What value series resistor is required for an LED connected to a 9 V supply?

2 What type of transformer would be required in a power supply unit and what turns ratio would be necessary to produce 6 V a.c. from the mains supply.?

3 Draw a diagram of a transformer, showing clearly the primary and the secondary coils. On your diagram include the waveforms at the input and the output for a step-down operation.

4 What is reactance of an inductor and how does it differ for a.c. and d.c.?

5 Calculate the reactance of an inductor of inductance 0.1 mH when a signal of (a) 25 Hz and (b) 2500 Hz passes through it. Which of these two signals would be filtered out if they were passing together?

6 Describe how you would use an inductor in a filter circuit and describe which frequencies would be most affected.

3.6 Active components

Active components are those in which an energy source is required for proper operation, the most well-known of which are transistors, thyristors, integrated circuits (ICs) and relays.

Transistors

The transistor is a semiconductor device which is made either as a separate component or as part of integrated circuits where many are packed together on a 'chip'. They are made from silicon or germanium, although today the silicon type is preferred as these can operate at higher temperatures.

Transistors are of two types, the **bipolar junction transistor** and the **field effect transistor** (FET) also known as the **unijunction transistor**, although the bipolar transistor is more commonly used. Figure 3.6.1 shows the symbols used to represent the various types of transistors described below.

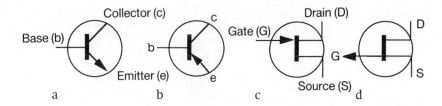

Figure 3.6.1 Transistor symbols: (a) npn-bipolar; (b) pnp-bipolar; (c) n-channel FET; (d) p-channel FET

Junction transistors are made from a single piece of semiconductor which has been divided into three regions by the addition of different impurities. One type of impurity increases the positive charge carriers (called **holes**)in that region of the crystal, thereby making it a **p-type** region. Another type of impurity produces an **n-type** region by increasing the number of negative charge carriers (called **electrons**).

The transistor has three terminals called the **collector**, the **base** and the **emitter**. The emitter region of the semiconductor emits electrons; these electrons are collected by the collector and the base controls the flow of electrons from emitter to collector. In an **npn transistor** the collector and the emitter are connected to regions of n-type semiconductor and the base to a region of p-type silicon. In a **pnp transistor** these connections are reversed.

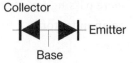

Figure 3.6.2 Transistor as two opposing diodes

Between the three regions of the transistor are two pn junctions and therefore the transistor can be considered as two diodes back to back as shown in figure 3.6.2. If the base region is unconnected then the two diodes oppose each other and no current can flow. For proper operation the base terminal of the transistor must be connected to the collector terminal through a resistor to limit the base current. The collector is then connected to the positive of the power supply in the case of an npn transistor or the negative of the supply in the case of a pnp transistor. The correct connections for both types of transistor is shown in table 3.6.1.

Table 3.6.1 Connections for npn and pnp transistors

Transistor type	Collector	Base	Emitter
npn	positive	positive	negative
pnp	negative	negative	positive

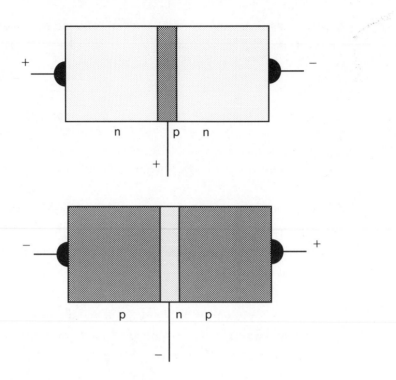

Figure 3.6.3   Transistor connections

How the transistor works   There are two paths in which current can flow in a transistor. These are from the collector to the emitter and from the base to the emitter, as shown in figure 3.6.4.

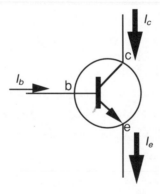

Figure 3.6.4   Transistor current flow

When the collector of a npn transistor is positive and the emitter negative no current flows. If the base is now made positive then the base-emitter junction will be forward-biased and the collector emitter junction will be reverse-biased. A small current will then flow in the forward direction from the base to the emitter. This current triggers the flow of a much larger current between the collector and the emitter and therefore the emitter current is the sum of the base current and the collector current. This can be expressed as emitter current = collector current current + base current

or in symbols

$$I_e = I_c + I_b$$

where I_e, I_c and I_b are the emitter current, collector current and base current respectively, as identified in figure 3.6.4. Conduction in a transistor is due to the flow of holes and electrons.

For a silicon transistor, 0.65 V is needed to forward bias the base-emitter junction. The base-emitter current then switches on and can control a much larger current flowing between the collector and the emitter.

Transistors are small, cheap and fast, being able to switch millions of times a second. They have no moving parts, and as a result they are very reliable and have an infinite life. Because of these properties, transistors are used in making high-speed switches; current, voltage and power amplifiers; and oscillators.

Modes of connection The description above deals with the transistor connected in such a way that the emitter is common to the base (input) and the collector (output). This is called the common-emitter mode and is shown in figure 3.6.5a. Other modes are common-collector, shown in figure 3.6.5b and common-base, shown in figure 3.6.5.c. Table 3.6.2 gives a brief summary of the three modes of connection.

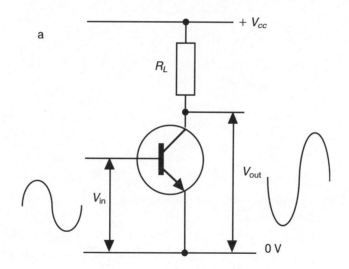

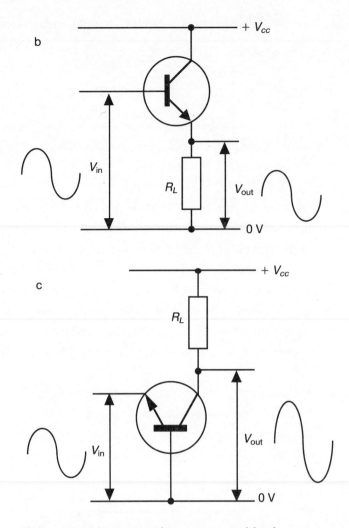

Figure 3.6.5 (a) npn transistor connected in the common-emitter mode; (b) npn transistor connected in the common-collector mode and (c) npn transistor connected in the common-base mode

Table 3.6.2 Summary of the three modes of connection for transistor amplifiers

Property	Common-emitter	Common-collector	Common-base
Voltage gain	High	Unity (1)	High
Current gain	High	High	Unity (1)
Power gain	Very high	Medium	Medium
Input resistance	Medium (few kΩ)	High (> several kΩ)	Low (< 100 Ω)
Output resistance	Medium/High	Low	Very high (∼ 1 MΩ)
Phase shift	180°	0	0

Transistor d.c. current gain (h_{FE})

This is the ratio of the collector current to the base current, i.e.

$$h_{FE} = \frac{\text{collector current } I_c}{\text{base current } I_b}$$

and is fairly constant for a particular transistor over a limited range of I_c. However, it varies enormously from one transistor to the next in the same family. For example, low-gain transistors might have current gains from say 10 to 100, whilst those with a higher gain may range from 200 to 1000. Data books and component catalogues often quote the minimum and maximum values of h_{FE} and it is important that the minimum value is used to determined the collector current when choosing a transistor for a particular circuit.

Transistor a.c. current gain (h_{fe})

This is defined as the change in collector current divided by the change in the base current, i.e.

$$h_{fe} = \frac{\text{change in collector current } (\Delta I_c)}{\text{change in base current } (\Delta I_b)}$$

where Δ represents the change in the value of the current, and in most circumstances this is almost the same as the d.c. current gain.

Transistor input and output resistances

These are usually defined for the a.c. condition of a circuit as

$$\text{Input resistance} = \frac{\text{change in base-emitter voltage } (\Delta V_{be})}{\text{change in the base current } (\Delta I_b)}$$

where Δ represents the change in the value of the voltage. For the common-emitter mode of connection this covers a range up to about 5 kΩ.

$$\text{Output resistance} = \frac{\text{change in collector-emitter voltage } (\Delta V_{ce})}{\text{change in collector current } (\Delta I_c)}$$

This is typically between 50 kΩ and 100 kΩ.

Transistor transition frequency (F_T)

This is the frequency at which h_{FE} is equal to 1.

Transconductance (g_m)

This relates the output current to the input voltage and is given by

$$g_m = \frac{I_c}{V_b}$$

The unit is A/V and is called the **siemens** (S).

Transistor parameters

Apart from the gain, the following parameters are commonly found in data books when describing transistors:

$I_{c\,max}$ maximum collector current that can be passed safely by a particular transistor;

$P_{T\,max}$ maximum power rating at a temperature of 25 °C and is the maximum energy dissipated in one second (i.e. the power) safely by the transistor;

V_{CEO} maximum d.c. voltage between the collector and the emitter when the base is open circuit;

V_{EBO} maximum d.c. voltage between the emitter and the base when the collector is open circuit;

V_{CBO} maximum d.c. voltage between the collector and the base when the emitter is open circuit.

The transistor amplifier

The circuit in figure 3.6.6 is a typical single-stage, fully stabilised transistor voltage amplifier.

R_1 and R_2 make up a potential divider whose function is to fix the base-emitter voltage at a value sufficient to forward bias the base-emitter junction so that there is a quiescent current to maintain the collector voltage at half the value of the supply. R_1 and R_2 are chosen so that the current flowing through them is about five to ten times greater than the quiescent base current. This is to prevent any changes to the base voltage if there is a change in the base current.

R_4 is the emitter resistor; its purpose is to ensure that any change in I_c is fed back, in the form of a voltage change, to the base of the transistor. This voltage change will in turn correct the change in I_c. If I_c increases then so does I_e, and as V_4 (voltage across R_4) = $I_e \times R_4$, V_4 also increases. The voltage across R_2 = $(V_{be} + V_4)$ is fixed by the potential divider. Therefore, an increase in V_4 will lead to a corresponding decrease in V_{be}; this leads to a decrease in I_b which restores I_c to its original value.

Capacitors C_1 and C_2 allow a.c. to flow into the amplifier whilst at the same time blocking d.c. and thereby maintaining the d.c. condition of the circuit. Capacitor C_3 allows an easy path for a.c. This prevents an a.c. voltage from developing across R_4 which would be fed back to the base of the transistor, thereby reducing the gain.

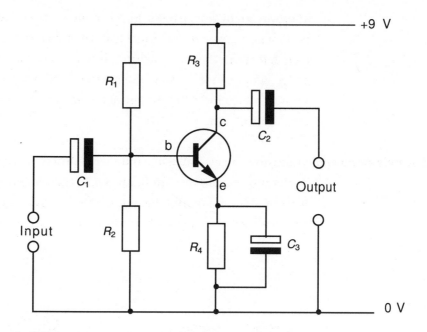

Figure 3.6.6 The transistor amplifier

Information for a particular transistor is shown as a code on the body of the transistor. The code usually contains a string of letters and numbers which, in Europe, is defined by the numbering system of the **Pro-Electron Organisation**. In this system the first letter of the code represents the type of semiconductor material used in the transistor

A   germanium
B   silicon
C   gallium arsenide
D   indium antimide

and the second letter indicates the main use of the transistor

C   audio frequency amplifier
D   audio frequency, power amplifier
F   low-power radio frequency amplifier
P   high-power radio frequency amplifier

while the rest of the code is used to identify the broad area of use of the transistor, e.g. whether they are general-purpose types for use in domestic appliances or more specialist types used in specific areas of industry. A three-figure number, as in BC109 or BC184L, for instance, is used to distinguish the general-purpose types, whilst the specialist types are recognised by a letter such as W, X, Y or Z.

There are many transistors which cannot be identified by the above system. This is because many manufacturers have their own codes and the use of a data book (generally from the manufacturer) is required for a full interpretation of the codes. American transistors use a system which begins with 2N followed by a number which indicates the age of the design – the higher the number the more recent the design.

Types of transistor casing Transistors are available in a number of different types of casings and pin configurations as shown in figure 3.6.7. Therefore it is essential to have a data book in order to identify the pins of the various types of transistors. The casings are identified by code numbers, the only exception being the E-line plastic type.

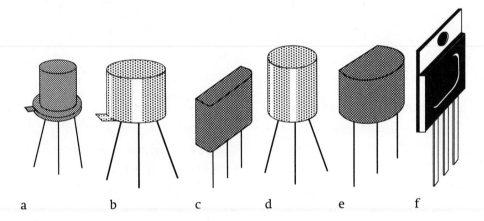

a   b   c   d   e   f

Figure 3.6.7 Types of transistor casings: (a) TO18; (b) TO39; (c) E-line; (d) TO1; (e) TO92; (f) TO220

Field effect transistors (FETs) Figure 3.6.8 shows the symbols for the field effect transistor, which is constructed in an entirely different way from that of a junction transistor.

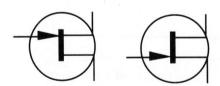

Figure 3.6.8   FET symbols

FETs have a single piece of either p-type or n-type silicon through which a current flows and as a result they are also called **unijunction transistors**. This single piece of conductor is called the **channel**, the ends of which are connected to two terminals called the **source S** and the **drain D**. Between these terminals is another region which has been doped (has had impurities added) so that it has charge carriers opposite to those in the channel; this region is joined to another terminal called the **gate G**. This results in a pn junction being created between the two regions. The pn junction has a region around it in which there are no charge carriers and therefore behaves as an insulator; this is called the **depletion layer**. When the pn junction is reverse-biased the depletion layer grows in size, the actual width being dependent on the the size of the reverse voltage.

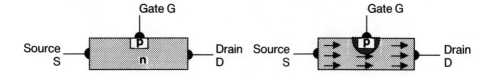

Figure 3.6.9 Structure of, and current flow in, unijunction transistor

When the drain is made positive with respect to the source, a current flows along the channel between the drain and the source. Only the majority carriers (electrons for an n-channel FET) are involved in this conduction. Due to the depletion layer the region at the middle of the channel is narrower and therefore effectively reduces the maximum current that can flow. If the gate is made negative relative to the source then the pn junction will be reverse-biased and the depletion layer will be increased, thus decreasing the width of the channel for conduction. The current flowing though the channel is called the **drain current** I_D, and for a particular drain-source voltage the drain current is controlled by the **gate-source voltage** V_{GS}.

Therefore a signal placed on the gate terminal of a FET will cause modification to the drain current according to the waveform of the signal. This current can be use to produce an output waveform identical to that of the input.

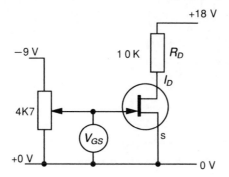

Figure 3.6.10 Circuit for investigating the FET characteristics

The circuit shown in figure 3.6.10 is used to investigate the FET; large negative gate voltage leads to zero drain-source current. As the gate voltage is increased, i.e. made more positive, the current flow from drain to source increases. This leads to a voltage drop across R_D resulting in a decrease in the drain voltage. A plot of I_D against V_{GS} is known as the **transfer characteristic**, shown in figure 3.6.11.

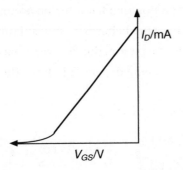

Figure 3.6.11   FET transfer characteristic

The gain of a FET is referred to as its **transconductance**, g_m, which is defined as

$$g_m = \frac{\text{change in drain current}}{\text{change in gate-source voltage}} = \frac{\Delta I_D}{\Delta V_{GS}}$$

Input resistance   As the pn junction of a FET is always reverse-biased very little input current flows. Typical input resistance for a.c. is of the order of 10^9 and above.

Like the bipolar transistor, FETs can be connected in three different configurations. These are **common source**, **common drain** and **common gate** and are shown in figure 3.6.12.

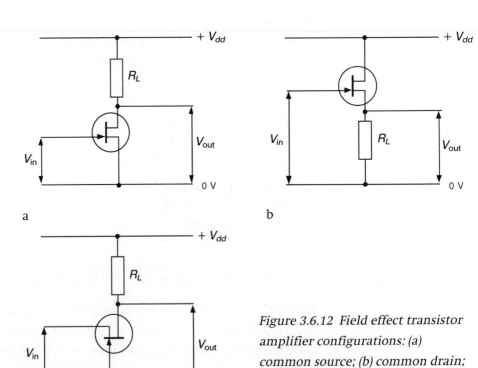

Figure 3.6.12 Field effect transistor amplifier configurations: (a) common source; (b) common drain; and (c) common gate

Thyristor

Figure 3.6.13   Thyristor symbol

The thyristor, whose symbol is shown in figure 3.6.13, is also known as the **silicon control rectifier** (SCR). It is made from a single piece of semiconductor in which impurities have been added to produce four regions of p-, n-, p- and n-type semiconductors as in the arrangement of figure 3.6.14. There are three connections, one joined to the first p-type region called the **anode** A, one attached to the second p-type region called the **gate** G, and one connected to the second n-type region called the **cathode** C.

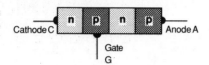

Figure 3.6.14 The thyristor

When the anode is positive and the cathode negative the thyristor is forward-biased. However, it does not conduct until the gate is made positive and this conduction continues even when this positive voltage is removed. The thyristor is switched off by disconnecting or reversing the supply voltage. The absence of a current when the supply is reversed indicates that the thyristor is essentially a diode and as a result it can only pass the positive half cycles and therefore half the power of a waveform.

Triac   This consists of two thyristors arranged in opposition and controlled by a single gate as shown in its symbol in figure 3.6.15. The purpose of this arrangement is to allow conduction to take place on both half cycles of a waveform and therefore to deliver full power when switched. The connections are called main terminal 1(MT1), gate (G) and main terminal 2 (MT2). Triggering is achieved by applying pulses between MT1 and the gate, and the triac can handle a gate current ranging from a few amps to 100 A.

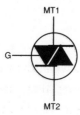

Figure 3.6.15 The triac symbol

Integrated circuits (ICs)

Integrated circuits are pieces of silicon on which a large number of discrete components have been fabricated. It is possible to have transistors, diodes, resistors and capacitors arranged together to perform a particular function.

ICs are commonly obtained in rectangular plastic packages having two rows of pins known as the **dual-in-line** (DIL) package; standard pin configurations have from 8, 14, 16, 18 and 20 pins up to 40 pins. Pin spacing is set at 2.5 mm (0.1 in) and each row is separated by either 7.5 mm for small ICs or 15 mm for larger ICs. The pins are numbered from left to right in an anticlockwise direction, pin number 1 being identified by a small circular notch, as shown in figure 3.6.16.

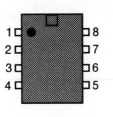 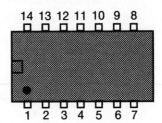

Figure 3.6.16 Integrated circuit packages, 8- and 14-pin DIL

Integrated circuits can be grouped according to the number of discrete circuits contained on a single chip. This grouping is referred to as the **scale of integration** and consists of the following:

SSI   small-scale integration, from 1 to 10 discrete circuits;
MSI   medium-scale integration, from 10 to 100 discrete circuits;
LSI   large-scale integration, from 100 to 1000 discrete circuits;
VLSI   very large scale integration, from 1000 to 10 000 discrete circuits; and
SLSI   super large scale integration, from 10 000 to 100 000 discrete circuits.

There are basically two groups of integrated circuits. Those that are composed of switches and are able to switch between two different voltage levels corresponding to the logic states **on** and **off** are known as **digital** ICs. The other main group, the **linear** ICs, operate on analogue signals, i.e. signals that vary continuously with the physical quantity they represent and which include all amplifier circuits.

Circuits involving ICs are on the whole cheaper, more reliable, smaller and involve fewer discrete components than comparative circuits constructed wholly of discrete components. However, there are a number of disadvantages. For example, apart from power amplifiers and voltage regulators, they cannot cope with high-current, high-voltage or high-power requirements and can be damaged by overloading or by fluctuating power supplies.

1 What are active components?

2 Describe the bipolar and the unipolar transistor and explain how they differ from each other.

3 Describe how a bipolar transistor works.

4 Write down the relationship between the collector current, emitter current and base current.

5 Explain the statement: 'Conduction in a transistor is due to the flow of holes and electrons'.

6 Draw diagrams showing the three modes of operations of the transistor and state which mode could be used as an amplifier with 180° phase shift.

7 Define h_{FE} of a transistor.

8 Describe the operation of the FET.

9 Define transconductance, g_m.

10 What is a thyristor and what could it be used for?

11 What is the meaning of the terms SSI, MSI, LSI and VLSI?

12 What are the main advantages and disadvantages of using IC in circuit designs?

The 555 timer IC

The 555 timer is an 8-pin DIL integrated circuit. When triggered it produces an output pulse (voltage which goes high and then after a time returns to its original value). It can be used as either a monostable (a timer) or an astable multivibrator (an oscillator) with times from a few microseconds to hours. It works on any d.c. supply from 3 to 15 V and can supply (source) or accept (sink) a current of up to 200 mA. This means that it can drive devices such as lamps and relays directly.

How the 555 works

In figure 3.6.17, pin 7 is an output pin which is controlled by a transistor inside the chip. Normally it is connected to ground.

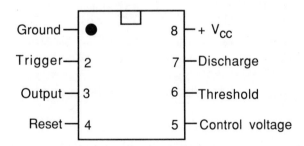

Figure 3.6.17 The 555 timer

When the voltage at pin 2 (the 'trigger') falls below $\frac{1}{3}$ of the supply V_s (by briefly connecting it to ground), the IC is triggered and the 'output' (pin 3) rises to near V_s (the supply). Grounding pin 2 also switches off the transistor, grounding pin

7 and thus allowing its voltage to rise. The capacitor, which is connected between this pin and ground, starts to charge. Pin 6 (the threshold) is an input to the chip and when its voltage reaches $\frac{2}{3}$ of the supply voltage it switches on the transistor causing pin 7 to return to ground again. The capacitor is discharged and will remain so until pin 2 is again triggered. The reset (pin 4) is used to reset the IC, i.e. it causes the output to return to zero volts if it is connected to zero volts. The control voltage ($\frac{2}{3}V_{cc}$) is brought out to pin 5 and therefore allows for a different control voltage to be applied or for it to be completely de-coupled to make the device more immune to noise (unwanted voltages).

The circuit of figure 3.6.18 is that of a monostable; R and C are external components whose values determine the time T (in seconds) for which the circuit is on. This time is given by

$$T = 1.1\,R \times C$$

When used as a timer the 555 is operating as a monostable. This means that it has one stable state, in this case the off state. The circuit will always revert back to this state after a period of time.

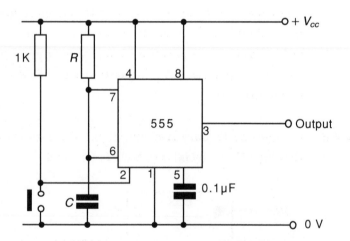

Figure 3.6.18 The 555 timer as a monostable

The astable multivibrator   The circuit for the astable is shown in figure 3.6.19. In the astable circuit pin 2 is connected to pin 6, so as soon as pin 6 returns pin 7 to ground this low voltage is fed back to pin 2, which then retriggers the chip. A second resistor is added between pins 6 and 7 to slow down the discharge of the capacitor.

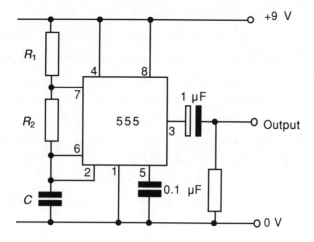

Figure 3.6.19. The 555 as an astable

The time for which the output is 'high', T_1, is given by

$$T_1 = 0.7 (R_1 + R_2) C$$

and the time for which it is 'low', T_2 is

$$T_2 = 0.7 \times R_2 \times C$$

Therefore the total period for the oscillation, T, is

$$T = 0.7 (R_1 + 2R_2) C$$

The frequency of the astable is determined by the external components, R_1, R_2 and C; it is given by the formula

$$f = \frac{1.45}{(R_1 + 2R_2)} \times C$$

If R_2 is much larger than R_1 then the mark/space ratio is approximately equal to one and the frequency is given by

$$f = \frac{0.72}{R_2 \times C}$$

The frequency is measured in hertz if the resistance is measured in ohms and the capacitance in farads.

Questions

1 What kind of electronic device is a 555?

2 Which pins are the positive, ground and output?

3 What are the two ways in which a 555 may be used?

4 What range of d.c voltages can be used to operate the 555?

5 (a) How is the 555 triggered? (b) What happens when it is triggered?

6 Which two components determine the 'on' time of the timer circuit?

7 What is the formula for the time (in seconds) for the timer circuit?

8 What is the meaning of monostable?

9 What is the meaning of astable?

10 Draw a diagram and identify each component of the timer circuit.

Op-amps

Operational amplifiers (op-amps) were originally used to carry out mathematical operations such as addition, subtraction, differentiation and integration. In the early days they were made from discrete components but are now in the form of integrated circuits in which transistors, resistors and capacitors are all contained on the same piece of silicon.

Operational amplifiers are called differential voltage amplifiers because they have two inputs and one output and they amplify the difference in the voltage between the two inputs. In general these amplifiers have the following properties.

1 A very high open-loop (without feedback) voltage gain. The symbol for this is A_0 and it is about 100 000 for d.c. and very low frequency a.c. (below 10 Hz). The open-loop gain decreases with increased frequency.

2 A high-input impedance, from 2 MΩ upwards. As a result they draw very little current from the supply and consequently have little effect on the input voltage.

3 An output impedance, usually below 100 Ω. This means that all the output voltage is transferred to any load connected to the amplifier.

4 A very wide bandwidth. This is the range of frequencies which are amplified by the amplifier without distortion. In fact the bandwidth is defined as the frequency at which the undistorted output voltage falls below 0.707 of its d.c. value.

5 A slew rate which should be large. This is the rate of change of output voltage with time and typically it should be between 0.2 V/μs and 15 V/μs.

6 A large common mode rejection ratio. This is the ratio of differential voltage gain to common mode voltage gain and is a measure of the amplifiers ability to amplify the difference voltage whilst ignoring common voltages on both inputs.

The symbol for the op-amp is shown in figure 3.6.20. The two inputs are called inverting ($-$) and non-inverting ($+$). In general a dual balanced power supply is needed if a.c. amplification is to be achieved. Most amplifiers can operate on a supply ranging from +3 V to +18 V.

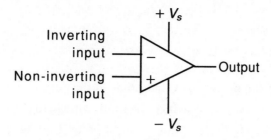

Figure 3.6.20 Operation amplifier symbol

The 741 operational amplifier, as shown in figure 3.6.21, is a very popular IC which is contained in an 8-in DIL package. It has an open-loop gain of 100 000, an input resistance of 2 MΩ, a bandwidth of 1 kHz at a gain of 1000, an output resistance of 150 Ω and a maximum load current of 10 to 13 mA.

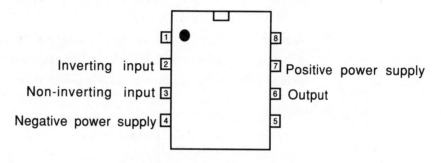

Figure 3.6.21   The 741 operational amplifier

Basic op-amp operation   If the non-inverting input voltage is more positive than the inverting input voltage then the output will be positive. If it is more negative than the inverting input then the output is negative. The voltage of the output changes in the same direction (in phase) as that of the non-inverting input. If the inverting input voltage is more positive than the non-inverting input voltage then the output voltage will be negative and if the inverting input is less positive then the output will be positive. In this case the output changes in antiphase to the inverting input voltage. If there is no difference between the two input voltages then the output voltage is zero.

Voltage gain   The voltage gain of an amplifier is the number of times the output voltage is bigger than the input voltage, given by

$$\text{voltage gain } (A_v) = \frac{\text{output voltage}}{\text{input voltage}}$$

where the input voltage is the non-inverting input voltage minus the inverting input voltage. The voltage gain A_v of a non-inverting amplifier with negative feedback is given by

$$\frac{V_{out}}{V_{in}} = 1 + \frac{R_2}{R_1} \qquad \text{therefore} \qquad A_v = 1 + \frac{R_2}{R_1}$$

The op-amp and negative feedback

This is the process by which some of the output voltage is fed back to the input in such a way as to reduce the input voltage to the amplifier. The result is a reduction in overall gain of the amplifier leading to a reduction in the output voltage. The operational amplifier can be connected to behave as a non-inverting amplifier or as an inverting amplifier. These two circuits are shown in figures 3.6.22a and 3.6.22b. In the non-inverting amplifier the feedback is achieved by the use of two resistors arranged as a potential divider, which splits up the output voltage so that a fraction can be sent back to the inverting input. This fraction when subtracted from V_{in} gives the amplifier input voltage. From figure 3.6.22a it can be seen that as V_{out} increases, the voltage across R_1 (the feedback fraction) also increases. As this is subtracted from V_{in} the amplifier input voltage will decrease leading to a decrease in the output voltage. This decrease will reduce the feedback fraction which is fed back to the input. The overall effect of the negative feedback is to stabilise the output of the amplifier.

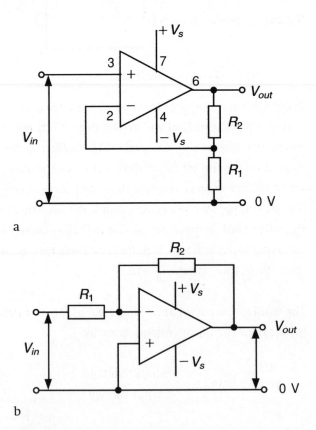

Figure 3.6.22 (a) Non-inverting amplifier and (b) inverting amplifier

The op-amp voltage comparator In this mode of operation the op-amp is used to compare the voltages at its inputs and produces an output when one voltage is larger than the other. The op-amp is used in the open-loop configuration (without negative feedback), which means that the output is either near the positive supply or near the negative supply. The general arrangement is to fix one of the input voltages, either by the use of a Zener diode or a potential divider network. The diagrams of figure 3.6.23 show a number of devices making use of a voltage comparator.

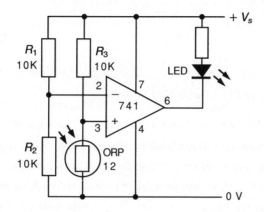

a

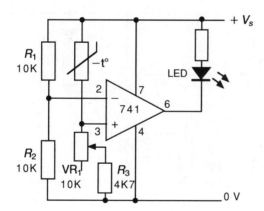

b

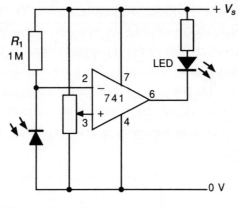

c

Figure 3.6.23 Comparator (a) as a light detector; (b) as a temperature indicator; and (c) as a light-operated switch.

The Schmitt trigger   A problem with comparator circuits is their speed of switching. This is usually fairly slow and may result in the output switching repeatedly between the on and off states before settling down. The Schmitt trigger is a circuit for converting this slow switching into a fast, sudden trigger action. It makes use of positive feedback, i.e. some of the output voltage is fed back to the non-inverting input of the 741.

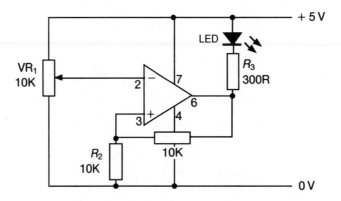

Figure 3.6.24 Schmitt trigger switching circuit

If input 2 of figure 3.6.24 is at low voltage then the output will be about 5 V. The two 10 kΩ resistors make up a potential divider network and at approximately 2.5 V will be fed back to the non-inverting input, which keeps the output at near 5 V.

If the voltage of input 2 is increased slowly then when it reaches 2.5 V the output will fall towards zero. This will pull down the voltage to the non-inverting input, thus increasing the difference between the two inputs and accelerating the change in the output voltage. If the output is slowly increased then the whole process is repeated in reverse and the output once again rises rapidly towards 5 V.

Questions

1 What is an operational amplifier?

2 List the properties of an ideal operational amplifier.

3 Draw the symbol and identify the pins of a standard 741 op-amp DIL package.

4 Define voltage gain and give the formula for the voltage gain of the non-inverting and the inverting amplifiers.

5 Draw a diagram of (a) the inverting amplifier and (b) the non-inverting amplifier.

6 Draw and explain the output characteristics of the (a) the inverting amplifier and (b) the non-inverting amplifier.

7 Draw a diagram showing the frequency response of an op-amp (a) without feedback and (b) with negative feedback. Explain the shape of the graph in each case.

8 Describe the use of the operational amplifier as a voltage comparator and draw a circuit to illustrate how it is used.

Relays   A relay is a mechanical switch used to switch other circuits on and off. It enables small currents in one circuit to control a much larger current in another circuit or the simultaneous switching of more than one circuit.

The basic structure of the relay is shown in figure 3.6.25a. The contacts are of three basic types, **normally open** (no), **normally closed** (nc) and **change-over** (c-o). In addition they can be either single-pole (sp) or double-pole (dp).

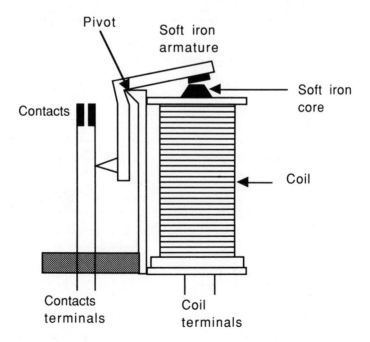

a

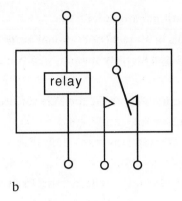

b

Figure 3.6.25 (a) Structure of a simple relay; (b) relay symbol

When a small current flows through the coil of the relay it becomes an electromagnet and attracts the soft iron armature. This movement is transmitted, via the pivot, to the contacts operating the other circuits. When the current flowing through the coil stops, the magnetic field collapses and the armature is able to return to its original position and in turn allow the contacts to return to their initial states.

A relay will have a nominal operating voltage, maximum current and voltage rating; however, in practice there are a range of voltages over which it will operate. For example, a 4.5 V relay can operate off a supply ranging from 3.2 V to 6.5 V.

The circuit in figure 3.6.26 shows one way in which a relay is used. The small current which flows through the collector of the transistor also passes through the coil of the relay. This enables it to switch on the external 12 V supply to operate the electric bell.

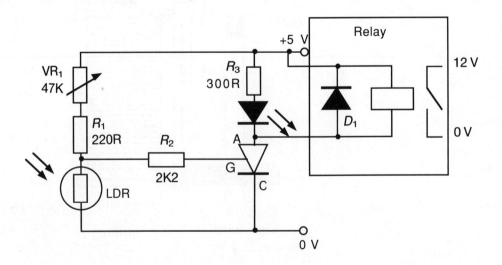

Figure 3.6.26 Light-operated relay switch

3.7 Transducers

Transducers take in energy in one form and send it out in another form. Energy comes in many different forms: electrical, sound, vibration, heat, light, motion and magnetic. In electronics either the input or the output is in the form of electrical energy. A transducer which changes non-electrical energy into electrical energy is called an **input transducer**. Conversely one that changes electrical energy into a non-electrical form is called an **output transducer**.

Transducers are used as the interface which takes in one of the many forms of energy within the environment for processing by electronic systems or to convert the electrical output from these systems into another energy form.

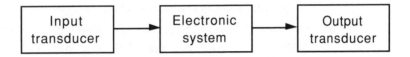

Figure 3.7.1 Transducers as input and output interfaces

Table 3.7.1 gives a list of transducers and the energy conversion which takes place in each. The thermistor, light-dependent resistor and the light-emitting diode were covered in section 3.5; the remainder of this section will look at the other transducers in more detail.

Table 3.7.1 Examples of input and output transducers

Energy	Input transducer	Output transducer
Heat	Thermistors	Heating coil
Light	Light-dependent resistor (LDR)	Light-emitting diode (LED)
Magnetic	Tape recorder head	Tape play-back head
Motion	Generator	Electric motor
Sound	Microphone	Loudspeaker
Vibrational	Record pick-up	

Microphones

Figure 3.7.2 Symbol of microphone

Figure 3.7.2 shows the symbol for the microphone. There are three different groups of microphones: the **velocity-dependent** group, sometimes referred to as having constant velocity; the **amplitude-dependent** group, sometimes referred to as having constant amplitude; and the **carbon microphone**.

Microphones have various properties which should be considered when deciding which to use. These are:

1 impedance – this is the total opposition to a.c. and it is important that this is closely matched to the input impedance of the amplifier it is being used with for efficient power transfer;

2 frequency response – this should cover the range from 20 Hz to 16.5 kHz which is the audio frequency range. In addition the microphone's sensitivity should be the same for all frequencies within the range; and

3 directional sensitivity, i.e. the responsiveness to sound coming from different directions.

A microphone may produce a larger voltage output for sounds coming from certain directions than for sounds coming from other directions. The diagrams in figure 3.7.3 are called polar diagrams. Since the length of line OA indicates the sensitivity in any particular direction, these diagrams can be used to define the directional sensitivity of microphones. The uni-directional microphone will have the pattern as in figure 3.7.3a showing a high sensitivity in one direction. The bi-directional microphone, represented by figure 3.7.3b, is very sensitive in two directions, whilst the omni-directional microphone is equally sensitive in all directions as is shown in figure 3.7.3c.

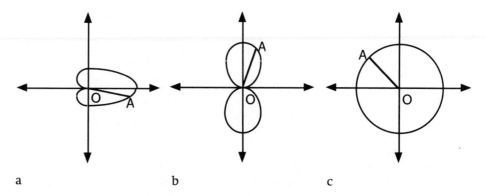

a   b   c

Figure 3.7.3 Polar diagrams showing directional sensitivity of the microphone: (a) uni-directional; (b) bi-directional; (c) omni-directional

Velocity-dependent microphones In these microphones, the output voltage is proportional to the velocity of vibration of the moving parts, which in turn depends on the intensity of sound received. Two such microphones, the moving-coil and the ribbon type, are shown in figures 3.7.4 and 3.7.5.

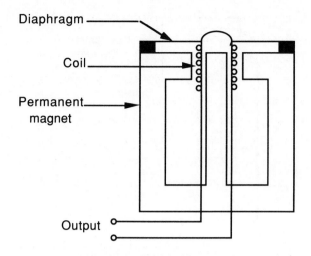

Figure 3.7.4 Moving-coil microphone

The **moving-coil microphone** is sometimes referred to as a **dynamic microphone**. It consists of a light disc called the **diaphragm** which is attached to a small coil of many turns of fine wire wound onto a tube called the **former**. When sound strikes the diaphragm, the coil moves up and down within the circular pole pieces of the permanent magnet. As a result of electromagnetic induction, an e.m.f. between 1 and 10 mV, varying at the same frequency as the sound, is generated within the coil.

Moving-coil microphones have impedances between 100 Ω and 200 Ω, and are either uni-directional or omni-directional. They are robust and have very good reproduction, and these properties together with their low cost make them very popular.

Ribbon type microphones consist of a corrugated aluminium ribbon which is suspended between the pole pieces of a permanent magnet. The arrangement is such that sound falling on the ribbon causes it to move within the pole pieces at the same frequency as the sound. This leads to the generation of an induced e.m.f. in the ribbon at the same frequency as the sound. Because of their construction, ribbon microphones are bi-directional. They have very low impedance and are not as robust as the moving-coil type although, in general, their reproduction quality is as good.

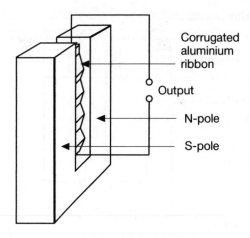

Figure 3.7.5 Ribbon type microphone

Amplitude-dependent microphones   In these microphones the output p.d. is proportional to the amount by which the sound waves displace the moving part from its rest position. Two examples of this type of microphone are the crystal type (figure 3.7.6) and the capacitor type (figure 3.7.7).

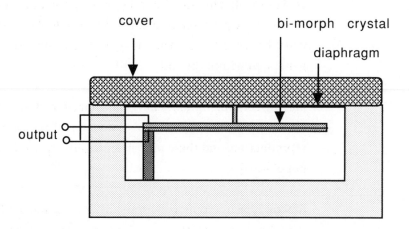

Figure 3.7.6 Crystal microphone

The **crystal microphone** makes use of the **piezoelectric** effect, in which a p.d. is developed across the opposite faces of a crystal when it is bent. It is constructed so that when sound strikes the diaphragm its movement causes deformation of the crystal surfaces. This leads to the production of an alternating e.m.f. at the frequency of the sound.

The crystal microphone is generally omni-directional, i.e. it has equal sensitivity in all directions. It has a very high impedance, usually over 1 MΩ, and a high output, around 100 mV. Its performance is not as good as the velocity-dependent microphone but is cheap and therefore has an application where quality is not so important.

The **capacitor** or **condenser type** of microphone consists of two metal capacitor plates. One plate is fixed but the other is free to move and therefore acts as a movable diaphragm. Sound causes vibration of the diaphragm causing the distance between it and the fixed plate to vary and as a result changes the capacitance. An e.m.f. in series with a resistor is connected across the capacitor and the charging and discharge current produced causes a varying p.d. to be produced across the series resistor. This p.d. is amplified before passing out of the microphone.

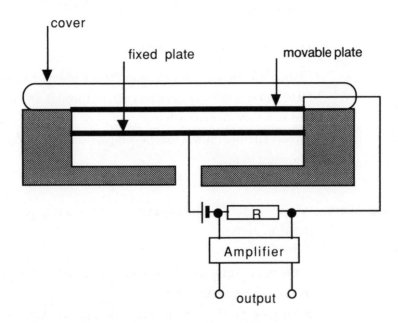

Figure 3.7.7   Capacitor or condenser microphone

Capacitor microphones can be made very small and are uni- or omni-directional. Because of their exceptionally high quality these microphones are used in broadcasting, on the stage and for public address systems.

Carbon microphones   Carbon microphones in their simplest form consist of a fixed piece of carbon shaped in the form of a cup, separated by a layer of carbon granules from another piece of carbon which is in the form of a dome and positioned at the bottom of a cone-shaped diaphragm (see figure 3.7.8). This piece of carbon is free to move and vibrates when sound waves strike the diaphragm. Compression of the granules decreases its resistance, whilst a decrease in pressure leads to an increase in the resistance.

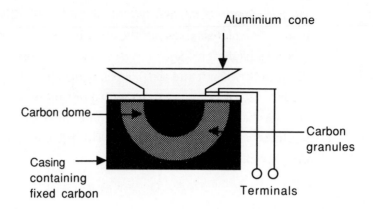

Figure 3.7.8 Carbon microphone

Carbon microphones are used in the telephone system. The system provides 50 V, and this drives a varying current through the microphone as the resistance varies in accordance with movements of the diaphragm. The quality of the carbon microphones is low in comparison with the other microphones described so far.

Loudspeakers When selecting a loudspeaker it is important to pay attention to the following three properties:

1 the impedance, which must match up to the impedance of the amplifier for maximum power transfer;
2 the power rating, i.e. the maximum power that the speaker can supply, above which it is possible to permanently damage the loudspeaker; and
3 the frequency response, which is the range of frequencies that the speaker can reproduce. For good speakers, it should be at the same level over the whole audiofrequency range.

The symbol for the loudspeaker is shown in figure 3.7.9. There are two main types of loudspeakers: the moving-coil type and the crystal type.

Figure 3.7.9 Speaker symbol

Moving-coil loudspeaker The basic construction is shown in figure 3.7.10. A varying current passing through the coil of the speaker causes it to vibrate in and out of the pole pieces of the permanent magnet. The cone of the speaker is attached to the coil and therefore vibrates at the same frequency. This in turn causes the surrounding air to vibrate and sound is produced at the same frequency as that of the a.c.

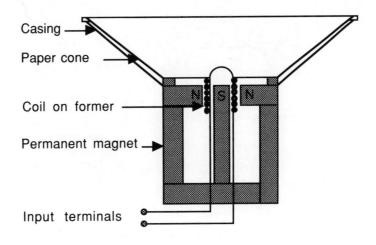

Casing

Paper cone

Coil on former

Permanent magnet

Input terminals

Figure 3.7.10 Moving-coil loudspeaker

For this type of speaker, common values for its impedance are 4 Ω, 8 Ω and 16 Ω, while the maximum value obtained is around 80 Ω.

Crystal-type loudspeaker This type operates on the principle that a varying p.d. applied across opposite faces of a crystal causes the crystal to vibrate and produce sound at the same frequency as the a.c. The construction is very similar to that of the crystal microphone of figure 3.7.6. Its impedance is of the order of about 1 kΩ and the frequency response is between 3 kHz and 40 kHz. This is the high-frequency end of the audio range and as a result it is used in multispeaker units as a tweeter to reproduce the treble (high-frequency) notes.

In general, speakers are not very good at converting electrical energy to sound energy. The smaller the speaker the more inefficient it is; small speakers are less than 20% efficient in many cases. For larger speakers the efficiency is around 50% at low power operation.

Record pick-up

Figure 3.7.11 Pick-up symbol

This transducer converts vibrations into electrical signals. The vibrations are produced by the grooves cut into the records and are the musical sounds stored on the disc.

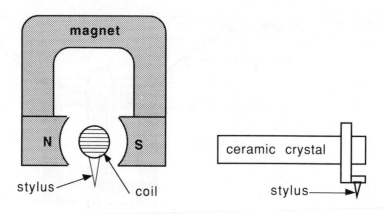

Figure 3.7.12 Magnetic and ceramic/crystal cartridges

Generally pick-ups consist of a **stylus** and a **cartridge** as shown in figure 3.7.12, both of which are contained in the pick-up arm of the turntable. The stylus fits into the groove and is made to vibrate by the wavy sides of the groove in the disc as the record revolves on the turntable. The vibrations of the stylus are translated into electrical signals by the cartridge, of which the **magnetic** and **ceramic** are the two basic types.

Magnetic cartridges These cover a whole range of different types: moving-coil, moving-iron, moving-magnet, induced-magnet and variable-reluctance types. They give excellent reproduction and depending on the design they can have a range of impedances from 50 Ω to 100 kΩ.

All these types of cartridges depend on the fact that relative movement is produced between the coil and a magnetic field, leading to the induction of an e.m.f. in the order of 5 mV to 10 mV. All magnetic types are known as velocity devices because the magnitude of the induced voltage depends on the velocity of the stylus movements rather than its amplitude.

The **moving-coil** type consists of a pair of tiny coils mounted on rockable mountings between the pole pieces of a magnet. Each coil picks up vibrations in one plane only. The coils are low-impedance coils, having few turns and therefore giving a very low output. As a result preamplification is needed to boost the output signal. The **moving-iron** method was used extensively in early mono pick-ups. Here the stylus causes movement of an armature which is enclosed between the pole of a permanent magnet. Movement of the stylus leads to changes of the field through the coil of the armature and the corresponding induction of a voltage.

Ceramic cartridges   These pick-ups make use of the piezoelectric effect and consist of two slices of material, such as barium titinate or lead zirconate titinate, set at an angle so that they are placed under stress by the stylus movement. The deformation of these crystals leads to the production of an e.m.f. of the order of about 100 mV. The e.m.f. is proportional to the amplitude of the recording signal. These cartridges generally have good frequency response and should be used with loads of between 1 MΩ and 2 MΩ.

Stereo pick-up   Stereo sound is recorded on both sides of right-angled grooves cut into the disc. One side carries the right-hand signal and the other side the left-hand signal. The pick-up is carried out by two cartridges housed in the same package and the audiofrequency signals are separated and amplified in different right and left channel amplifiers; see figure 3.7.13.

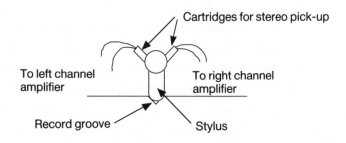

Figure 3.7.13   Stereo pick-up

Compact disc pick-up   The disc consists of clear polycarbonate plastic. Audio signals are recorded on it in the form of tiny pits of varying lengths and spacing in the surface of the disc. The disc is silvered and covered with a protective material. A beam of laser light is passed through a partly reflecting mirror and is focused onto the pits on the disc from the other side through the coating. The reflected beam is focused onto a photodiode which converts the information contained in the pits into digital electrical signals. The tracks start from near the centre of the disc and end just before reaching the edge. The disc rotates at between 200 and 500 r.p.m., the pick-up moving across the disc reading the encoded information.

Record and playback heads   These are found on tape recorders and cassette players. Both of these devices make use of the sound stored by magnetising the iron oxide or chromium oxide layer of a plastic tape. Each head unit consists of two coils wound onto a ring-shaped magnetic core so that they operate in antiphase. The front of the ring has a gap (pole pieces) which is filled with a non-magnetic material called **shim**; see figure 3.7.14.

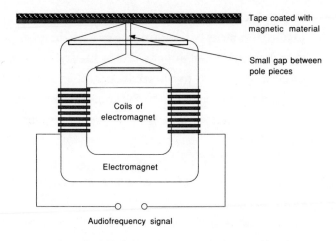

Tape coated with
magnetic material

Small gap between
pole pieces

Coils of
electromagnet

Electromagnet

Audiofrequency signal

Figure 3.7.14 Record/playback head

Sound picked up by a microphone is converted into audiofrequency electrical
signals. This signal is fed into the coils of the record head to produce a magnetic
field which varies in strength and causes magnetisation of the tiny particles in
the tape. The strength of the magnetisation depends on the amplitude of the
signal as that particular part of the tape passes the tape head. The magnetised
tape can be considered as having regions of tiny magnets as shown in figure
3.7.15, the length of the individual magnets being dependent on the frequency
of the a.c. Low frequencies and high tape speeds produce longer regions than
high frequencies and low tape speeds.

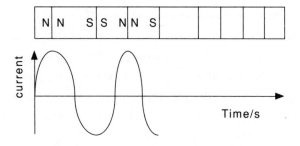

Figure 3.7.15 Magnetised tape

As the magnetisation curve (shown in figure 3.7.16) possesses non-linear regions
it is essential to have some form of biasing to avoid distortion of the audio
signal recorded on the tape. This is commonly done by superimposing an a.c.
waveform of much higher frequency than the highest audiofrequency onto the
waveform being recorded. The result of this is to allow the recording signal to
operate in the linear region of the magnetisation curve; the high-frequency a.c.
is not recorded.

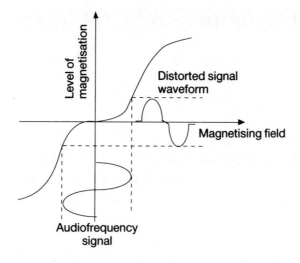

Figure 3.7.16 Distortion of signal due to magnetisation curve

Playback can be achieved by using the same head or a separate playback head. The magnetised tape must run over the head at the same constant speed as during the recording process. Any variation in the speed will lead to variation in the pitch of the sound, causing distortions such as **wow** (low-frequency variations) and **flutter** (high-frequency variations). In passing over the head a varying e.m.f. is induced, at the same frequency as the recording frequency, in the coils of the electromagnet. This voltage is then amplified and used to reproduce the original sound.

A separate head is required to erase information on a tape. It contains an electromagnet in which there is a much larger gap so that much more tape can be covered. The erase head is placed before the record head (and is fed with the same bias a.c. signal) and the gradually decreasing amplitude of the signal demagnetises the tape.

Questions

1 What is (a) an input transducer and (b) an output transducer?

2 List a number of transducers and state the energy changes involved in their operation.

3 Describe the operation of one velocity-dependent and one amplitude-dependent microphone.

4 Describe, with an appropriate diagram, the operation of a moving-coil loudspeaker.

5 What properties should be considered when selecting a loudspeaker?

6 Name two transducers used in record players and describe their operation.

7 Describe the operation of record/playback heads of a tape recorder.

8 What are 'flutter' and 'wow' and how are they produced?

4 Measuring instruments and techniques

4.1 Types of meters

Measurement is necessary in electronics to obtain information about a particular circuit. The three basic electrical quantities, voltage, current and resistance, are measured using various instruments, the symbols of which are shown in figure 4.1.1.

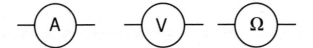

Figure 4.1.1 Meter symbols: ammeter, voltmeter and ohmmeter

Voltage, e.m.f. and p.d. are measured using a **voltmeter**, millivoltmeter, microvoltmeter or a **multimeter**, set to the appropriate range. Current is measured using an **ammeter**, milliammeter, microammeter or a **multimeter**, set to the appropriate range, and resistance is measured using an **ohmmeter** or a **multimeter**, set to the appropriate range.

Another very important instrument is the **oscilloscope**, sometimes referred to as the **cathode ray oscilloscope** (CRO). This can be used to measure voltage, frequency and phase difference or to display a waveform.

Ammeters and voltmeters

Most ammeters and voltmeters are of the moving-coil type. They have a rectangular coil which rotates within the field of a permanent magnet when a current passes through it. Attached to the coil is a very light pointer which moves relative to a fixed scale and a small hair-spring which is used to return the coil to its undeflected position. The meter is designed so that the deflection of the coil is directly proportional to the current flowing through it and if the resistance is constant it is also proportional to the voltage placed across it.

Moving-coil meters have what is called a 'basic movement' that has two electrical properties related to it. These are the **coil resistance** and the **full-scale deflection** (f.s.d.) current (the current needed for the needle to swing from zero to the other end of the scale). The **sensitivity** of a meter is related to the amount of current required to produce f.s.d. A perfect ammeter should offer no **impedance** (opposition) to current flow, so therefore the tiniest current would cause a deflection. A good voltmeter is one which has a very high impedance and therefore requires very little current to operate. The **sensitivity** of a voltmeter is the total resistance per unit volt, more commonly expressed as ohms per volt, and is calculated using the following formula:

$$\text{sensitivity} = \frac{\text{total meter resistance}}{\text{voltage needed for f.s.d.}} \text{ ohms/volt}$$

The ohmmeter

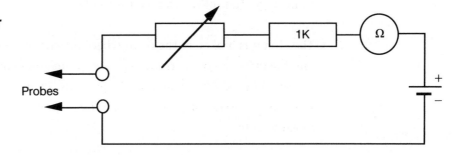

Figure 4.1.2 The ohmmeter

An ohmmeter consists of a 1.5 V or 3 V battery which drives a current through the component under test. The value of the current depends on the resistance of the component and therefore with a properly calibrated scale the position of the pointer gives the resistance of the component.

The multimeter The multimeter is a single meter that can be used to measure voltage, current and resistance. Most types can also measure both alternating (a.c.) and direct (d.c) currents and voltages. In addition, they contain a range switch which allows precise readings to be taken. Multimeters are either of the moving-coil type or of the digital type.

Moving-coil multimeters are somewhat difficult to use and therefore it is essential that the user notes the mode, the range setting for that mode and the correct meter scale to read. The range used depends on the mode/range switch, a multiposition rotary switch, whose position determines the mode (current, voltage or resistance) and hence the range. The scales on the meter are arranged as follows: ohms on the top with zero at the far right and infinity at the extreme left. Next is either the a.c. scale (red) or the d.c. scales (black), both of which measure from left to right, i.e. zero on the left and the maximum of that range on the right.

Digital multimeters have no moving parts. They consist of an **analogue-to-digital** converter (A/D converter) with a very high input resistance. Readings are displayed directly on a liquid crystal display (LCD) and both mode selection and range setting are selected by push switches.

4.2 Measuring current, voltage and resistance

Measuring current

Current is measured using either an ammeter or a multimeter and is measured in amps, milliamps or microamps. The way in which current is measured is the same, regardless of which meter is used.

The circuit is broken at the point where the current measurement is required and the meter is connected in series with the other components of the circuit as shown in figure 4.2.1. Note that the positive terminal of the meter is connected to the positive side of the circuit and the negative terminal is connected to the negative side.

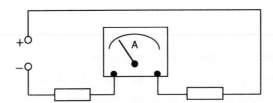

Figure 4.2.1 Measuring current

Measuring voltage

In electronics most voltage measurement is in fact a measure of the difference in voltage between two regions of a circuit. This is called the **potential difference** or **p.d.** and is measured in volts. Potential is measured with respect to zero, ground or the negative side of the circuit.

To measure a voltage or a p.d. the voltmeter is connected across (in parallel with) the component, as shown in figure 4.2.2. Note that the negative side of the meter is connected to the negative side of the component and the positive side of the meter to the positive of the component.

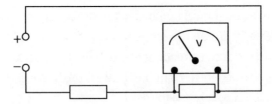

Figure 4.2.2 Measuring voltage

Measuring resistance

Resistance is the opposition presented by a component to the flow of a current. It is measured in ohms and is usually measured using a multimeter.

To measure resistance, the meter is first switched to the highest ohms range. It is zeroed by touching the two leads together and turning the zero adjust of the meter until the pointer is on zero. The component is connected between the leads and the position of the pointer noted. If the pointer is not approximately in the middle of the scale then the range should be changed to bring the pointer into the middle. It is important to zero on the new range before reading the scale. The resistance is the scale reading multiplied by the range setting. A meter set to measure resistance should never be connected across a component in which a current is flowing.

Using a digital multimeter, the resistance mode is set and different ranges are selected until the reading is displayed. The reading is either in ohms or in kilohms.

Comparison of analogue and digital multimeters

Analogue meters are more difficult to read and hence are more likely to result in reading errors, particularly when the pointer is resting between scale markings. With an analogue meter the reading is continuous on a continuous scale and is capable of displaying slow input changes. The input resistance varies with the range but is of the order of a few kilohms. This means that the meter will take some current from the circuit for its operation. Batteries are needed for when the meter is used in the resistance mode only.

Digital meters are much easier to read and so reading errors are less likely. The input is discontinuous and is based on the sample rate of the A/D converter. The reading displayed changes by a single digit. Input resistance is usually very high for d.c., about 10 MΩ, and somewhat lower for a.c. but still much higher than for analogue meters. Batteries are needed for *all* operations of the meter, including the display, and they therefore need replacing much more frequently than those used in analogue meters.

4.3 The oscilloscope

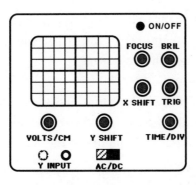

Figure 4.3.1 A typical oscilloscope

The oscilloscope as shown in figure 4.3.1 is sometimes called the **cathode ray oscilloscope** (CRO). It is used to produce a trace of voltage connected to its inputs on a screen and to enable measurements to be conducted on the trace.

A CRO consists of a cathode ray tube which produces and projects a beam of electrons onto a phosphor screen where it produces a spot of light. The design of the tube allows the beam to be focused and the brilliance to be controlled. There is also a power supply and two sets of deflection plates which are controlled by electronic circuits. One set of plates, called the 'Y' plates, causes the electron beam to move up and down, whilst the other set, the 'X' plates, produces horizontal movement of the electron beam.

How it works

The voltage to be measured, called the input voltage, is connected to the input terminals of the oscilloscope. The spot which is produced moves steadily across the screen from left to right. As it moves across the screen, it is moved up and down by the input voltage supplied. This results in the spot tracing out a graph.

The spot is moved from left to right by the 'X' deflection plates. These are supplied by a 'ramp' voltage, produced by the electronics inside the oscilloscope, which causes the spot to jump back to the left whenever it reaches to the extreme right. The new trace produced falls on top of the previous trace and because of the persistence of vision one stationary graph is seen, as in figure 4.3.2.

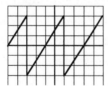

Figure 4.3.2 Ramp voltage

Using the oscilloscope

With no signal connected to the input terminals, switch on using the on/off switch and wait a few minutes for the oscilloscope to warm up. A line or a spot going from left to right should be seen.

If no trace appears, turn up the intensity using the **brilliance** control and adjust the **X shift** and **Y shift** controls until the trace is found. If a LOCATE button is present then pressing this will point out the current position of the trace.

When the trace is obtained on the screen, it should be centred and the intensity reduced as much as possible. It should then be focused using the focus control to give a sharp line or spot.

If there is an AC/DC switch then press DC even if it is desired to measure a.c. The AC setting is used only if it is required to separate a small a.c. from a large d.c.

Connect the voltage to the input terminals in order to see the shape of the voltage. It might be necessary to adjust the **trigger level** in order to make the trace stationary. Then adjust the VOLTS/CM (or VOLTS/DIV) control, so that the trace covers about half to two-thirds the height of the screen, and adjust the TIME/DIV (or **time base**) control, so that the trace shows from three to six cycles.

4.4 Measuring with the CRO

The oscilloscope screen is covered with a 1 cm × 1 cm grid which can be treated as a piece of graph paper with the axes running through the middle. The vertical direction measures voltage and the horizontal direction measures time.

Measuring voltage

The VOLTS/CM or VOLTS/DIV setting determines the number of volts represented by each centimetre division in the vertical direction. For instance, if the setting is on 0.2 V, then 1 cm upwards measures 0.2 V.

To measure a voltage, connect the oscilloscope probes on either side of the component across which the p.d. is required. Note the height (in centimetres) of the trace produced by the input voltage and multiply this by the setting of the VOLTS/CM control.

An alternative way to do this is to switch off the time base so that the trace is no longer moving across the screen. A vertical line should be obtained which should be centred by adjusting the X shift. The height of this vertical line is the **peak–peak voltage**. Use the grid to measure the height of the line, divide this value by two and multiply by the VOLTS/CM setting.

For example, the traces in figure 4.4.1 show a wave with a total height 6 cm. If the VOLTS/CM setting is 0.5 V/div then the peak–peak voltage is 0.5 × 6 = 3.0 V and the peak voltage is half of this, 1.5 V.

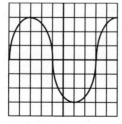   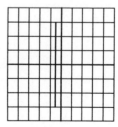

a   b

Figure 4.4.1 Waveform (a) with time base on; and (b) with time base off

Measuring time   The TIME/DIV or TIME/CM setting determines the amount of time represented by each centimetre division in the horizontal direction. For instance, if the setting is on 1 ms, then 1 cm horizontally measures 1 ms.

To measure the time taken for one cycle (i.e. the period), having obtained a steady trace, measure the number of centimetres occupied by one cycle of the trace and multiply this by the TIME/DIV setting. For example if one cycle takes up 4.5 cm and the TIME/DIV is set on 100 μs, then the total time for the cycle is 4.5×100 μs $= 450$ μs, i.e. 0.45 ms, or 0.00045 seconds.

Measuring frequency   The frequency is actually calculated from the relationship

$$\text{frequency} = \frac{1}{\text{period}} \quad \text{or} \quad f = \frac{1}{T}$$

where f is the frequency in Hz and T is the period in seconds. Using the above example,

$$\text{frequency} = \frac{1}{0.00045} = \frac{1000}{0.45} = 2222.22 \text{ Hz}$$

Measuring phase difference   The phase difference between two waveforms of the same frequency can be obtained by measuring the time period between similar points on the two waves, for example between the two peaks.

This is done as outlined above by counting the number of divisions separating one peak from the other and multiplying by the TIME/DIV setting. If the period of the waveform is also obtained then the phase difference can be given as a fraction of a cycle either in radians or in degrees. The formula for this is given below:

$$\text{phase difference (radians)} = \frac{\text{time between peaks}}{\text{period of waveform}} \times 2\pi \text{ radians}$$

$$\text{phase difference (degrees)} = \frac{\text{time between peaks}}{\text{period of waveform}} \times 360 \text{ degrees}$$

In figure 4.4.2 the peaks of the two waves are separated by 1 cm or one division. If the time base was set on 0.1 ms/div and the period of this waveform was 0.4 ms, then using the formulae above, the phase difference would be $(0.1/0.4) \times 2\pi = \pi/2$ radians, or $(0.1/0.4) \times 360 = 90$ degrees.

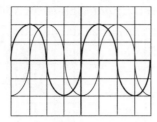

Figure 4.4.2 Two waves with a phase difference of 90°

Phase relationships using the X and Y inputs

The traces shown in figure 4.4.3 are obtained if sine waves of the same frequencies and amplitudes are simultaneously applied to the X and Y inputs of the oscilloscope, with the time base turned off.

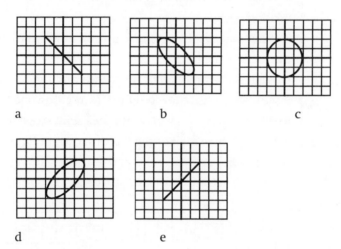

a   b   c

d   e

Figure 4.4.3 Phase difference between waves having the same frequencies: (a) zero; (b) 45°; (c) 90°; (d) 135°; (e) 180°

Lissajous figures

If the sine waves are of different frequencies then the traces are called Lissajous figures (see figure 4.4.4). The figures can be used to determine the frequency ratio of the two waves, i.e. the frequency of one divided by the frequency of the other, given by the following formula:

$$\frac{\text{frequency of Y input signal}}{\text{frequency of X input signal}} = \frac{\text{number of loops touching } y \text{ axis}}{\text{number of loops touching the } x \text{ axis}}$$

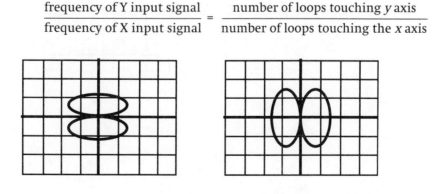

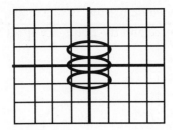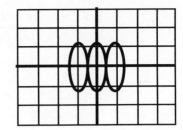

Figure 4.4.4 Lissajous figures

Questions

1 What is the purpose of the cathode ray tube in the oscilloscope?

2 What is the function of the 'X' and the 'Y' deflection plates within the oscilloscope?

3 What makes the spot move up and down as it moves across the screen of the oscilloscope?

4 What is the function of the X shift and the Y shift?

5 Describe in full how to set up the oscilloscope for use.

6 Describe how you would use the oscilloscope to measure a voltage.

7 Describe how each of the traces shown in figure 4.4.5 is produced; state whether they are a.c. or d.c. and estimate the value of the voltages if the VOLTS/DIV settings are (a) 0.5; (b) 0.4; (c) 1.0 V/div.

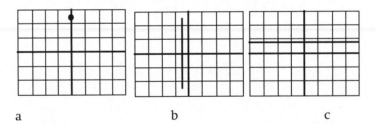

a   b   c

Figure 4.4.5

8 Work out the voltages (peak–peak and r.m.s. voltages) shown in figure 4.4.6.

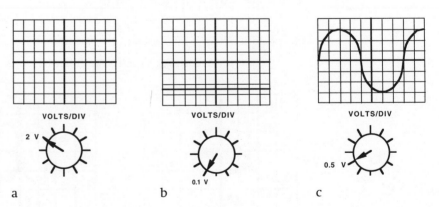

VOLTS/DIV   VOLTS/DIV   VOLTS/DIV

2 V   0.1 V   0.5 V

a   b   c

Figure 4.4.6

9 Describe how you would use the oscilloscope to measure frequency.

10 Work out the period and the frequency of the waveforms shown in figure 4.4.7.

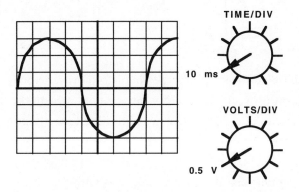

a

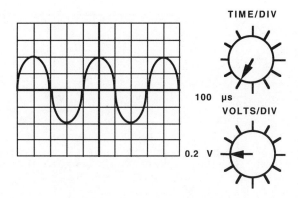

b

Figure 4.4.7

11 Describe how you would use the oscilloscope to measure phase difference and calculate the phase difference in the traces shown in figure 4.4.8 .

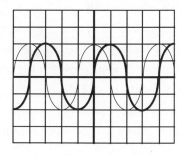   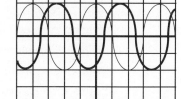

a   b

Figure 4.4.8

12 Work out the frequency ratio for the Lissajous figures shown in figure 4.4.4 above.

5 Construction techniques and fault finding

5.1 Prototype board Construction on prototype boards can prove to be tricky for many students due to the difficulty in relating the rows of holes on the board with actual points on a circuit diagram. The method outlined here is simple to apply and is also suitable for copper stripboard and veroboard constructions.

Prototype board construction starts with the circuit diagram, as shown in figure 5.1.1.

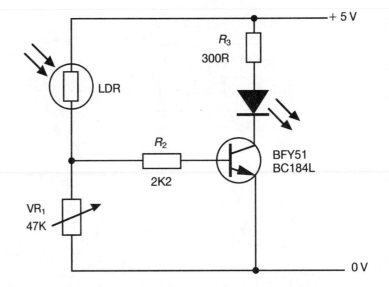

Figure 5.1.1 Circuit to be constructed on a prototype board

First, each junction is identified and a ring is drawn around it. A junction is any place on the circuit diagram where two or more components are connected either together or to wires leading to or from the circuit. Once identified and ringed, as shown in figure 5.1.2, each junction is carefully numbered. Generally '1' is used to identify the junction with the positive supply rail, and junctions of components having multiple legs, such as transistors, are numbered consecutively, with due regard to the physical arrangement of the legs (e.g. see junctions 4, 5 and 6).

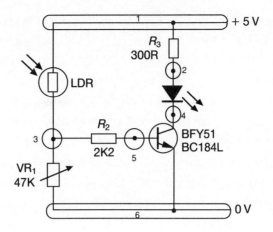

Figure 5.1.2 Circuit diagram with junctions identified, ringed and numbered

On completion of this process the number of rows of holes required on the prototype board is determined as being the same as the number of junctions. The rows of holes should then also be numbered, but note that it is not essential to number every row, since if this is done the board will be very cramped. It is therefore more common to number every other row of holes or every third row if the length of the component leads will allow it.

The components as identified in figure 5.1.3 can then be added to the board as described below.

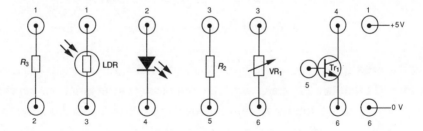

Figure 5.1.3 The components showing track numbers to which they are attached

Starting with the resistors:

1 R_3 goes across from junction 1 to junction 2 and therefore should be connected across from row 1 to row 2 of the prototype board.

2 R_2 goes from junction 3 to junction 5 and therefore rows 3 and 5.

3 VR$_1$ goes between junctions 3 and 6.

4 The LDR is inserted from junction 1 to junction 3 and therefore goes from row 1 to row 3.

5 The LED is inserted between junctions 2 and 4 and is therefore connected between rows 2 and 4.

6 The three legs of the transistor are connected to junctions 4, 5 and 6. If the length and orientation of the legs allow, the transistor can be inserted with its legs in the respective rows of the board. However, if this is difficult to do directly, the transistor can be placed in an entirely different part of the board, using three consecutive rows of holes for each, and then single-stranded wire can be used to link the respective legs to the appropriate rows of the main circuit.

7 Row 1, corresponding to the first junction, could in fact be the positive supply rail. Alternatively, as it is easier not to do this, row 1 can be linked to the positive supply rail and similarly row 7 to the negative supply rail with pieces of single-stranded wire. Coloured wires are then used to link these rails to the positive and the negative of the power supply respectively. The whole construction is shown in figure 5.1.4.

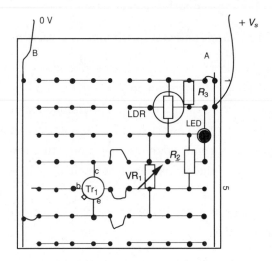

Figure 5.1.4   Prototype board layout diagram

Using the prototype board for IC circuits

A circuit centred around an integrated circuit (IC) is constructed in a slightly different way. The numbering of the junctions depends on the number of pins on the IC chip and also must allow for the fact that the chip makes use of both sides of the prototype board.

For the circuit shown in figure 5.1.5 the board can be divided into two halves, say A and B. Four rows of holes on side A are needed for pins 1, 2, 3 and 4 and on side B another four rows are needed for pins 5, 6, 7 and 8. Therefore, additional junctions will have to be made using rows above or below those used for the IC pins. If the rows containing the IC pins are A1 to A4 and B1 to B4 then row A5 could be used for the only additional junction. In the circuit shown in figure 5.1.5 only one additional junction is required, that between the R_3 resistor and the LED. Note, though, that the numbering used here need bear no relationship to the numbering on the prototype board, since it is arbitrary. This example simply attempts to illustrate the process to be adopted when setting up circuits on a prototype board.

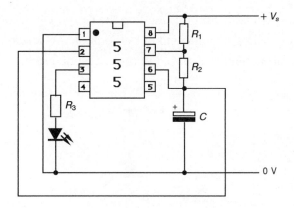

Figure 5.1.5 Simple circuit using the 555 timer IC

In the circuit shown in figure 5.1.5, pin 2 of the IC is connected to pin 6. This connection could be made using a piece of single-stranded wire placed in row A1, linking across to row B3 (see figure 5.1.6a). However this is untidy and prevents easy access to the chip. A neater solution, as shown in figure 5.1.6b, would be to take the wire down to row A6, place another piece across the dividing channel to row B6 and then take a third piece from this row up to row B3.

Pin 1 and the negative side of the LED should be linked directly to the negative supply rail. Capacitor *C* should have its positive terminal placed in row B6 and its negative terminal placed directly into the negative rail. IC pin 8 should be connected to the positive by linking row A1 to the positive supply rail. The completed construction is shown in figure 5.1.6b.

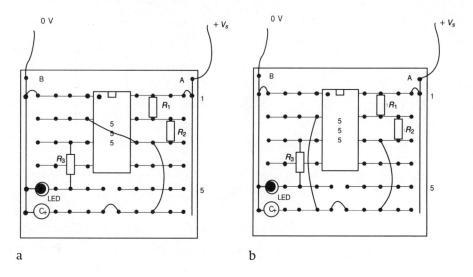

Figure 5.1.6 Prototype board layout with IC circuit: (a) preventing easy access to the chip; and (b) a neater solution utilising row B6

5.2 Matrix board

Many students find this method the easiest when constructing a circuit, because the physical arrangement of the components resembles, in a very precise way, the arrangement depicted in the circuit diagram.

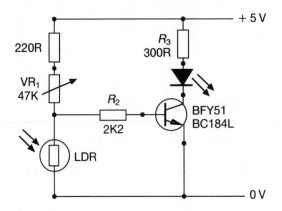

Figure 5.2.1 Circuit layout diagram with junctions marked with dots

Crosses or dots are used to mark the positions on the circuit diagram (see figure 5.2.1) where components are joined together or where components are joined to wire conductors. **Press-fit terminal pins** are pushed in at roughly these positions on a piece of blank matrix board as shown in figure 5.2.2.

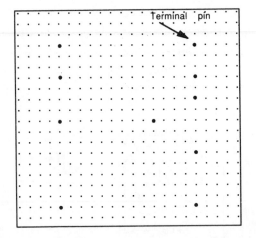

Figure 5.2.2 Matrix board with terminal pins in place

Conductor paths are then linked using either bare copper wire or single-stranded insulated wire soldered to the terminal pins, and the components positioned to match the circuit diagram, care being taken to ensure correct polarity on all relevant components. Components which are to be mounted off the board should have multi-stranded wires soldered to their terminals and connected to the relevant terminal pins on the board. Finally multi-stranded power supply leads (colour-coded red-positive and black-negative) are fitted. The completed circuit is shown in figure 5.2.3.

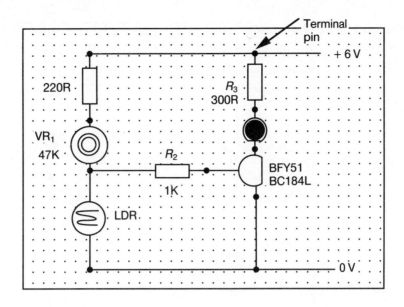

Figure 5.2.3 Completed circuit laid out on a matrix board

5.3 Copper stripboard

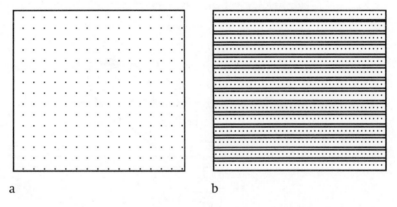

a   b

Figure 5.3.1 Copper stripboard (a) top side and (b) reverse side

Like prototype board construction this type starts by identifying and numbering the junctions on the circuit diagram. Each copper strip is then numbered from 1 up to the number of junctions and marked using a fine-tipped felt pen. Components are then connected between strips, being mounted from the non-copper side of the board and soldered onto the copper tracks below. Single-stranded tinned copper wire is used to link tracks and should be mounted in the same way as all components. It is usual, although not essential, to mount components by starting with wire links, followed by resistors and other passive components and then finally components which are more delicate, such as transistors and ICs. Components can be fitted so that they are resting on the surface of the board and great care should be taken to ensure correct polarity of components such as diodes, electrolytic capacitors, transistors and thyristors. The circuit of the light-operated switch is used to illustrate this method of construction and the process is shown in figures 5.3.2 and 5.3.3.

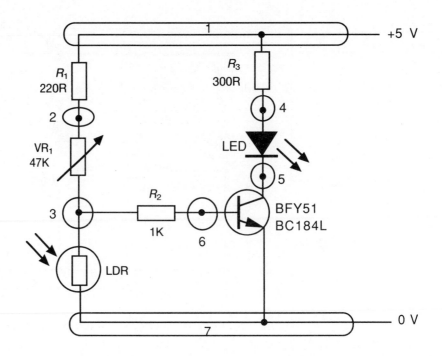

Figure 5.3.2 Light switch circuit with junctions identified

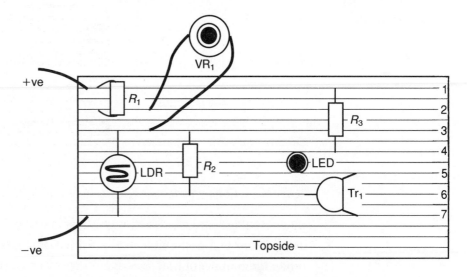

Figure 5.3.3 Copper stripboard layout diagram of light switch

Constructing IC circuits making use of **DIL (dual in line) packages** begins with the positioning of the IC socket(s) so that each pair of legs sits on a single track, the whole IC occupying a number of parallel copper tracks. As each pin has to be isolated from all others it is necessary to break the track linking each pair of pins as in figure 5.3.4. This is done using either a drill or a specialist tool called a **spot face cutter.** Care should be taken to ensure that breaks are clean and that no debris exists between tracks.

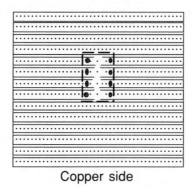

Copper side

Figure 5.3.4 Mounting of an 8-pin DIL IC on copper stripboard

Off-the-board components are connected to the board using multi-stranded insulating wire. Multi-stranded wires are also used for power supply connections and for linking boards.

5.4 Printed circuit board

Of all the circuit construction methods this requires the greatest amount of thinking and skill in its preparation. Small-scale production is usually achieved in one of the following three ways:

1 The first and perhaps the simplest is to draw the track layout directly onto the cleaned surface of the copper clad board and to cover over the lines with etch-resist ink from an **etch-resist pen**. The board is then left to dry before immersion in the etch tank.

2 The second method involves the use of **etch-resist transfers** to mark out the layout tracks onto the surface of the board. The result is neat precise artwork which when etched gives a very professional finish.

3 The third and last method, known as the **photographic** method, involves the use of specialist equipment such as an **ultra-violet exposure unit** and special **photo-resist boards**. As a result this is a more costly way of producing prototypes. However, it does enable multiple boards to be produced and also allows for modifications in the artwork. The artwork is produced as neatly as possible using p.c.b. transfers to re-create the track layout diagram on a transparency. This is then placed on the glass screen of the UV unit with the photo-resist board placed on top. The lid of the unit is closed and the board exposed for three to four minutes. Then the board is removed and placed in a developing tank containing sodium hydroxide for a short period, between a minute and a minute and a half, after which time it is removed and thoroughly washed under running water. Finally the board is etched by immersing it in the etch tank for between ten and twenty minutes depending on the strength of the solution.

For all three methods the etch tank contains a ferric chloride solution, which is kept about 10 °C above room temperature.

Producing the layout diagram and the p.c.b. artwork is perhaps the most difficult aspect of this method of construction. A simple way to begin this task is explained in steps 1 to 7 below and illustrated in figures 5.4.1 to 5.4.7. If the circuit consists of ICs then a transfer should be used to correctly position the IC pins on the board and it is essential that this is done as early as possible. Once the ICs are positioned then the tracks can be drawn free-hand with the etch-resist pen or constructed from the etch-resist transfers.

1 Position a piece of tracing paper above the circuit diagram and draw in the position of the junctions.

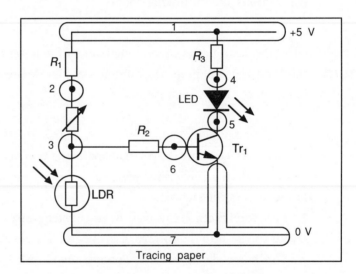

Figure 5.4.1 Marking out the junctions from the circuit diagram

2 Remove the circuit diagram and check the junctions and tracks drawn on the tracing paper.

110

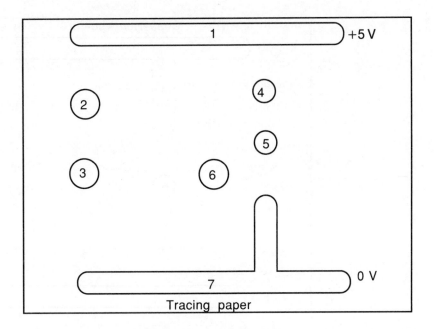

Figure 5.4.2 Tracing paper showing the positions of the junctions

3 Reverse and invert the tracing paper as shown in figure 5.4.3 to create the diagram to be transferred to the copper clad board.

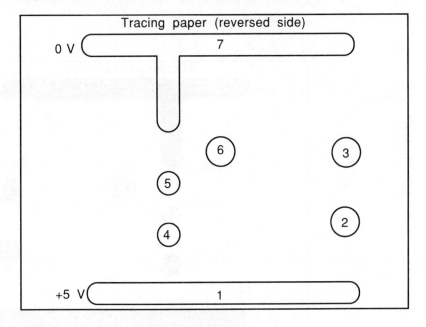

Figure 5.4.3 Tracing paper reversed and inverted

4 Transfer the drawing as shown in figure 5.4.4, to the clean copper clad board by either (a) placing a piece of carbon paper between the board and the tracing paper and tracing over it, or (b) copying the drawing directly onto the circuit board.

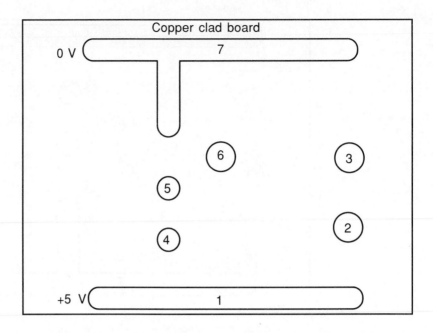

Figure 5.4.4 Junctions transferred onto a piece of copper clad board

5 Cover the tracks with ink from an etch-resist pen. Allow the board to dry and then place it in the etching tank. Once etched, remove it and thoroughly wash it under running water. Then dry the board and clean off the etch-resist using an appropriate solvent.

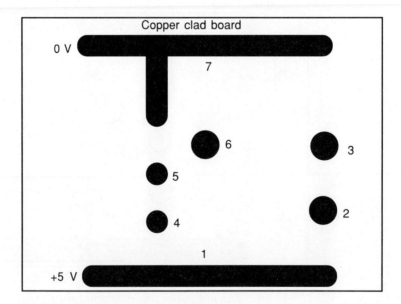

Figure 5.4.5 Etch-resist used to mark the tracks

6 Drill holes using a 0.1 mm drill bit at the positions where the components are to be mounted.

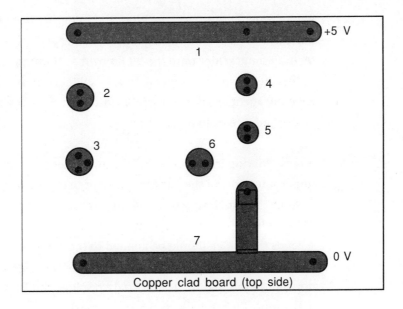

Figure 5.4.6 Holes drilled into the copper tracks for mounting the components

7 After cleaning the board, mount the components from the top side and solder onto the tracks below.

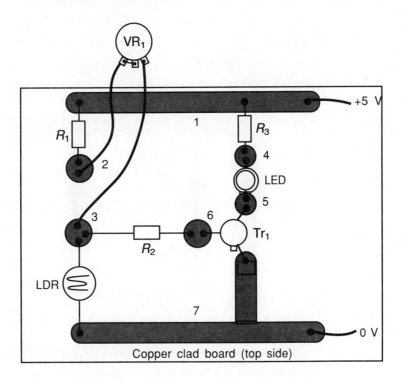

Figure 5.4.7 Components mounted onto the top side of the printed circuit board

5.5 Soldering   Soldering should be performed with due regard to safety. It should be carried out using a low-voltage soldering iron, operated from a transformer connected to the mains. The soldering iron should have a holder and the work should be placed on a heat-proof mat.

Before starting to solder, the **bit** of the soldering iron must be cleaned. This is done when it is hot by wiping it across a wet sponge or fine abrasive paper. Melting some solder onto the bit (known as **tinning**) and wiping that off in the sponge helps this cleaning process, as solder contains cores of flux, which is a cleaning agent. For a successful result all parts of the board to be soldered must be dry and free from dirt and grease.

A hot soldering iron is essential if good solder joints are to be produced. It is important to make the joint hot but not to overheat it, as overheating can cause damage. The soldering iron should be placed so that it is touching both the lead to be soldered and the copper track to which it is to be joined. After a few seconds the solder should be applied to the track; it will melt onto the track and flow up around the base of the lead forming a wedge. Solder flows from cold to hot and therefore if the lead is cold no solder will flow around it or the solder may form a blob (see figure 5.5.1). Similarly, if the track is cold the solder will form a blob around the leg of the component. If the solder is not hot enough then the blob formed is dull and it is referred to as a **dry joint**. A dry joint is one which has failed to bond sufficiently strongly with the copper track and as a result it provides a poor conducting path for current. It can be put right by applying a clean soldering iron to the joint and leaving it long enough for it to melt the solder so that it flows properly. On the other hand a good solder joint as shown in figure 5.5.1 should have a mound of solder tapering up from the copper track around the leg of the component; the solder should look smooth and shiny when cooled.

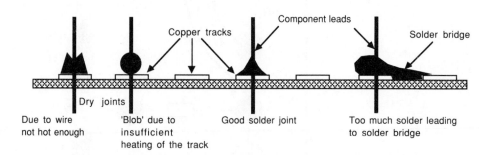

Figure 5.5.1 Examples of good and bad solder joints

Apart from dry joints, another problem to avoid is **solder bridges** linking tracks. This happens when too much solder is applied to a joint and an adjacent track is heated at the same time as the joint, perhaps by using a soldering iron bit which is too large. This situation should be dealt with immediately if it does occur. There are a number of ways of removing solder bridges, the simplest being to use a solder sucker or a desolder braid to remove the hot solder. If these are not available then you can try to make the solder flow away from the gap between the tracks by heating one or other of the tracks, tilting the board slightly and removing the excess solder on the tip of the soldering iron. This should then be wiped away and the process repeated until all the solder bridging the tracks has been removed.

Multi-stranded wires should be twisted and tinned before soldering. This prevents the individual fine strands from splaying out and so increasing the risk of shorting due to cross-linking.

Transistors can be damaged by excessive heat and therefore care should be taken not to heat these for too long a time when soldering. Better still a **heat shunt** or a pair of pliers should be used to grip the leg being soldered or desoldered to stop heat flowing into the body of the transistor.

When soldering is completed the board should be checked visually and by running a small screwdriver between the tracks to ensure that all the tracks are free, and that there are no dry joints which will undermine the proper functioning of the board.

5.6 Circuit faults

Circuit faults are of two main types: short-circuit and open-circuit faults. A **short-circuit fault** is one which is due to an unwanted connection which allows current to flow along a path (or paths) which are not part of the circuit design. The new path(s) might re-route some or all the current from the true path resulting in that region of the circuit failing to work correctly. An **open-circuit fault** is caused by a break in the circuit which prevents the flow of current to that part of the circuit. Both short-circuit and open-circuit faults can be caused by failure of individual components within the circuit as well as problems with connections.

Short-circuit faults

Short-circuit faults result from part of the circuit having a resistance lower than that of the surrounding components. This can be due to:

1 the failure of a component, leading to it having an abnormally low resistance;
2 the touching of uninsulated parts of the component terminal; or
3 the effects of moisture lying between conducting paths which create links of lower resistance than the components.

Short-circuit faults can be identified by the fact that the circuit, or that section of the circuit, draws an unusually large amount of current and, secondly, the voltage between two points joined by a short-circuit will be the same and may be significantly lower than expected.

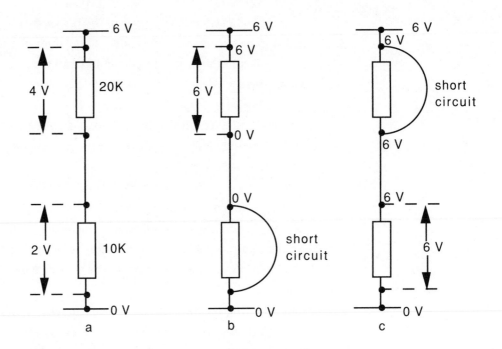

Figure 5.6.1 Short-circuit faults

Figure 5.6.1 illustrates short-circuit faults with resistors. The arrangement in figure 5.6.1a is the normal circuit; figures 5.6.1b and 5.6.1c show the voltage changes corresponding to a short-circuit across either of the two resistors.

Open-circuit faults

Open-circuit faults result from a part of the circuit having an extremely high resistance. This could be due to:

1 a break in the circuit;
2 the failure of a component leading to it having an unusually high resistance; or
3 an increase in the insulation at certain points, caused by dirt, grease or corrosion.

Open-circuit faults are identified by the fact that the current in that part of the circuit will be zero or very much reduced from the value expected and, secondly, the voltage difference across an open-circuit will be very high or significantly higher than that expected. Open-circuit faults for resistors are shown in figure 5.6.2.

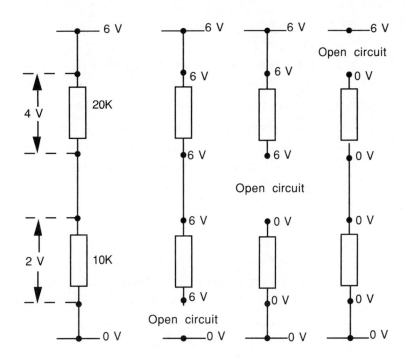

Figure 5.6.2 Open-circuit faults

5.7 Circuit testing

Having completed construction, the first thing to do is to carry out a thorough test of the circuit. This will involve a number of different procedures ranging from a **visual check** for faults to using equipment such as **meters**, **signal injectors** and **oscilloscopes** to test the circuit against the design specifications.

Testing a circuit is a painstaking exercise and it is important to persist until the fault is found. A step-by-step, logical approach should be used and notes should be kept of the tests carried out and the outcome of each test. The testing should follow the order: visual, power supply, active components and passive components.

Visual check

This should be done before power is connected to the circuit and attention should be paid to the following:

1 All components should be properly connected and the right way round (particularly transistors, LEDs, diodes and electrolytic capacitors) in the circuit.
2 All wire links should be located in the right places.
3 Power supply leads should be properly positioned on the board and of the correct polarity.
4 Check for dry solder joints (all joints should appear shiny and should be firmly holding the components' leads to the copper tracks of the circuit board).

117

5 Check for solder bridges (if in doubt run the blade of a screwdriver between the tracks).

6 Check for small pieces of copper between the tracks, particularly at the edges of freshly cut boards.

7 Breaks (both intentional and those that are not intentional) in the copper tracks should be checked.

If all is well then switch on the power to the circuit. If it doesn't work then follow through the remaining tests.

Testing the power supply   The above checks would have ensured proper connections of the power supply (positive and negative) to the board and therefore any further tests must employ some means of testing for a voltage level. A voltmeter or a logic probe is suitable for this and should be used to trace the voltage from the supply to the appropriate points on the board or terminals of components directly connected to the power supply (see figure 5.7.1).

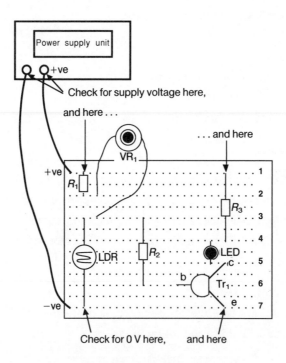

Figure 5.7.1 Checking voltage levels

If the expected voltage is not found at any of the points indicated in figure 5.7.1 then check for faulty wire(s) or connections back to the point where a voltage was last observed. Replace suspected wire(s) and remake connections as necessary. If the circuit is still not working then continue with the testing.

Testing active components

If the circuit contains a transistor as in the circuit of figure 5.7.1, then it is possible that this could be faulty. A piece of wire connected across the collector to the emitter as shown in figure 5.7.2 will short out the transistor.

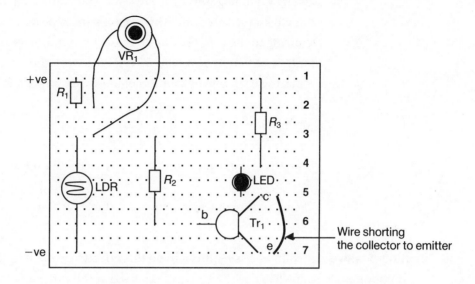

Figure 5.7.2 Testing transistor fault by shorting the collector–emitter terminals

If the output now works then the fault might lie with (a) the transistor or (b) the part of the circuit feeding the transistor. If the output stage did not work then all connections leading from the collector of the transistor should be checked. In the case of the circuit in figure 5.7.2 it is quite likely that the LED is faulty and should be replaced with a new one. To eliminate the transistor, check if it turns on when a 2.2 kΩ resistor is connected between its base and the positive supply (see figure 5.7.3).

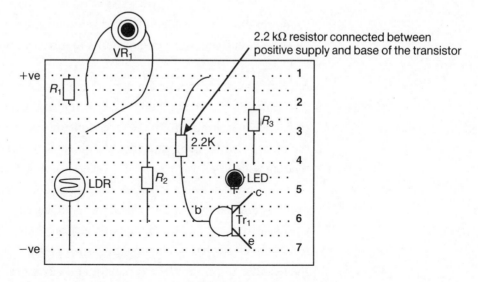

Figure 5.7.3 Testing that the transistor is still under the control of the base

119

If it does then the problem lies with the part of the circuit feeding the base and not with the transistor. However, if it still doesn't work, before concluding it is the transistor, disconnect the base by snipping close to the board and testing again by clipping the 2.2 kΩ resistor, still connected to the positive supply, directly to the base lead. This is to ensure that the base connection is not shorting to the zero line; in this case if the transistor doesn't switch on then it is faulty and should be replaced. If it does work then check for shorting before replacing it; if none is found then move on to next test.

An output which is on all the time indicates a short between the collector and the emitter of the transistor. This is either internal, in which case the transistor is faulty, or external and should be checked for on the board.

The procedure outlined above is suitable for testing all active components.

Testing passive components

A voltmeter is required to do this effectively and it is also useful to have some knowledge of the voltages expected at the various points in the circuit. If we continue to work with the circuit of figure 5.7.1 then we check the voltage across the resistors by connecting the negative terminal of the meter to the zero volt line of the circuit board and touch the positive meter lead to the side of the resistor connected to the positive side of the circuit. Starting with the LDR, check that the side that is connected to the zero volt line gives a zero reading on the voltmeter. Touch the other side of the LDR with the voltmeter lead and check that there is a voltage across it and that this varies as the intensity of light falling onto the LDR varies. Check that this voltage is being transmitted through to the base of the transistor.

When conducting this kind of test it is important to use the information above on short-circuit and open-circuit faults to interpret the result.

Apart from voltage measurements, resistance measurements can also be used to test components such as diodes and capacitors. A good diode should give a high resistance measurement in one direction and a low resistance measurement in the other, whilst a good capacitor should give an infinitely high resistance reading whichever way round. However, it is worth noting that an electrolytic capacitor must be connected the correct way round in the circuit to work properly and a meter in the resistance mode has an internal battery in which the negative is connected to the positive lead of the meter. Therefore when testing an electrolytic capacitor the positive lead of the meter should connect to the negative terminal of the capacitor and vice versa.

120

If the circuit makes use of an integrated circuit then the first thing to check is the power supply to the positive and negative pins. A voltmeter is required to check the input and output signals to and from the chip. For digital circuits it is better to use a logic probe for fault-finding and testing. The probe is a small hand-held device consisting of three light-emitting diodes which are used to indicate the logic state at the tip of the probe. These logic states are either 0 and 1 corresponding to low and high voltages of a relatively long duration. The third LED is used to indicate short duration pulses and relies on the use of additional circuitry to enlarge or stretch the pulse long enough to light the LED. The probe does not have an independent power supply and needs to be clipped onto the positive supply rail and the ground rail of the circuit. To test a digital IC, the point of the probe is touched onto the appropriate pins. A high voltage (logic 1) is indicated by the red LED; a low voltage (logic 0) by the green LED and the amber LED detects the logic level of a pulse train.

Component failure is due either to open-circuit or to short-circuit faults. If a component is suspected as the cause of the circuit failure then it should be removed and checked with a multimeter set on the ohms range to see if its resistance agrees with that expected. The component should then be replaced with a new component or with one which is known to be working correctly even if the above tests prove inconclusive.

Questions

1 Copy the circuit of figure 5.7.4 and identify and number each of the junctions.

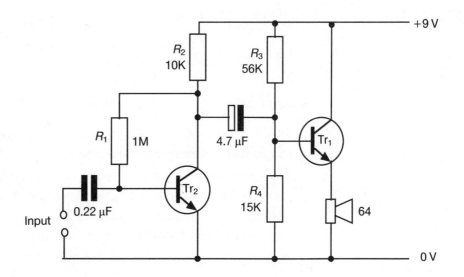

Figure 5.7.4

2 Draw the layout diagram for construction of the circuit from question 1 onto a prototype board.

3 Draw the varoboard layout diagram for the same circuit.

4 Describe the precautions you would take to ensure the safe construction of the circuit.

5 Describe the tests you would carry out to ensure that there are no faults with the circuit before switching on the power supply.

6 Describe what you would do if, after switching on the power and with a suitable input signal, there was no output from the speaker.

7 How would you test if the 15 kΩ resistor was shorting? What would be the effect on the output?

8 Design the printed circuit board artwork for the circuit in figure 5.7.4 and describe the processes involved in the construction of the p.c.b.

9 Look at the circuit of figure 5.7.5 and identify and list the obvious faults.

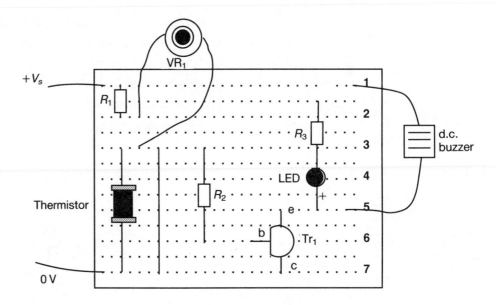

Figure 5.7.5

10 Draw the layout diagram for the circuit of question 9 with all the components properly in place and with all the faults removed.

11 If after connecting the circuit to the power supply and heating up the thermistor the circuit of question 9 doesn't work, describe how you would eliminate (a) the buzzer, (b) the LED and (c) the transistor from suspicion.

12 Describe what additional tests you would carry out to test the circuit of question 9 and suggest possible faults which would lead to the circuit still not working.

6 Component exercises

These are a series of exercises to enable you to practise the use of the prototype board for circuit construction and to develop your skill in the use of various instruments for measurement. They will also enable you to gain a practical understanding of some of the components studied in chapter 3.

The exercises would be of greater benefit after you have read chapter 3; however if you wish to start here then chapter 3 can be used for reference to support any of the exercises.

Carry out each exercise carefully by doing all the practical activities and answering as many questions as possible.

6.1 Resistors and resistance

Exercise 1
Identifying resistors

This a simple exercise designed to help you use the resistor colour codes to work out resistor values.

Materials

You will need a box of assorted fixed-value resistors having either four or five coloured bands and the resistor colour code (see section 3.5).

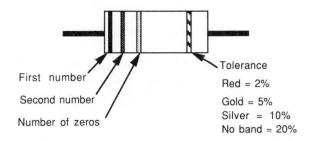

Figure 6.1.1   Colour marking on fixed-value resistors

Method

1 Obtain the box of resistors provided.
2 Copy out table 6.1.1 and write 1 in the first column.
3 Taking the first resistor, read the bands from left to right as in figure 6.1.1, and write in the colours of the first, second and third bands in the appropriate columns of the table.

4 Using the colour code, work out the value of the resistor and enter this in the table using the BS 1852 code.

5 Repeat this exercise for each of the remaining resistors, writing 2, 3, 4 etc. in the first column each time.

Table 6.1.1 Table needed for exercises 1 and 2

Resistor	Band			Value Ω	
	1st	2nd	3rd	Coded	Measured

Exercise 2
Measuring resistance

This exercise will help you practise measuring resistance, using first an analogue (moving-coil) multimeter and then a digital multimeter.

Materials

You will require a box of resistors, an analogue multimeter and a digital multimeter.

Figure 6.1.2 Measuring resistance

Method: using a
moving-coil multimeter

1 Connect the red lead to the positive terminal of the meter (identified by VAΩ) and the black lead to the negative or common terminal.

2 Set the meter to measure resistance by switching it to the resistance setting (identified by OHM, Ω or R).

3 Identify the resistance scale of the meter; the needle should be to the far left, which is the infinity setting. Whenever nothing is connected between the two leads the resistance is infinitely high.

4 Now touch the two leads together; the needle should go to the right and should rest on the zero of the scale. If this does not happen, then, with the leads still touching, alter the 'zero adjust' control until the needle is on zero.

5 Using the same set of resistors as in exercise 1, clip the first resistor between the two terminals of the meter and measure its resistance. It may be necessary to change the range switch until the needle is somewhere in the middle of the scale. The resistance is the reading on the scale multiplied by the range setting. Write this value in the last column of your copy of table 6.1.1.

6 Repeat for the remaining resistors.

Method: using a digital multimeter
This is somewhat easier than using the moving-coil meter. There is no scale or moving needle and all measurements are given directly using either a seven-segment display or a liquid crystal display.

1 Identify the mode select switch and switch to the resistance mode. With the leads in the correct terminals the display may show a '1' when nothing is connected. This '1' represents an infinitely large resistance. On touching the leads together '0' should be displayed, indicating that there is no resistance between the two leads.

2 Measure resistance in the same way as above using different range settings until a number giving the resistance in ohms or kilohms is displayed on the screen.

Exercise 3 Resistance and current
This exercise looks at how the current flowing in a circuit varies as the resistance in the circuit increases.

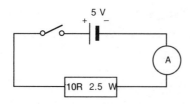

Figure 6.1.3 Resistance and current flow

Materials
This exercise will require a prototype board, a simple toggle switch or a push switch, a supply capable of producing 5 V, an ammeter or a multimeter (switched to the d.c. current range) and, in addition to the resistor shown in figure 6.1.3, a box containing the following fixed-value resistors: 22 Ω, 47 Ω, 100 Ω, 470 Ω, 1 kΩ.

Method
1 Using the prototype board, set up the circuit shown in figure 6.1.3. The ammeter or multimeter should be connected so that it is in series with the other components in the circuit, its positive going to the positive of the circuit and its negative to the negative of the circuit.

2 Copy table 6.1.2 into your notebook and write in the value of each resistor in the first column of the table.

3 Starting with the resistor shown in the diagram measure the current flowing

in the circuit when the switch is pressed. Record your readings in the second column of the table.

4 Repeat by replacing the resistor with each of the values shown above, starting with the 22 Ω and finishing with the 1 kΩ.

5 Look at the current measurements you have obtained and describe what you noticed about the current when the resistance in the circuit was increased. What would you say is one function of a resistor in a circuit?

Table 6.1.2 Table needed for exercise 3

Resistance R/Ω	Current I/A
10 Ω	
22 Ω	
47 Ω	
100 Ω	
470 Ω	
1 kΩ	

You should find that:
- the greater the resistance the smaller the current flowing in that circuit; and
- the amount of current which flows in any circuit depends on the total resistance of that circuit.

Exercise 4 Resistance and power

This exercise is to help you understand the power rating of a resistor and to see how it is calculated. Therefore before doing this exercise it is important to read section 3.5 on resistors, paying special attention to the section on power in a resistor.

Materials

You will need a 0.25 W, 0.5 W, 1.0 W and a 2.0 W 10 Ω resistor, a supply capable of providing 5 V d.c., a prototype board and a switch.

Method

1 Using the equation

$$\text{power} = (\text{current})^2 \times \text{resistance}$$

calculate the power dissipated by the 10 Ω resistor when a current of 0.5 A is flowing through it.

2 Which, if any, of the power ratings shown above would you use?

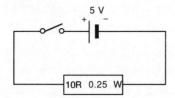

Figure 6.1.4 Resistance and power dissipation

3 Set up the circuit shown in figure 6.1.4 starting with the 0.25 W resistor. Close the switch and describe what happens.

4 Repeat step 3 using the 0.5 W, 1.0 W and 2.0 W resistors in turn. In each case describe fully what happened and state if this is what was expected.

5 Use your understanding of electrical power to explain your observations in steps 3 and 4 above.

Supplementary exercise 4 You are required to set up a circuit in which a 5 V supply is driving a current through a 100 Ω resistor.

Materials You will require the same materials as in exercise 4 above.

Method **1** Using the equation

$$\text{power} = (\text{voltage})^2/\text{resistance}$$

work out the power rating of the resistor to be used.

2 Choose the right resistor and set up the circuit on the prototype board.

3 In your notebook, draw a diagram of the circuit giving details of the colour code of the resistor used and its power rating.

You should find that:
• the smaller the power rating, the smaller the amount of current that can safely pass through the resistor without it overheating;
• a consideration of the rating is important when choosing resistors for a particular job;
• using the equation to calculate power, you will get a value of 0.25 W and therefore your selected resistor must not have a power rating lower than this.

Exercise 5 Resistance and voltage This exercise is based on Ohm's Law (see section 2.4), which states that the current flowing through a resistor is directly proportional to the voltage across it, providing the temperature remains constant. It is given by the equation

$$\text{voltage} = \text{current} \times \text{resistance}$$

This exercise will help you to practise voltage and current measurement and also the use of the oscilloscope, which was dealt with in section 4.4.

Materials The following apparatus is required for this exercise: a prototype board, a power supply capable of providing 5 V d.c., a switch, an ammeter (or multimeter set to measure d.c. current), a voltmeter (or multimeter set to measure d.c. voltage), a rheostat, a 100 kΩ potentiometer and a 10 Ω, 47 Ω and 100 Ω 2.5 W resistor.

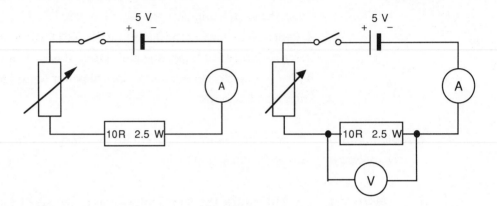

Figure 6.1.5 Confirmation of Ohm's Law

Method **1** Set up the circuit shown in figure 6.1.5 on the prototype board.

2 Copy table 6.1.3 into your notebook and write in the resistor value.

3 Close the switch and adjust the rheostat so that the current passing through the resistor is at a minimum.

4 Measure the current and write its value in the table.

5 Using this current, calculate the voltage across the resistor and record this in the table.

6 Now measure the voltage across the resistor using first a multimeter (switched to d.c. volts) connected in parallel with it, and then an oscilloscope. Remember that the positive lead of the multimeter must be connected to the positive side of the resistor and the negative lead to the negative side. The leads of the oscilloscope are connected in the same way as those of the multimeter and the voltage is measured by counting the number of divisions by which the trace has been displaced and multiplying this by the volts/division setting of the oscilloscope.

7 Write both of these readings in the last two columns of the table.

Table 6.1.3 Table needed for exercise 5

		Voltage V/V		
		---	---	---
Resistance R/Ω	Current I/A	Calculated	Measured (multimeter)	Measured (oscilloscope)

8 Adjust the rheostat and repeat steps 4 to 7, using different values of current.

9 Replace the resistor using, in turn, the 47 Ω and the 100 Ω resistors and repeat steps 4 to 7.

10 In all cases compare the measured voltages with the calculated values and state whether or not this exercise confirms Ohm's Law.

Supplementary exercise 5   A potentiometer is a device for producing a varying voltage, ranging from zero voltage to that of the supply.

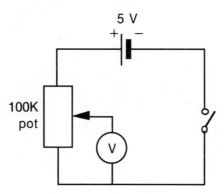

Figure 6.1.6 The potentiometer

Method   **1** Set up the circuit shown in figure 6.1.6.

2 Carry out a number of measurements following steps 6 and 7 in exercise 5 above to confirm that the variable resistor is behaving as a potentiometer.

You should find that:

• the voltage across a resistor is the product of the current flowing through the resistor and the resistance of the resistor;

• the voltage across a resistor depends on the size of the resistance; the larger the resistance the larger the share of the total voltage. Two identical resistors in series would have the same voltage across them. The voltage across each resistor is the fraction of the total resistance it represents multiplied by the supply voltage (V_s). For two resistors in series the voltage across R_1 is given by:

$$R_1 = \frac{R_1}{R_1 + R_2} \times V_s$$

• a variable resistor arranged as a potentiometer will produce a voltage which varies from zero to that of the supply.

Exercise 6 Resistor combinations

Resistors can be combined so that they are arranged in series or in parallel. Figures 6.1.7a and 6.1.7b show both of these types of arrangements. The total resistance for resistors in series is given by:

$$R_{total} = R_1 + R_2 + R_3$$

and the total resistance for resistors in parallel is given by:

$$\frac{1}{R_{total}} = \frac{1}{R_1} + \frac{1}{R_2} + \frac{1}{R_3}$$

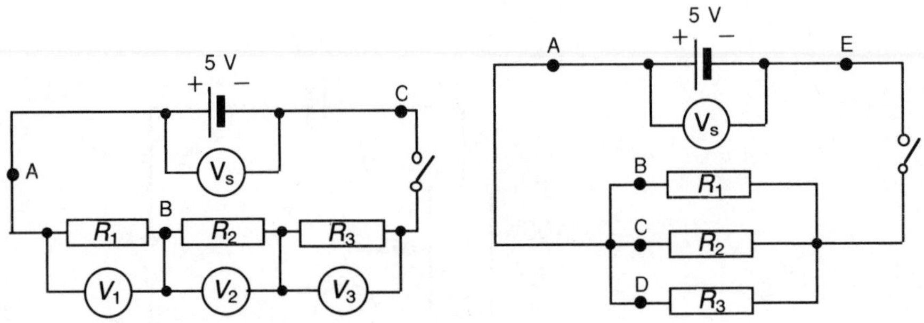

a   b

Figure 6.1.7 (a) Series and (b) parallel circuits

Materials

You will require a box of assorted fixed-value resistors, a voltmeter, an ammeter, a switch, a prototype board and a voltage supply.

Method

1 Copy table 6.1.4 and, choosing three resistors from the box, write in the values of resistors R_1, R_2 and R_3.

2 Work out the total resistance of the three resistors you have chosen. Write this value in the table.

Table 6.1.4 Table needed for exercise 6

R_1/Ω	R_2/Ω	R_3/Ω	$R_1+R_2+R_3/\Omega$	Measured value/Ω

3 Using the prototype board, set up the series circuit shown in figure 6.1.7a, where R_1, R_2 and R_3 are your chosen resistors.

4 Now measure the resistance of the combination using a multimeter and again write the value in the table.

5 Compare the calculated value with the measured value. Are they the same? Should they be the same? Explain your answer.

6 Using the multimeter, measure the current at points A, B and C. Write these into your copy of table 6.1.5 and describe what you notice about the currents you have measured.

Table 6.1.5 Table needed for exercise 6

Position	Current I/A
A	
B	
C	

7 Again using the multimeter, measure the voltages V_1, V_2 and V_3 across the three resistors when the switch is closed. Write these into your copy of table 6.1.6 and describe what you notice about the voltages you have measured.

Table 6.1.6 Table needed for exercise 6

Position	Voltage V/V
V_1	
V_2	
V_3	
V_s	

8 Add V_1, V_2 and V_3 together and compare the sum to that of the supply voltage V_s. What do you notice?

9 Using the values for the total voltage and the total current, use Ohm's Law to check the value for the total resistance.

You should find that:
- the total resistance of resistors in series is the sum of the resistances of the individual resistors;
- the measured sum is close to but not the same as the calculated sum – this is because each resistor has a tolerance which means that the stated value is different from the actual value;
- the current flowing through all resistors in series is the same;
- the voltage across resistors in series varies in size according to the size of the resistance – a small resistor has a smaller voltage across it than a larger one, and resistors of the same value would have the same voltage drop; and
- the sum of the voltages across the individual resistors in series is equal to the voltage of the supply.

Supplementary exercise 6

Method **1** As before, select three resistors from the box and set up the parallel circuit shown in figure 6.1.7b.
2 Copy table 6.1.7 and write in the resistor values.
3 Using the reciprocal ($1/x$) button of the calculator, find the sum for the three resistors you have chosen. Write this value in the table.
4 Measure the resistance of this parallel combination and record this in the table.

Table 6.1.7 Table needed for supplementary exercise 6

R_1	R_2	R_3	$\dfrac{1}{R_1} + \dfrac{1}{R_2} + \dfrac{1}{R_3}$	Measured value
/Ω	/Ω	/Ω	/Ω	/Ω

5 Compare the calculated value with the measured value. Are they the same? Should they be the same? Explain your answer.
6 Measure the currents at points A, B, C, D and E. Copy table 6.1.8, write in the value of the current and describe what you notice about the readings. Are they what you might have expected?

Table 6.1.8 Table needed for supplementary exercise 6

Position	Current I/A
A	
B	
C	
D	
E	

7 Measure the voltage across each resistor and across the supply when the switch is closed. Write these down into your copy of table 6.1.9. Describe what you notice about the potential differences and how they compare with that of the supply voltage.

Table 6.1.9 Additional table needed for supplementary exercise 6

Position	Voltage V/V
V_1	
V_2	
V_3	
V_s	

8 Use Ohm's Law to confirm the value of the total resistance of the circuit.

You should find that:
• when resistors are connected in parallel the combined resistance is less than that of any of the individual resistors;
• the current going through each branch of a parallel circuit is inversely related to the resistance in that branch – this means that the higher the resistance of a branch the smaller the current and vice versa;
• the total current in the circuit is the sum of the currents in the individual branches; and
• the voltage across all the resistors in parallel is the same as that of the supply.

Exercise 7
Resistor tolerance
The tolerance is the percentage by which the resistance is larger or smaller than the stated value. This percentage is given by the colour of the fourth or fifth band on the resistor. The tolerance code is as follows:

no fourth band	=	20%
silver	=	10%
gold	=	5%
red	=	2%

A 470 Ω resistor with a 10% tolerance has a value of 470 ± 10%, which is between 470 − 47 = 423 Ω and 470 + 47 = 517 Ω.

Alternatively the BS 1852 code gives the tolerance as:

F = ± 1%,
G = ± 2%,
J = ± 5%,
K = ± 10% and
M = ± 20%.

To calculate 10% of 1000 Ω, multiply the 1000 by 10 and divide the result by 100. The answer (100 Ω) is then added to 1000 to give the maximum value (1100 Ω) and subtracted from the 1000 to obtain the minimum value (900 Ω).

Method **1** Using the resistors as in exercise 1, identify the tolerance from the fourth or fifth band and calculate the maximum and minimum value of the resistance.
2 Copy out and fill in table 6.1.10 and for each resistor say whether the measured values lie within the calculated range.

Table 6.1.10 Table needed for exercise 7

Resistance /Ω	Tolerance %	Coded value /Ω	Maximum /Ω	Minimum /Ω	Measured /Ω

Exercise 8 Resistance and circuit faults

Before carrying out this exercise, please read section 5.6 on circuit faults. Circuit faults are of two types: short-circuit and open-circuit. Short-circuit faults lead to an area of low resistance and low voltage whilst an open-circuit fault leads to an area of high resistance and high voltage. This exercise should further illustrate the point.

Materials You will need a prototype board, a 5 kΩ and a 10 kΩ resistor and a 5 V d.c. supply.

Method **1** Set up the two resistors in series as in figure 6.1.8a and make a copy of table 6.1.11.

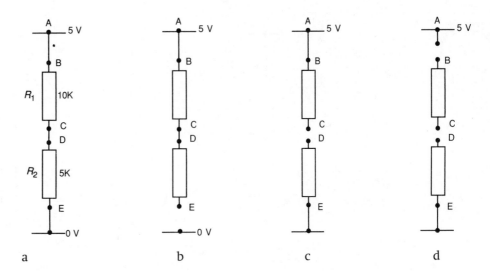

Figure 6.1.8 Resistor combinations showing open-circuit faults

2 Using either the multimeter or the oscilloscope measure the voltage drop at points A, B, C, D and E and write these measurements in the appropriate column of your table.

3 Now break the circuit as in figure 6.1.8b to create an open-circuit fault and repeat the measurements.

4 Repeat step 3, using the arrangements in figures 6.1.8c and 6.1.8d, each time measuring the voltages and entering the readings in the table.

Table 6.1.11 Table needed for exercise 8

Position	Voltage/V			
	Circuit a	Circuit b	Circuit c	Circuit d
A				
B				
etc.				

Supplementary exercise 8

Method **1** Set up the circuit as shown in figure 6.1.9a and short out R_2 by connecting a piece of insulated wire from one of its leads to the other as shown in figure 6.1.9b.

2 Measure the voltage at A, B, C, D and E. Copy table 6.1.12 and write in the values you have obtained.

3 Remake the circuit of figure 6.1.9a, short out R_1 as shown in figure 6.1.9c and repeat.

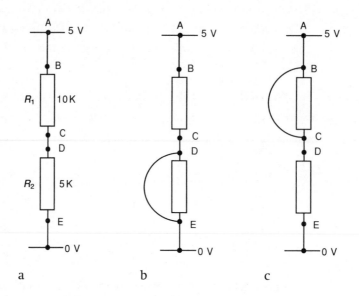

Figure 6.1.9 Resistor combinations showing short-circuit faults

Table 6.1.12 Table needed for supplementary exercise 8

Position	Voltage/V		
	Circuit a	Circuit b	Circuit c
A			
B			
etc.			

4 Using figure 6.1.9, calculate the voltages across R_1 and R_2. Compare these with the measured voltages. Are they the same? Should they be the same?

5 Look at the readings obtained in tables 6.1.11 and 6.1.12 and explain with reasons whether or not these are reasonable for the conditions shown in figures 6.1.8 and 6.1.9.

You should find that:

• in an open-circuit fault there was no current flow and therefore there is no voltage drop across the resistors – this means that at all points on the 5 V side of the break will give a reading of 5 V, whilst points on the 0 V side of the break will give a reading of 0 V.

• when there is a short-circuit fault the current which is flowing by-passes the resistor, leading to the absence of a voltage drop across it – this means that a voltmeter connected across it will read 0 V as there will be no potential difference across the resistor. Thus a circuit with a short-circuit fault behaves as though there is no resistance in that part of the circuit.

Exercise 9 Special resistors

Two special resistors commonly encountered in electronics are the light-dependent resistor (LDR) and the thermistor (see section 3.5). These two exercises should help you to find out more about these components.

Materials

For this exercise you will need an LDR (ORP12) and a prototype board.

Method

1 Using a multimeter measure the resistance of the LDR provided under the lighting conditions shown in table 6.1.13 and enter your measurements in your copy of the table.
2 Look up the symbol for the LDR and draw a circuit for measuring the current passing through it using a 6 V d.c. supply.
3 Measure the current flowing under the three lighting conditions used above and enter the values obtained in your table.

Table 6.1.13 Table needed for exercise 9

Lighting condition	Resistance/Ω	Current/A	Voltage/V
Daylight			
Artificial lighting			
Darkness			

4 Connect the multimeter to the LDR and measure the voltage across it under the same lighting conditions and enter these results in your table.
5 Summarise your results by stating what happened to the resistance, current and voltage under the various lighting conditions.
6 On the basis of the work done earlier in this section state whether or not these results were expected.
7 What is an LDR and why is it a special resistor?

Supplementary exercise 9

Materials

Replace the LDR with a thermistor.

Method   1 Using a multimeter measure the resistance of the thermistor provided under the temperature conditions shown in table 6.1.14 and enter your measurements in your copy of the table.

2 Look up the symbol for the thermistor and draw a circuit for measuring the current passing through it using a 6 V d.c. supply.

3 Measure the current flowing under the three temperature conditions used above and enter the values obtained in your table.

Table 6.1.14 Table needed for supplementary exercise 9

Temperature condition	Resistance/Ω	Current/A	Voltage/V
Room temperature			
Hot water			
Cold water			

4 Connect the multimeter to the thermistor and measure the voltage across it under the same temperature conditions and enter these results in your table.

5 Summarise your results by stating what happened to the resistance, current and voltage under the various temperature conditions.

6 On the basis of the work done earlier in this section state whether or not these results were expected.

7 What is a thermistor and why is it a special resistor?

6.2 Capacitors and capacitance

Exercise I Capacitor colour code

Materials   For this exercise you will need a box of assorted polyester capacitors.

Method   1 Use the diagram in figure 6.2.1 to work out the values of a number of different polyester capacitors obtained from the box provided.

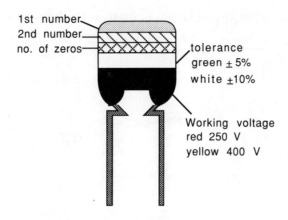

Figure 6.2.1 Capacitor colour code

2 Copy table 6.2.1 and fill in the columns for all capacitors used.

Table 6.2.1 Table for exercise 1

Capacitor	Colours			Tolerance	Working	Value
	1st	2nd	3rd		voltage/V	/pF

3 Use the information on the tolerance of each capacitor to work out the maximum and minimum value for each capacitor identified and complete a copy of table 6.2.2.

Table 6.2.2 Table needed for part 3 of exercise 1

Capacitance /pF	Tolerance %	Coded value /pF	Upper limit /pF	Lower limit /pF

Exercise 2 Capacitors and capacitance

Capacitance is the charge storage capacity of a capacitor. It is measured in farads or more commonly microfarads, nanofarads or picofarads.

Materials

For this exercise you will need a single-pole double-throw switch, a 390 Ω resistor, an LED, a power supply capable of producing 6 V d.c., a prototype board and capacitors of 220 μF, 470 μF, 1000 μF and 2200 μF.

Method **1** Set up the circuit shown in figure 6.2.2 on the prototype board.

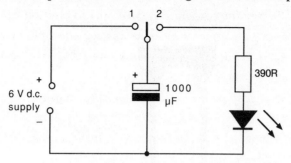

Figure 6.2.2 Charge storage capacity of a capacitor

2 Charge up the capacitor by placing the switch in position 1 and discharge it through the LED by switching to position 2. Note the time for which the LED is on.

3 Replace the capacitor with the 220 μF, 470 μF, 1000 μF and 2200 μF in turn, each time noting the time for which the LED is on.

4 Look at your observations and answer the following questions.

(a) How does the size of the capacitor affect the length of time that the LED is on?

(b) What causes the LED to light and how is this related to the capacitance of the capacitors?

You should find that:

• the time that the LED is on depends on the size of the capacitance – the larger the capacitance, the longer the time that the LED is on; and

• the capacitor stores charge which flows as a current through the LED – the larger the capacitor, the longer the time the current flows.

Exercise 3 Capacitance and voltage

You will need a single-pole double-throw switch, a 390 Ω resistor, an LED, a power supply capable of producing 6 V d.c., a prototype board, a voltmeter or multimeter and capacitors of 220 μF, 470 μF, 1000 μF and 2200 μF.

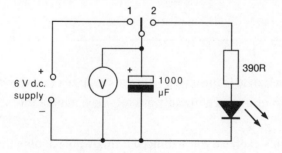

Figure 6.2.3 Voltage and capacitor discharge

Method 1 Set up the circuit as in figure 6.2.3.

2 Charge the capacitor by switching to position 1 for a short time.

3 Using a voltmeter measure and note down the voltage across the capacitor.

4 Start the discharge by switching to position 2 and observe the change in voltage throughout the discharge.

5 Repeat steps 2 to 4 for each of the remaining capacitors.

6 Use your observations to answer the following questions.

(a) What can you say about the voltage across the capacitor at the start of the discharge compared with the supply voltage?

(b) What happens to the voltage across the capacitor as it discharges through the LED?

You should find that:

• the voltage across the capacitor at the start of the discharge is the same as that of the supply; and

• this voltage decreases as the capacitor discharges.

Exercise 4 Capacitor and series resistor The rate at which a capacitor charges not only depends on its capacitance but also on the value of the series resistance. This and the following exercises look in more detail at the factors affecting the rate of both charging and discharging capacitors.

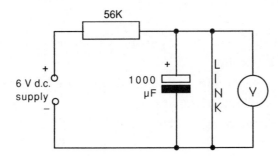

Figure 6.2.4 Capacitance and series resistor

Materials You will need a piece of single-stranded wire link, a power supply capable of producing 6 V d.c., a prototype board, a voltmeter or multimeter and resistors of 56 kΩ, 100 kΩ, 220 kΩ and 470 kΩ.

Method 1 Set up the circuit in figure 6.2.4 on the prototype board with the wire link in place and the voltmeter connected as shown.

Table 6.2.3 Table needed for exercise 3

Time/s	Voltage/V			
	56 kΩ	100 kΩ	220 kΩ	470 kΩ

2 Remove the wire link and record the increase in the voltage across the capacitor at ten-second intervals in a copy of table 6.2.3 until there is no further change in the voltage.

3 Replace the resistor with the 100 kΩ, 220 kΩ and 470 kΩ resistors in turn, each time reading the voltage at ten-second intervals and entering the readings in the appropriate column of the table.

4 Use your results to plots a series of graphs of voltage (vertical axis) against time (horizontal axis) for each of the resistors used.

Supplementary exercise 4a

Materials As well as those outlined above, you will need capacitors of 220 μF, 470 μF and 2200 μF.

Method **1** Set up the circuit in figure 6.2.4 again, using the 100 kΩ series resistor and the 220 μF capacitor.

2 Remove the wire link and again measure the voltage across the capacitor at ten-second intervals.

3 Copy and complete table 6.2.4.

Table 6.2.4 Table needed for supplementary exercise 4a

Time/s	Voltage/V		
	220 μF	470 μF	2200 μF

4 Repeat by using the 470 μF and the 2200 μF capacitors in turn.

5 Use the results you have obtained to plot a series of graphs of voltage against time for each of the capacitor values used.

6 Look at the results you have obtained and answer the following questions:

(a) What do you notice about the time taken for the capacitor to charge up as (i) the value of the series resistor increases and (ii) the value of the capacitance increases?

(b) What factors would you say determine the rate of charging of a capacitor?

You should find that:
- when the wire link is removed the capacitor begins to charge and the charging continues until the voltage across the capacitor is just below that of the supply – it will not reach the supply because of the resistance of the voltmeter;
- the time taken for the capacitor to charge up depends on the size of the series resistance and the size of the capacitance – it depends on the product $C \times R$, which is called the **time constant** of the capacitor–resistance circuit; and
- the plots of voltage–time for the charging process show an exponential growth, as shown in figure 6.2.5, and that the smaller the time constant the steeper the curve.

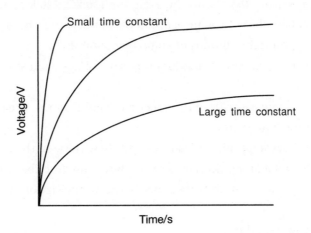

Figure 6.2.5 Voltage–time curves for a charging capacitor

Supplementary exercise 4b

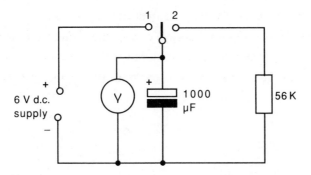

Figure 6.2.6 Series resistor and capacitor discharge

Method   1 Set up the circuit shown in figure 6.2.6.

2 Charge up the capacitor by switching to position 1 and discharge it through the resistor by switching to position 2.

3 Measure the voltage at ten-second time intervals until there is no further change in the voltage.

4 Copy and complete table 6.2.5.

Table 6.2.5 Table needed for supplementary exercise 4b

Time/s	Voltage/V			
	56 kΩ	100 kΩ	220 kΩ	470 kΩ

5 Replace the resistor by using the 100 kΩ, 220 kΩ and 470 kΩ resistors in turn. Repeat the voltage measurements at ten-second intervals and complete the appropriate columns of your copy of table 6.2.5.

6 Use your results to plot graphs of voltage against time for each resistor value used.

7 Set up a circuit to investigate the effect of the size of the capacitance on the rate of discharge.

8 Take appropriate readings and show these in the form of a table.

9 Plot a graph similar to those above and describe as fully as you can the dependence of the rate of discharge on the size of the capacitance.

You should find that:

• when the wire link is removed the capacitor begins to discharge and the rate of discharge depends on the size of the series resistor and on the size of the capacitance, i.e. the rate of discharge depends on the time constant for the circuit ($T = C \times R$);

• the plots of voltage against time for the discharge show a series of curves called exponential decay curves, where the decrease in voltage starts very large but gets smaller and smaller over the period of time (as shown in figure 6.2.7), and the smaller the time constant the steeper the curve.

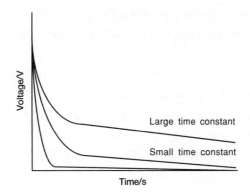

Figure 6.2.7 Voltage–time curves for a discharging capacitor

Exercise 5 Current in
C–R series circuits

This series of exercises looks at how the current changes in charging and discharging *C–R* circuits.

Materials

You will need a piece of single-stranded wire link, a power supply capable of producing 6 V d.c., a prototype board, a milliammeter or multimeter, a double-throw single-pole switch and a 56 kΩ resistor.

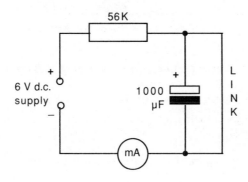

Figure 6.2.8 Current in C–R circuit

Method

1 Set up the circuit of figure 6.2.8 on the prototype board.

2 Connect the milliammeter or multimeter (switched to the milliamp range).to measure current.

Table 6.2.6 Table needed for exercise 5 and supplementary exercise 5

Time/s	Current/mA	
	Charge	Discharge

3 Remove the wire link and record the change in current every ten seconds in a copy of table 6.2.6 until there is no further change in the current.

4 Using your results, plot a graph of current against time and compare this plot with the one obtained for voltage against time for the similar circuit in exercise 4 above.

5 Use your graphs to answer the following questions:

(a) How has the voltage changed with time?

(b) What is the name of the curve obtained?

(c) How is this curve different from that of voltage against time?

(d) When is the rate of flow of current (gradient of the curve) at a maximum and when is it at a minimum?

Supplementary exercise 5

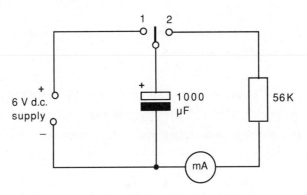

Figure 6.2.9 Current change in discharging C–R circuit

Method
1 Set up the circuit shown in figure 6.2.9.

2 Charge the capacitor by switching to position 1 and discharge it by switching to position 2.

3 Measure the current every ten seconds and record the value in your copy of table 6.2.6.

4 Continue measuring the current until there is no further change.

5 Again plot a graph of current against time and compare this with that for voltage against time obtained for the similar circuit in exercise 4b.

You should find that:

• when the capacitor is charging the current flowing decreases with time;

• the current against time curve is an exponential decay whilst the voltage grows exponentially with time (see figure 6.2.10);

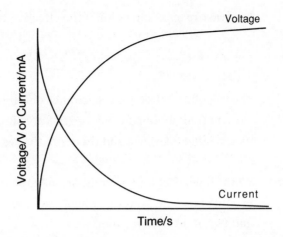

Figure 6.2.10 Current and voltage curves for a charging C–R circuit

• the rate of change of current is greatest at the start of the charging process and diminishes to almost nothing when the capacitor is fully charged;
• when a capacitor is discharged the voltage decays exponentially with time whilst the current grows exponentially with time (see figure 6.2.11).

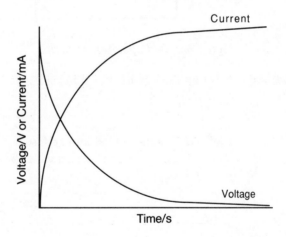

Figure 6.2.11 Current and voltage curves for a discharging C–R circuit

Exercise 6 Capacitor combinations Capacitors can be connected together in series or in parallel. This exercise investigates the effects on the total capacitance of both of these ways of connecting two capacitors.

The effective capacitance of two capacitors in series is given by

$$\frac{1}{C_e} = \frac{1}{C_1} + \frac{1}{C_2}$$

For two capacitors in parallel the effective capacitance is given by

$$C_e = C_1 + C_2$$

The calculated effective capacitance obtained from the time constants should be close to that obtained using the relationships above. However, these capacitors have a large tolerance and therefore the two values will not agree.

Materials You will need a piece of single-stranded wire link, a power supply capable of producing 6 V d.c., a prototype board, a voltmeter or multimeter plus one 56 kΩ and two 1000 μF capacitors.

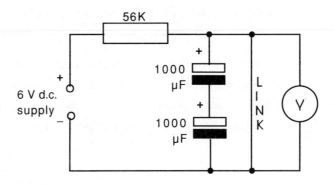

Figure 6.2.12 Capacitors in series

Method **1** Set up the circuit shown in figure 6.2.12 on the prototype board and copy table 6.2.7.

Table 6.2.7 Table needed for exercise 6

Time/s	Voltage/V	
	One capacitor	Two capacitors

2 Note the voltage in your copy of the table at time 0.
3 Remove the wire link, and record the voltage in the table every ten seconds until there is no further change in the voltage.
4 Remove one of the capacitors and repeat steps 2 and 3.
5 Plot graphs of voltage against time for both sets of readings.
6 Calculate 63% of the supply voltage and using the graphs find the time constants for both circuits.

7 The time constant is given by $T = CR$ and $C = T/R$, where, in this case, C is the effective resistance. Use the time constants obtained from step 6 above to calculate the effective capacitance of the two capacitors in series and for the single capacitor, and answer the following questions:

(a) Are these calculated values what you would expect?

(b) If not, are they larger or smaller?

Explain.

Supplementary exercise 6

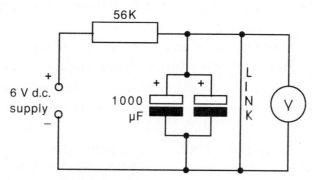

Figure 6.2.13 Capacitors in parallel

Method

1 Set up the parallel circuit of figure 6.2.13.

2 Repeat steps 2 to 4 in exercise 6 on page 148.

3 Plot the graph of voltage against time and find the time constant for the circuit.

4 Use this to calculate the effective capacitance of the circuit.

5 Compare the calculated value to the capacitor values used in the circuit and answer the following questions:

(a) Is this what was expected?

(b) Is there a relationship between the two values?

You should find that:

• the time constant for the two capacitors in series is shorter than for the single capacitor and the effective capacitance of the two capacitors is less than for the single one;

• the time constant of two capacitors in parallel is longer than for that of a single capacitor and the effective capacitance is the sum of the capacitance of the individual capacitors.

Exercise 7 Capacitor and circuit faults

Although capacitors are usually very reliable, failure does occur. This takes one of four basic forms:

1 short-circuit faults;

2 open-circuit faults;

3 too large leakage current (the current that flows from one plate to another through the dielectric); and

4 reduction in the capacitance.

Testing for short-circuit faults

The simplest way of doing this is to connect a multimeter, set to measure resistance, across the terminals of the capacitor. Remember that an electrolytic capacitor must be properly polarised and therefore it is important to realise that the positive of the battery inside the multimeter is connected to the negative terminal, i.e. the one containing the black lead, and therefore this terminal should be connected to the positive lead of the electrolytic capacitor.

Materials

You will need a multimeter and a box of assorted capacitors.

Method

1 Choose a capacitor from the box and connect it to the appropriate terminals of the multimeter which has previously been set to the lowest resistance range.

2 Describe your observations.

3 Describe what you would expect to see if the capacitor had a short-circuit fault.

Testing for open-circuit failure

If a capacitor is open-circuit, no charge can flow onto its plates when it is first connected to the supply. Therefore a simple test for open-circuit failure would be to connect a multimeter, set on its resistance mode, across the terminals of the capacitor. This should be done by clipping on one of the leads first, and then whilst watching the needle, touching the other lead. If the capacitor is good, then the needle will swing briefly to indicate the charging of the plates, whilst if there is an open circuit the meter needle will not move. Note that the current in a very small capacitor might be too brief to have any noticeable effect on the needle and therefore this test will not be conclusive when used on very small capacitors.

Test for excessive leakage current

This test can also be used as a confirmation of a short-circuit fault.

Method

1 Choose several different electrolytic capacitors from the box and use the RS (Radio Spares) catalogue to find either the leakage currents or an expression to calculate the leakage currents.

2 Using

minimum resistance = operating voltage/maximum leakage current

calculate the minimum resistance of each capacitor.

3 Copy table 6.2.8 and note your results.

Table 6.2.8 Table needed for exercise 7

Capacitor/μF	Leakage current/μA		Resistance/Ω	
	Calculated	Measured	Calculated	Measured

4 Measure the resistance of each of the capacitors.

5 Compare your measurements with the resistance calculated at step 2 and answer the following questions.

(a) Are the two sets of results the same?

(b) Is this what was expected?

Explain.

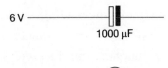

Figure 6.2.14 Measuring the leakage current of a capacitor

6 Set up the circuit shown in figure 6.2.14.

7 First the multimeter should be set to the milliamp range and the circuit connected to the supply. The charging current should fall and the meter should then be switched to the microamp range. Wait until the current has stabilised and record its value. This is the leakage current of the capacitor.

8 Compare the leakage current found with the value given in the catalogue.

9 Repeat steps 6 to 8 for a number of other capacitors.

10 What information should you be able to obtain from the above? Give a full explanation of your findings and your general conclusions.

Testing for reduction in capacitance   For large capacitors this can be done by measuring the time constant using a fixed resistance and comparing it with the calculated time constant for the capacitor. Write your own detailed description of how this could be done, including details of all calculations needed.

Another method which is applicable for all capacitors is to connect the suspected capacitor in series with a capacitor of known value. If a known voltage is connected across the two and the voltage across the suspected capacitor measured, then its capacitance can be calculated. The calculation is based on the fact that the charge stored on both capacitors is the same and is given by

$$\text{charge} = \text{capacitance} \times \text{voltage}$$

Therefore,

voltage across suspect capacitor $V_{sus} = V_{sup} \times (C_{good}/C_{sus} + C_{good})$

Rearranging in terms of capacitance, we get

$$C_{sus} = \{(V_{sup} \times C_{good}) - (V_{sus} \times C_{good})\}/V_{sus}$$

where V_{sup} is the supply voltage, V_{sus} is the voltage across the suspect capacitor, C_{sus} is the suspect capacitance, and C_{good} is the good capacitance.

The calculated value is then compared with the stated value having allowed for the tolerance of the capacitor.

You should find that:
• when testing for short-circuits the readings of the multimeter flicker before settling to show infinite resistance – this is due to the momentary flow of current as the capacitor is charged from the meter battery;
(A capacitor which has a short-circuit fault will have a fairly low resistance due to the current path between the two plates of the capacitor. In fact most short-circuit faults are not apparent at voltages much lower than the operating voltage of the capacitor.)
• it is possible to measure the leakage current and compare it to that recommended by the manufacturers – an excessive leakage current is also an indication of short-circuit failure; and
• open-circuit faults produce no reading on the multimeter as there is no direct current path to charge or discharge the capacitor.

6.3 Diodes

Please read the information on the diode in section 3.5 before carrying out these exercises.

Exercise I
Diode resistance

When the anode of a diode is positive and the cathode negative the diode is said to be forward-biased and when the anode is negative and the cathode positive the diode is said to be reverse-biased.

Material You will need a switch, a diode (1N4001), a power supply unit and a multimeter.

Method 1 Set the multimeter to the highest resistance range and adjust for zero by touching the two leads together and turning the 'zero adjust'.

2 Connect the anode of the diode to the positive terminal and the cathode to the negative. Write down the resistance in your notebook.

3 Reverse the connections to the diode and again note down the resistance.

4 State whether or not these readings are what you would expect to obtain.

You should find that:

• the resistance is low when the anode is connected to the positive of the meter battery (the black lead) and the cathode to the negative (the red lead);

• the resistance is high when the connections are reversed; and

• this test is a simple way of testing the condition of a diode – a failed diode will give either a low resistance or a high resistance in both directions .

Exercise 2
Function of a diode

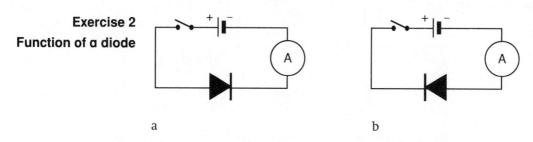

a   b

Figure 6.3.1 Diode (a) forward-biased and (b) reverse-biased

Method 1 Use the prototype board to set up the circuits of figure 6.3.1.

2 Describe what happens in each case when the switch is pressed and state the condition for a diode to conduct.

You should find that:

• the diode allows a current to flow when the anode of the diode is positive and the cathode negative, but not when the anode is negative and the cathode positive.

Exercise 3 Diode
transition voltage

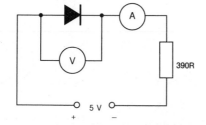

Figure 6.3.2 Measuring the diode transition voltage

Method
1 Set up the circuit shown in figure 6.3.2 on the prototype board.
2 Connect the multimeter across the diode and set it to measure voltage.
3 Use the potentiometer of the power supply to slowly increase the voltage across the circuit and note the voltage at which the diode starts to conduct.
4 Continue to increase the voltage to a maximum of 10 V.

You should find that:

• the diode conducts at around 0.6–0.7 V, and this voltage remains constant regardless of the supply voltage. This level of voltage indicates that the diode is made from silicon. A voltage of around 0.15 V would suggest a diode made from germanium.

Note: This voltage is called the diode transition voltage; it is the minimum voltage at which the diode starts to conduct.

Exercise 4 Diode forward characteristic

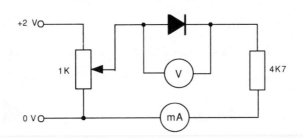

Figure 6.3.3 Circuit for investigating diode forward characteristic

Method
1 Set up the circuit shown in figure 6.3.3 using first the germanium diode.
2 Adjust the potentiometer so that the voltage across the diode is zero.
3 Set the meter ranges to 1.5 V and to 10 mA and slowly adjust the potentiometer until the diode starts to conduct.

Table 6.3.1 Table needed for exercise 4

Current/mA	Voltage/mA		
	Silicon diode	Germanium diode	Resistor

4 Make a copy of table 6.3.1 in your notebook to record the voltage readings for currents of 1, 2, 4, 6, 8 and 10 mA.
5 Repeat steps 1 to 4 using the silicon diode.
6 Replace the diode with the 1 kΩ resistor and repeat steps 1 to 4.

7 Using all three sets of results plot graphs of current (vertical axis) against voltage (horizontal axis) and answer the following questions:

(a) Describe the graphs obtained and state the difference between the graph for the silicon diode and that for the germanium diode.

(b) What are the main features of the graphs which distinguish the diodes from the resistor?

8 Use the graph for the silicon diode to find the resistance of the diode when it is passing various amounts of currents, and state what happens to the resistance of the diode when the current it is passing is increased.

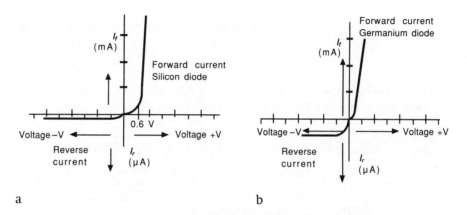

a   b

Figure 6.3.4 Diode forward characteristic for (a) silicon and (b) germanium diodes

You should find that:

- the graphs you obtained look like those shown in figure 6.3.4 but without the reverse current;
- a higher voltage is needed to make a silicon diode conduct; and
- a higher current is passed by the silicon diode than by the germanium diode.

Note: The reverse current is obtained when the diode is reverse-biased and is usually very much smaller than the forward current. For silicon diodes this is in the region of microamperes and for germanium diode nanoamperes. If the reversed voltage becomes too high then the diode will break down and there will be a sudden dramatic increase in the reverse current.

The graph for the resistors, shown in figure 6.3.5, is that of a straight line passing through the origin (the steepness of the line depending on the value of the resistance). This means that the voltage is proportional to the current and indicates an ohmic conductor (one obeying Ohm's Law). The graphs for the diodes are curves, which means that they do not obey Ohm's Law and are therefore non-ohmic in behaviour.

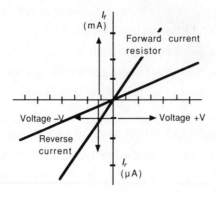

Figure 6.3.5 Plots of voltage against current for resistors

Exercise 5 Investigating the Zener diode

Zener diodes are designed to break down at a fixed and predictable voltage which remains constant over a wide range of current.

Materials

For this exercise you will need a BZX85, 5.1 V, 1.3 W Zener diode, a prototype board and a d.c. power supply unit.

Method

1 Using the formulae

$$\text{max diode current} = \frac{\text{power}}{\text{Zener voltage}}$$

and

$$\text{series resistance} = \frac{\text{supply voltage} - \text{Zener voltage}}{\text{max diode current}} \; \Omega$$

calculate the series resistance for supply voltages 6 V, 8 V, 10 V and 12 V.
2 Copy table 6.3.2 and write in your results.

Table 6.3.2 Table needed for exercise 5

Supply voltage /V	Series resistance /Ω	Voltage across diode /V	Diode current /mA
6			
8			
10			
12			

3 Calculate and select the correct resistor to be used in the circuit of figure 6.3.6.

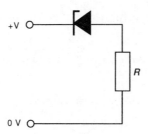

Figure 6.3.6 Zener diode and series resistor

4 Set up the circuit shown in figure 6.3.6 and measure the voltage across the diode using each value of the supply voltage given above. Note these readings in column 3 of your table.

5 Set up the circuit using each of the resistance values calculated in turn and measure the current for each of the supply voltages. Write these readings in column 4 of your table.

6 Finally using the highest value of the resistance calculated, measure the current as the voltage is increased from 6 to 12 V.

7 Describe what you have noticed about the diode voltage as the supply voltage is increased.

8 Compare the ammeter readings with that calculated and answer the following questions:

(a) Do the two sets of readings agree?

(b) Are these what you expected?

(c) What happens to the diode current as the supply voltage is increased?

You should find that:

• the Zener voltage remains constant over a range of supply voltages and diode currents.

Exercise 6 Zener diode and stabilisation

Materials You will need a BZX85, 5.1 V, 1.3 W Zener diode, a prototype board, a d.c. power supply unit and a 100 Ω resistor.

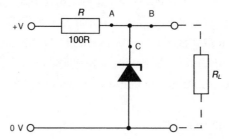

Figure 6.3.7 Zener diode and voltage stabilisation

Method   1 Set up the circuit shown in figure 6.3.7 on the prototype board initially without the load resistor.

2 With the supply set at 9 V measure the voltage across the Zener diode and the current flowing through it.

3 Copy table 6.3.3 and note down these values.

Table 6.3.3 Table needed for exercise 6

Load /Ω	V Zener/V	I_A/A	I_B/A	I_C/A	$(I_B + I_C)$/A
No load					
10K					
4K7					
1K					
470					
390					
220					
100					
68					
47					

4 Start by inserting the 47R load resistor and again measure the voltage across the Zener diode.

5 Measure the current at positions A, B and C and write these readings in the appropriate columns of your table.

6 Repeat by using, in turn, each of the load resistors shown in the first column of the table.

7 For each resistor value add the current readings at B and C together and enter this in the last column.

8 Look carefully at the results you have written down in the table and answer the following questions:

(a) What do you notice about the diode voltage as the load current increases?

(b) Which is the supply current and what do you notice about it as the load current increases?

(c) What do you notice about the diode current as the load current increases?

(d) Look at the last column and compare the readings with those in the third column. What do you notice about them? Is this what you expected?

9 Investigate the effect of having a very low load resistance. Describe what you did, the measurements taken and what you found.

You should find that:
• the diode voltage remains fairly constant over the range of load resistance used;

- the diode current is constant throughout;
- this constant current divides to supply the load and the diode; and
- the more the load current the lower the diode current.

Note: When the load resistance is very low, nearly all the supply current is diverted through it with the result that the diode current is too low to maintain conduction in the reverse breakdown mode. The consequence of this is that the diode voltage and hence the load voltage is no longer constant at 5.1 V.

6.4 Transistors

These exercises should be carried out either after reading section 3.6 on transistors or at the same time as going through the section.

Exercise 1 Identifying transistors

Materials   For this exercise you will need a box of assorted transistors.

Method   **1** Select a number of different transistors from the box of components provided.
2 Copy table 6.4.1 and enter these as numbers 1 to n (n is the number of transistors selected) in the first column of the table.

Table 6.4.1 Table needed for exercise 1

Transistor no.	ID no.	Material	Case	Uses	Pt /mA	I_c/mA	h_{FE}
1							
2							
3							

3 For each of the transistors note down the identification number in the appropriate column of the table.
4 Use a catalogue to find each of your transistors and to fill in the details of the other columns of the table.

Exercise 2 Transistor resistance

As described in section 3.6 the transistor is effectively two pn junctions, i.e. two diodes connected in series. In the last section it was observed that the resistance of the junction was high when the diode was reverse-biased and low when it was forward-biased and therefore this can be used to check the transistor condition.

Before doing this exercise please make sure that you know how to measure resistance (see section 6.1). The resistance is measured using a multimeter set to the resistance mode and it is important to remember that on this setting the positive terminal of the multimeter battery is connected to the negative (black) terminal of the multimeter and the negative of the battery is connected to the positive (red) terminal.

Method 1 From your table in exercise 1, select one npn and one pnp transistor and in conjunction with the diagram of figure 6.4.1 use these to carry out the following investigation.

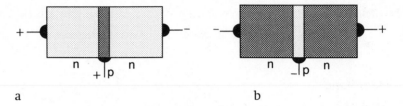

a   b

Figure 6.4.1 (a) npn and (b) pnp junctions

Table 6.4.2 Table needed for exercise 2

Connection mode	(npn) resistance/Ω	(pnp) resistance/Ω
1 Red lead to base. Common lead (black) to collector.		
2 Red lead to base. Common lead to emitter.		
3 Common lead to base. Red lead to collector.		
4 Red lead to collector. Common lead to emitter		
5 Common lead to collector. Red lead to emitter.		

2 Make a copy of table 6.4.2.

3 Connect the multimeter leads to the terminals of first the npn transistor as described for the first connection mode and measure the resistance. Write this value in the appropriate column of the table.

4 Repeat step 3 for the remaining modes of connection numbered 2 to 5 in the table.

5 Replace the transistor with the pnp type and repeat steps 3 and 4, filling in column three of the table.

6 Look carefully at your results and using what you already know about the pn junction in diodes, state with reasons whether or not your findings are what you expected.

You should find that:

• the base emitter and the base collector junctions give a high resistance reading for the npn transistor and a low resistance reading for the pnp transistor when the base is negative and the collector/emitter is positive – in the case of the npn transistor the two junctions are reverse-biased and for the pnp transistor the two junctions are forward-biased;

• when the meter is connected to the collector and the emitter of both transistors, a high resistance is obtained whatever the polarity of the leads – this is because the two np junctions making up the transistor are arranged so that a voltage between the collector and the emitter causes one of the junctions to be forward-biased and the other to be reverse-biased, the reverse-biased junction resulting in the high resistance reading between the collector and the emitter.

Note: Table 6.4.2 can be used to test the conditions of all transistors.

Exercise 3 Basic transistor action (as a switch)

Materials You will need two 6 V, 60 mA bulbs with holders, a 1 kΩ resistor, an npn transistor, a prototype board and a piece of wire to use as a 'flylead'.

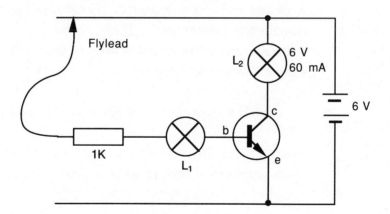

Figure 6.4.2 Simple transistor switch

Method 1 Set up the circuit shown in figure 6.4.2 on the prototype board.
2 Make a copy of table 6.4.3.

Table 6.4.3 Table needed for exercise 3

Flylead	L_1	L_2
+ve		
−ve		
+ve		

3 Connect the flylead to the positive supply line and record the state of L_1 and L_2.

4 Now connect the flylead to the negative supply and again note the state of L_1 and L_2.

5 Remove L_1 from its holder, connect the flylead to the positive supply line and note the state of L_2.

You should find that:
• when the flylead was connected to the positive supply line lamp L_2 came on and lamp L_1 remained off;
• when the bulb of L_1 was removed from its holder L_2 remained off;
• measurement of the currents indicates a small base current is insufficient to light L_1 but is necessary for L_2 to light;
• the current flowing through L_2, the collector current, should be much larger than the base current; and
• the emitter current should be the sum of the collector current and the base current. This can be stated as

$$\text{emitter current } I_e = \text{collector current } I_c + \text{base current } I_b$$

Basically the transistor requires a small base current to switch on and control a much larger flow of current between the collector and the emitter.

Exercise 4 Transistors and voltages

Materials You will need a prototype board, two voltmeters or multimeters, a 10 kΩ resistor, a 100 kΩ potentiometer and a d.c. power supply unit.

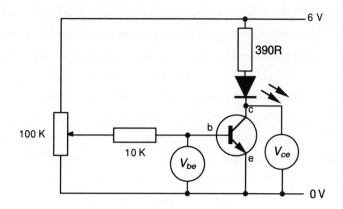

Figure 6.4.3 Simple transistor switching circuit

Method **1** Using the prototype board, set up the circuit shown in figure 6.4.3 and adjust the potentiometer so that V_{be} reads zero volts.

Table 6.4.4 Table needed for exercise 4

V_{be}/V	V_{ce}/V	I_b/mA	I_c/mA

2 Copy table 6.4.4 and record the voltages V_{be} and V_{ce} in the appropriate column.

3 Slowly adjust the variable resistor until the LED lights and again record the voltages V_{be} and V_{ce}.

Supplementary exercise 4

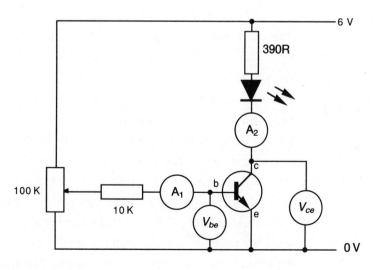

Figure 6.4.4 Investigating the transistor switch

Method

1 Modify the circuit to include ammeters as shown in figure 6.4.4.

2 Repeat the experiment but this time for each small increase in the base-emitter voltage note the corresponding change in the base current (I_b), collector voltage (V_{ce}), and collector current (I_c).

3 Record these readings in your copy of table 6.4.4.

4 Using your results, answer the following questions:

(a) From your results what can you say about the collector-emitter voltage when the transistor is off (LED off)?

(b) What is the base-emitter voltage when the transistor just switches on?

(c) What is the collector voltage when the transistor is on? Is this voltage the same for all base-emitter voltages after the transistor has switched on?

5 Use the readings in your copy of table 6.4.4 to plot two graphs, one of collector voltage (vertical axis) against base voltage (horizontal axis) and the other of collector current (vertical axis) against base current (horizontal axis).

6 Explain both graphs as fully as you can. Find the curve in each case and explain the meaning of each.

You should find that:

- when the LED is off (transistor off) V_{ce} is similar to that of the supply.

Note: The transistor switches on when the base-emitter voltage (V_{be}) is between 0.6 V and 0.7 V for an npn transistor. When switched on, the collector voltage falls as more and more current passes through the transistor and reaches a minimum when the maximum current is passing. This maximum current is called the **saturation current** and, as the transistor and load resistor are in series, when this is flowing the maximum voltage is dropped across the load resistor (almost equal to that of the supply) and thus V_{ce} is close to zero.

$$V_s = I_c R_L + V_{ce}$$

where V_s is the supply voltage.

The two graphs you were asked to draw are shown in figures 6.4.5 and 6.4.6. They are known as transistor characteristics and are plots of current–current, current–voltage and voltage–voltage relationships for the transistor. In figure 6.4.5 V_c is seen to fall over a very short range of input (base) voltages to a constant value just above zero volts. The curve of this fall is the gain of the transistor. Figure 6.4.6 is known as the **transfer characteristic**. It shows that I_c increases linearly as I_b is increased and then levels off at a constant value which is independent of I_b. This constant value is the saturation current which flows when the transistor is fully on (bottomed). The curve of this graph is I_c / I_b (the d.c. or static current gain of the transistor). This quantity is known as h_{FE}.

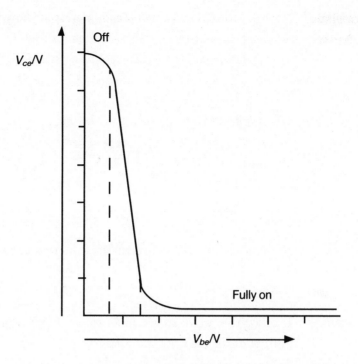

Figure 6.4.5 Graph of V_{ce} against V_{be} for an npn transistor

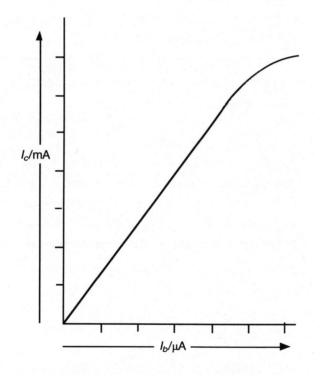

Figure 6.4.6 Transistor transfer characteristic

Exercise 5 Transistor input characteristic

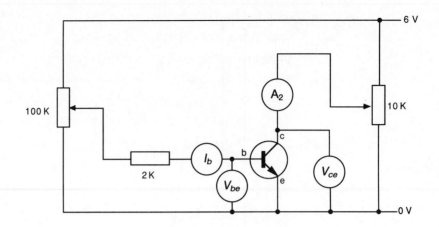

Figure 6.4.7 Circuit for investigating the input characteristic of a transistor

Method

1 Set up the circuit shown in figure 6.4.7 on the prototype board using a multimeter to measure the voltages.

2 Copy table 6.4.5.

Table 6.4.5 Table needed for exercise 5

V_{be}/V	I_b/μA

3 Using the 10 kΩ potentiometer to keep V_{ce} constant adjust the 100 kΩ potentiometer to give a series of values for I_b and V_{be}.

4 Enter each of these values in the appropriate column of your copy of the table.

5 Use your results to plot a graph of I_b (vertical axis) against V_{be}.

6 The input resistance of the transistor is given for d.c. by

$$R_1 = \frac{V_{be}}{I_b} \ \Omega$$

and for a.c. by

$$R_1 = \frac{\Delta V_{be}}{\Delta I_b} \ \Omega$$

where ΔV_{be} and ΔI_b are the changes in V_{be} and I_b respectively. Use your graph to find the maximum and minimum values of the input resistance.

You should find that:

- your graph resembles that of figure 6.4.8;
- looking at the graph, I_b remains zero until V_{be} rises above 0.65 volts, after which small changes in V_{be} produce large variations in I_b; and
- the curve of the graph is very steep, which means that V_{be} remains fairly close to 0.65 V regardless of the base current.

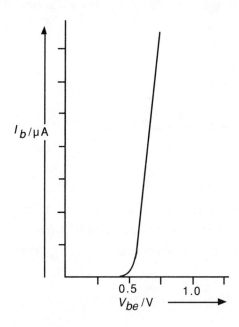

Figure 6.4.8 Input characteristic

Supplementary exercise 5a: Transistor output characteristic

This is the relationship between I_c and V_{ce}.

Method
1 Set up the circuit shown in figure 6.4.7 again and adjust I_b to about 10 μA.
2 Copy table 6.4.6.and record the values of I_c and V_{ce}.

Table 6.4.6 Table needed for supplementary exercise 5a

V_{ce}	I_{ce}

3 Using the potentiometer VR_2 obtain a number of readings for V_{ce} and the corresponding values of I_c. Enter these in your copy of the table.

4 Increase I_b to 20 μA and again obtain a series of readings for V_{ce} and I_c.

5 Repeat step 4 for I_b having values of 30, 40, 50 and 60 μA.

6 Use your results to plot a series of curves of I_c (vertical) against I_b (horizontal).

7 Describe the curves and give an explanation, in terms of the action of the transistor, of the main features. The output resistance of the transistor is given by

$$R_{out} = \frac{\Delta V_{ce}}{\Delta I_c}$$

where ΔV_{ce} is the change in V_{ce} and ΔI_c is the change in I_c. Use the section of the curve below the 'knee' to calculate the output resistance of the transistor.

You should find that:

- your curves resemble the one shown in figure 6.4.9 . From these curves you will see that Ic changes linearly with V_{ce} over a very limited range of V_{ce} Beyond this range there is little increase in I_c as V_{ce} continues to increase.

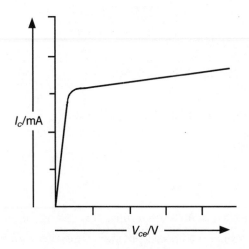

Figure 6.4.9 Output characteristic

Supplementary This is a plot of I_c against V_{ce} when there is a load connected to the collector of
exercise 5b: The load line the transistor.

Method **1** Using the equation $V_{ce} = V_{cc} - I_c R_L$, with $V_{cc} = 6$ V and $R_L = 1$ kΩ calculate V_{ce} for each of the values of I_c measured in exercise 5a.

2 Draw a table and enter the value of I_c and the calculated values of V_{ce}. Use these values to plot a graph of I_c against V_{ce}.

3 A simpler way of plotting the load line is to locate two points, one on the V_{ce}

axis when $I_c = 0$ and therefore $V_{ce} = 6$ V, the other on the I_c axis where $V_{ce} = 0$ and therefore $I_c = V_{cc}/R_L$. Using the curves of figure 6.4.10, draw on the load line as described above.

4 The load line can be used to fix the quiescent operating point of an amplifier. (The quiescent operating point is that d.c. load current that flows through the transistor even when there is no input. It is usually chosen to be near the centre of the load line.) Using this information, what is the V_{ce}, I_c and I_b at the operating point of this transistor?

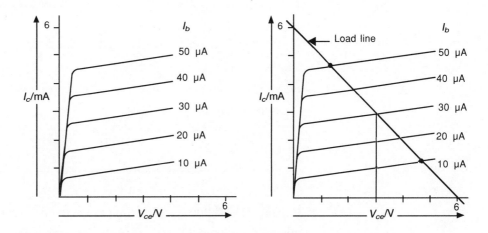

Figure 6.4.10 Use of the output characteristics to determine the load line

Exercise 6 The transistor current gain (h_{FE})   The d.c. current gain of a transistor, h_{FE}, is given by

$$h_{FE} = \frac{\text{change in collector current}}{\text{change in base current}}$$

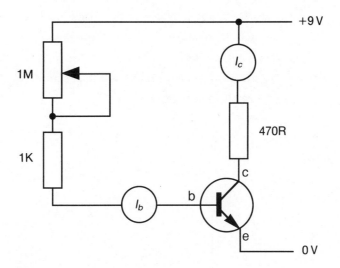

Figure 6.4.11 Circuit for investigating the current gain of the transitor

169

Method   1 Set up the circuit shown in figure 6.4.11 on the prototype board.
2 Copy table 6.4.7.

Table 6.4.7 Table needed for exercise 6

ZTX300	I_b/mA	
	I_c/mA	
BFY51	I_b/mA	
	I_c/mA	
BC184L	I_b/mA	
	I_c/mA	

3 Using the ZTX300 transistor, measure the base current and the collector current for a range of settings of the variable resistor and enter your results in your copy of the table.
4 Use your results to plot a graph of I_b (horizontal axis) against I_c (vertical axis).
5 From your graph find the change in base current and the corresponding change in collector current, and use these to determine the current gain of the transistor.
6 Repeat steps 3 to 5 for the remaining two transistors: BFY51 and BC184L.

You should find that:
- a small change in base current leads to a large change in collector current;
- an increase in the base current leads to an increase in the collector current and vice versa; and
- h_{FE} has a range of values which differ markedly from one transistor to the next regardless of the type.

Exercise 7 The transistor amplifier

Please read section 3.6 before carrying out this investigation.

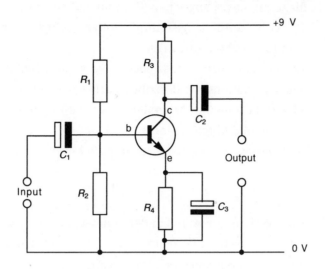

Figure 6.4.12 The transistor amplifier

Materials

You need a prototype board, a signal generator, a dual-beam oscilloscope, resistors R_1 = 10 kΩ, R_2 = 1.5 kΩ, R_3 = 470 Ω, R_4 = 1 kΩ, and capacitors $C_1 = C_2$ = 10 µF and C_3 = 100 µF.

Method

1 Set up the circuit shown in figure 6.4.12 on a prototype board using the component values given above.

2 Connect a signal generator to the input. Also connect a dual-beam oscilloscope so that input 1 is on the input and input 2 is on the output.

3 Set the signal generator to produce a sine wave with frequency of 1 kHz and obtain the trace of the input by adjusting both the signal generator output, the time base and the volts/cm setting of the oscilloscope.

4 Note down the volts/cm setting in your notebook and calculate (a) the peak voltage, (b) the peak-to-peak voltage and (c) the r.m.s. voltage of the input signal.

5 Draw a picture of the input signal and use the oscilloscope trace to work out the period and the frequency of the signal (see section 2.3). Note these values under the picture you have drawn.

6 Without any changes to the input signal or to the oscilloscope settings obtain the output signal. Draw a picture of this in your notebook.

7 Adjust the oscilloscope until a clear trace of the output is obtained. Note down the volts/cm setting and the time-base setting and use these to calculate (a) the peak voltage, (b) the r.m.s. voltage and (c) the frequency of the output signal.

8 Does the output wave form resemble that of the input? If not, what are the main differences between the two?

9 Slowly reduce the output of the signal generator and describe, with diagrams, any changes to both the input and output signals.

10 Slowly increase the output of the signal generator and again describe, with diagrams, any changes to both input and output.

11 Work out the range of input voltages which can be amplified by the amplifier without distortion.

12 Use your calculations above to work out the gain of the amplifier. Show all your calculations and describe clearly what you are doing.

13 Repeat steps 3 to 12 for a number of different transistors, both of the same type and of different types.

14 Investigate the gain of the amplifier over a range of frequencies for two different transistors and report on your findings.

6.5 The 555 IC The 555 timer is covered in detail in section 3.6, which should be read before carrying out this investigation. It is an 8-pin DIL integrated circuit and has the pin connections shown in figure 6.5.1.

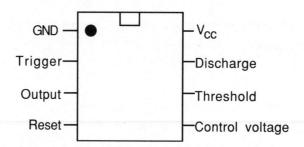

Figure 6.5.1 The 555 timer

The circuit of figure 6.5.2 is that of a monostable; R and C are external components whose values determine the time T (in seconds) for which the circuit is on. This time is given by

$$T = 1.1R \times C$$

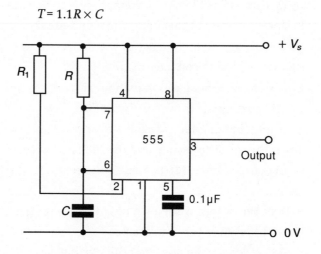

Figure 6.5.2 The 555 timer as a monostable

Exercise I The 555 monostable

Materials You will need a 555 timer, a 100 μF capacitor, a 0.1 μF capacitor, a push-to-make switch, a d.c. buzzer, a prototype board, a power supply and the following resistors: 1 kΩ, 10 kΩ, 47 kΩ, 100 kΩ, 470 kΩ.

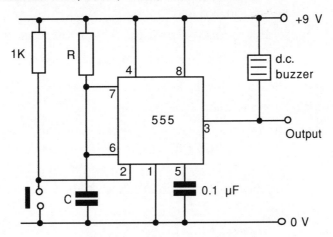

Figure 6.5.3 The monostable timer

Method 1 Set up the circuit shown in figure 6.5.3.

2 Using the formula given on page 172, work out the time T for each of the following resistor values: 1 kΩ, 10 kΩ, 47 kΩ, 100 kΩ, 470 kΩ. In all cases $C = 100$ μF.

3 Copy table 6.5.1 and enter the resistor values with the corresponding calculated times.

Table 6.5.1 Table needed for exercise 1

	Time/s	
Resistance/Ω	Calculated	Measured
1000		
10 000		
47 000		
100 000		
470 000		

4 Using each resistor in turn, start the timer and measure the length of time for which the circuit is on. Enter these times in the table.

5 Compare the calculated times with the measured times and answer the following questions:

(a) Are the calculated and measured time the same? Should they be the same?

(b) How would you explain the difference, if any, between the calculated and the measured times?

(c) How would you make the timer more accurate?

Exercise 2 The 555 astable multivibrator

The circuit for the astable is shown in figure 6.5.4. The time for which the output is 'high', T_1, is given by

$$T_1 = 0.7 (R_1 + R_2) C$$

and the time for which it is 'low', T_2, is

$$T_2 = 0.7 \times R_2 \times C$$

Therefore the total period for the oscillation, T, is

$$T = 0.7 (R_1 + 2R_2) C$$

The frequency of the astable is determined by the external components, R_1, R_2 and C; it is given by

$$f = \frac{1.45}{(R_1 + 2R_2)} \times C$$

If R_2 is much larger than R_1 then the mark/space ratio is approximately equal to one and the frequency is given by

$$f = \frac{0.72}{R_2 \times C}$$

The frequency is measured in hertz if the resistance is measured in ohms and the capacitance in farads.

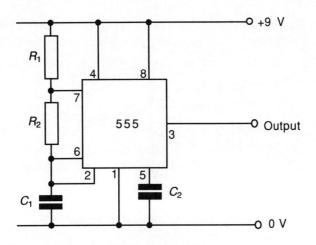

Figure 6.5.4 The 555 as an astable.

Method　**1** Set up the circuit of figure 6.5.4 on the prototype board and copy table 6.5.2 in your notebook.

2 Let $R_1 = R_2$ and have the following values: 1 kΩ, 10 kΩ, 47 kΩ, 100 kΩ and 470 kΩ and $C_1 = C_2 = 0.1$ µF. Use the appropriate formula to calculate the frequency using each of the resistor values given and enter this in the table.

3 Using either a frequency meter or an oscilloscope, measure the frequency for each resistor value and also enter these in the table.

4 Compare the calculated frequency with the measured frequency and answer the following questions:

(a) Are the measured and the calculated values the same? Should they be the same?

(b) How would you explain the difference between the calculated and the measured frequencies?

(c) What changes would you suggest to improve the accuracy of the oscillator?

Table 6.5.2 Table needed for exercise 2

	Frequency/Hz	
Resistance /Ω	Calculated	Measured
1 000		
10 000		
47 000		
100 000		
470 000		

6.6 The 741 IC   Please read section 3.6 on the 741 IC before carrying out these exercises.

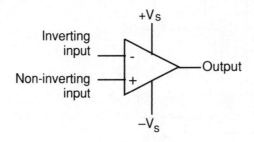

Figure 6.6.1 Operational amplifier symbol

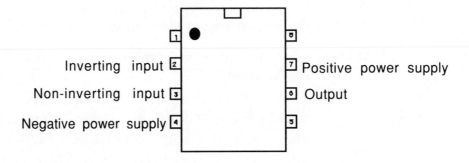

Figure 6.6.2   The 741 operational amplifier

Exercise 1 The 741

Materials   For this exercise you will need a prototype board, a balanced d.c. supply unit or some means of obtaining a balanced supply, a 741 operational amplifier and a voltmeter or a multimeter.

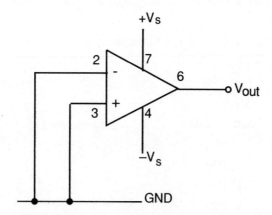

Figure 6.6.3 Differential input of the 741

Method   1 Set up the circuit shown in figure 6.6.3, ensuring that the two inputs are connected to ground (0 V).

2 Measure and note the voltage at the output of the chip (pin 6).

3 Remove each input in turn noting any change in the output produced as a result.

4 From what you know of the 741 is this what you expected? Explain your answer.

You should find that:

- the output voltage is either the positive supply or the negative supply; and
- the removal of one or other of the inputs may lead to no change in the output or a full reversal in the sign of the output voltage.

Note: The grounding of both inputs makes the difference in the input voltage zero and this should have produced zero output voltage. However, there is a small offset voltage on one of the inputs which produces a small differential input voltage, the sign of which cannot be determined. This voltage is amplified by the very large open-loop gain causing the output to be quickly saturated. Changing the voltage to one or other of the inputs will bring about a change in the sign of the differential input voltage, which will cause the output to saturate in the other direction.

Exercise 2 The 741 offset voltage

The offset voltage is used to make the output zero when there is zero input voltage. This offset voltage is controlled by the use of a potentiometer connected between pins 1 and 5 of the chip. The wiper of the potentiometer is connected to the negative supply rail of the amplifier.

Materials In addition to those listed for exercise 1, a 10 kΩ potentiometer is needed.

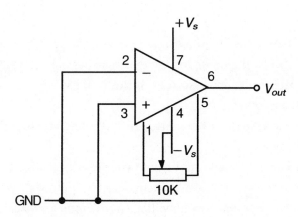

Figure 6.6.4 Investigating the offset voltage of the 741

177

Method 1 Set up the circuit shown in figure 6.6.4 and use a voltmeter to monitor the output voltage as the offset voltage is adjusted with the potentiometer.
2 Note your observations in your notebook.

You should find that:
- it is impossible to obtain zero voltage at the output.

Note: The reason for this is the very large open-loop gain, which means that the tiniest offset voltage will lead to either positive or negative saturation.

Exercise 3 The operational amplifier and negative feedback

This is the process by which some of the output voltage is fed back to the input in such a way as to reduce the input voltage to the amplifier. The result is a reduction in overall gain of the amplifier leading to a reduction in the output voltage. The operational amplifier can be connected to behave as a non-inverting amplifier (figure 6.6.5) or as an inverting amplifier (figure 6.6.7).

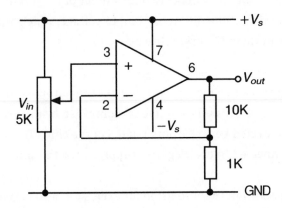

Figure 6.6.5 Non-inverting amplifier with variable input voltage

Method 1 Set up the circuit of figure 6.6.5 on the prototype board.
2 Adjust the input voltage to zero using the potentiometer and check that the output voltage is also zero. If this is not so adjust to zero using the offset potentiometer.
3 Increase the input voltage in stages and measure the corresponding output voltage.
4 Draw up a table and record your results.
5 Repeat steps 2 to 4 by increasing the input voltage in the reverse direction.
6 Plot a graph of input voltage (horizontal axis) against output voltage (vertical axis).
7 Inspect your graph and say what information can be obtained from it.

You should find that:

• your graph looks like that shown in figure 6.6.6, showing that the output voltage varies linearly within a range of input voltages and reaches saturation as the input goes beyond the range.

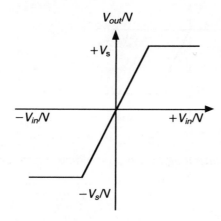

Figure 6.6.6. *Output against input voltage characteristic for the non-inverting amplifier*

Supplementary exercise 3a

Method 1 Remove the feedback resistor and repeat steps 2 to 6 in exercise 3.

2 Describe and explain your findings.

Supplementary exercise 3b

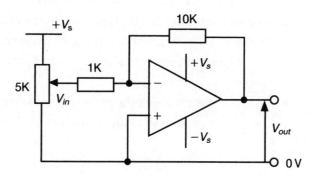

Figure 6.6.7 *Inverting amplifier with variable input voltage*

Method 1 Set up the circuit of figure 6.6.7 and repeat the procedures carried out in the previous exercise.

2 Tabulate your results and plot another graph of input voltage (horizontal axis) against output voltage (vertical axis).

3 Compare your graph with that shown in figure 6.6.8.

179

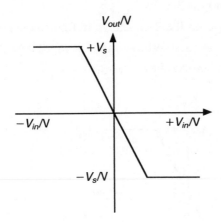

Figure 6.6.8 Output against input voltage characteristic for the inverting amplifier

Exercise 4 The op-amp and voltage gain

The voltage gain A_v of a non-inverting amplifier with negative feedback is given by the formula

$$A_v = \frac{V_{out}}{V_{in}} = 1 + \frac{R_2}{R_1}$$

Method

1 Set up the circuit of figure 6.6.5.

2 Adjust the potentiometer to give an input voltage of 0.5 V.

3 Measure the output voltage and use the formula above to calculate the voltage gain.

4 Use the resistor values to calculate the gain.

5 Draw up a table and tabulate your results.

6 Keeping the input voltage fixed, change the value of the feedback resistor, using the 22 kΩ, 47 kΩ, 68 kΩ, 82 kΩ and 100 kΩ resistors in turn. Each time use V_{out}/V_{in} to measure the gain and $A_v = 1 + R_2/R_1$ to calculate the theoretical gain.

7 Tabulate all your results.

8 What can you say about the measured gain compared to the calculated gain?

9 What conclusion can you draw with regard to this?

Supplementary exercise 4

Method

1 Set up the inverting amplifier shown in figure 6.6.7 and repeat steps 2 to 5 of exercise 4.

2 The gain of the inverting amplifier can be calculated using

$$A_v = -\frac{R_F}{R_{in}}$$

Calculate the gain using the resistor values given in step 6 of exercise 4 and tabulate your results.

3 Use the ratio of the input and output voltages to measure the actual gain of the circuit.

4 Again, compare the theoretical gain with the actual gain and state what conclusions can be drawn.

You should find that:

• the measured gain is very close to the theoretical gain and that it is independent of the actual property of the amplifier circuit; and

• the gain is only dependent on the ratio of the two resistors.

Exercise 5 The op-amp and frequency response

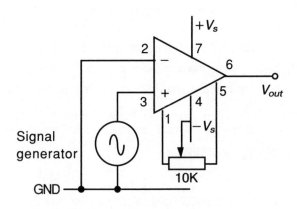

Figure 6.6.9 Frequency response of the 741

Method

1 Set up the op-amp circuit of figure 6.6.9 with a signal generator connected to the non-inverting input.

2 Connect the multimeter, set to the a.c. voltage range, to the output.

3 Measure the voltage when there is no input signal.

4 Set the generator to sine wave output and adjust the frequency to a very low value.

5 Draw up a table of frequency against output voltage.

6 Slowly increase the frequency in steps of 1 kHz up to the maximum of the generator, each time noting the output voltage in your notebook.

Method   **1** Set up the non-inverting amplifier circuit with negative feedback, using a 10 kΩ feedback resistor.

2 Repeat the procedure of exercise 5 for different values of the feedback resistor (22 kΩ, 47 kΩ, 68 kΩ, 82 kΩ and 100 kΩ).

3 Draw up another table to tabulate these results.

4 Use your results to plot a graph of output voltage (vertical axis) against frequency (horizontal axis) and explain the shape of the graph.

You should find that:
- when in the open-loop configuration the amplifier has very poor frequency response, the gain falling off significantly with frequency; and
- the greater the negative feedback the smaller the overall gain and the better the frequency response of the amplifier.

Exercise 6 Op-amp cut-off frequency   The cut-off frequency of an amplifier is the frequency at which the gain has fallen to 0.707 of its d.c. value.

Method   **1** Work out the cut-off frequency for the open-loop circuit and for each of the feedback circuits used in exercise 5 above.

2 What can you say about the cut-off frequency as the gain of the amplifier is decreased?

3 Suggest how you would use the op-amp to amplify frequencies within the audiofrequency range.

Exercise 7 The Schmitt trigger   This circuit is used for speeding up the switching action of many operational amplifier comparator circuits.

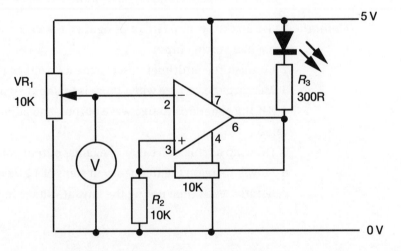

Figure 6.6.10 The Schmitt trigger switching circuit

Method

1 Set up the circuit shown in figure 6.6.10.

2 Adjust the potentiometer to its minimum position and note whether the LED is off or on.

3 Measure the output voltage and confirm that it is near that of the supply.

4 Measure the voltage at pin 3 and confirm that it is about 2.5 V.

5 Slowly increase the voltage on pin 2 by adjusting the potentiometer until the LED lights up.

6 Measure the voltages at pins 2 and 3 and the output voltage at pin 6.

7 Use your observations to describe how the circuit works.

You should find that:

• when the voltage at pin 2 is low the voltage at pin 6 (the output) is high and the LED is off; the voltage at pin 3 is near 2.5 V; and

• when the voltage at pin 2 is increasing the LED comes on suddenly, with the voltage at pin 6 falling quickly to near 0 V

7 Power supplies

7.1 Batteries

Why batteries are used The past few years have seen a reduction in the size and also the power requirement of electronic circuits. This has led to smaller, more portable devices and consequently to the need for small, relatively cheap, independent power supplies. Many such supplies take the form of batteries or dry cells and during the past few years there have been major advances in the development of these batteries, both in their capacity and in their size.

Batteries are ideal for satisfying the power requirement of modern electronic circuits. On the whole they are small (and getting smaller), fairly cheap and can maintain a reasonably constant d.c. voltage, at low load currents, for an appreciable length of time. Also they need no maintenance and can be replaced by anyone.

Many of us are familiar with the use of batteries for powering transistor radios, torches and toys. However, as a result of the growth of modern technology it is now commonplace for batteries to be found in cameras, watches, calculators, portable tape recorders, video cameras, computer games and many other devices.

Batteries do have a number of disadvantages. For instance they have to be replaced on a fairly regular basis and this can be costly over a period of time. Old batteries have a tendency to leak chemicals, which will corrode electrical contacts and therefore disrupt the proper operation of the device. Batteries for providing large currents are not only very expensive but also very heavy, thus making it more difficult to have a truly portable piece of equipment.

Power supply units In many applications the power supply unit (PSU) provides a respectable alternative to the battery and in fact many modern portable devices come equipped with their own built in PSU. Power supply units are mains-driven and the device will require a mains connecting cable to connect to the normal domestic electricity supply. All PSUs need a transformer to reduce the mains voltage to that necessary to operate the particular device. This is usually built into the PSU within the device and is supplied as part of the mains connecting cable.

Power supply units provide d.c. at constant voltage and/or constant current and because they are connected to the mains they can reduce the operating cost of an electronic device enormously. However, such a device, although still portable, is no longer mobile and therefore it must be supplied with batteries if it is to continue working when in transit. PSUs are therefore very useful when the device is to kept in one place for a period of time and should be seen as a complement to the battery and not as a replacement.

What is a battery?   A battery consists of a number of cells connected in series as in figure 7.1.1.

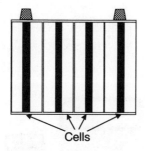

Figure 7.1.1 A typical battery   *Figure 7.1.2 Symbol for the battery*

The potential difference or voltage between the two terminals of a battery is called the **electromotive force (e.m.f.)**. The e.m.f. is at a maximum when the battery is new and decreases over time; the rate of decrease depends on the rate at which current is drawn from the battery.

The **current rating** of a battery is the amount of discharge current it can produce for a specified period of time with the output voltage not falling below a minimum level. The rating most commonly used is the **ampere-hour** (Ah). The specified discharge time is usually eight hours and therefore a 200 Ah battery can deliver 200 A in eight hours or 200/8 = 25 A per hour. If the current being drawn is greater then the battery will be discharged in a shorter period of time and if it is smaller then it will take longer to discharge. Current ratings are stated for particular temperatures; usually this is around 80 °F (27 °C). Higher temperatures increase the current capacity and lower temperatures decrease it. The ampere-hour capacity is reduced by approximately 1% for each 1 °F decrease in temperature. Starter motors usually require around 300 Ah from a battery.

The cells of the battery are made from a chemical, called the **electrolyte**, which reacts with the electrodes to produce energy. Therefore a battery changes *chemical* energy to *electrical* energy. The chemicals offer certain resistance to the flow of current, called the **internal resistance** of the battery, and this tends to increase in value over the life of the battery. The cells making up a battery are two main types, called **primary** and **secondary**.

Primary cells   These are the ones which are thrown away when they are exhausted. They are sometimes referred to as **dry cells** due to the fact that the electrolyte, although moist, is sealed and cannot be spilled. Batteries consisting of dry cells are called A, B and C batteries according to their original uses in pre-transistor radios, using valve technology:

'A' type batteries, rated at 4.5 V or 6 V with a current rating in excess of 150 mA, were used to heat the filament in valves to produce thermionic emission of electrons;
'B' type batteries, rated at 9 V, are used to provide the collector–emitter voltage for npn transistors and integrated circuits; and
'C' type batteries, rated at 1.5 V, were used to produce the small d.c. grid voltage within certain valves.

Figure 7.1.3 Types of primary cells and batteries: from left to right D, C, AA, PP9 and PP3

Secondary cells   These can be recharged on reversal of the chemical reaction within the cell. When the cell drives a current through a load it is discharging and this is associated with the neutralisation of the ions within the electrodes. When the current is reversed the process is reversed, thereby reforming the electrodes and charging the cell. The charging current must be a steady d.c. current which is obtained from an external voltage source. The most common secondary cell is the lead-acid type found in cars and motorcycle batteries. In addition, the much smaller nickel-cadmium cells are increasingly replacing primary cells in many applications.

Whether a cell is charged or discharged can be determined by measuring the **specific gravity** of the electrolyte. The specific gravity is a measure which compares the weight of the liquid in the battery (dilute sulphuric acid) with that of a similar volume of water and is measured using a **hydrometer**. In a fully charged battery the dilute sulphuric acid has a specific gravity of 1.28 at room temperature. When discharged fully the specific gravity falls to 1.15. Specific gravity is related to the e.m.f. in the following way:

e.m.f. = specific gravity + 0.84

Comparison of primary and secondary cells

Table 7.1.1 summarises the main differences between primary and secondary cells.

Table 7.1.1 Comparison of primary and secondary cells

Primary cells	Secondary cells
Cheap	Expensive
Small	Small to large
Sealed	Sealed and non-sealed
Short life	Relatively long life
Non-rechargeable	Rechargeable
Fairly lightweight	Usually heavier

Types of batteries

The last few years have seen a growth in the range and types of cells/batteries commonly available. These are summarised in table 7.1.2.

Table 7.1.2 Commonly available cell types

Name of cell	Type of cell	e.m.f./V
Zinc-carbon	Primary	1.5
Manganese-dioxide alkaline	Primary/Secondary	1.5
Mercury-oxide	Primary	1.35
Zinc-chloride	Primary	1.5
Silver-oxide	Primary	1.5
Lead-acid	Secondary	2.1
Nickel-cadmium	Secondary	1.25
Silver-cadmium	Secondary	1.1
Silver-zinc	Secondary	1.5

Zinc-carbon cell

The most common primary cell is the **Leclanche** type, of which the zinc-carbon (shown in figure 7.1.4) is perhaps the best known. The negative electrode of this cell is made of zinc and the positive electrode is made of manganese dioxide powder. The carbon rod is in contact with the manganese dioxide and is used to collect the current. It is not involved with the chemical reaction. When the cell is being used hydrogen gas is released and collects around the carbon electrode. The process is called **polarisation** and it leads to a reduction in the output voltage of the cell. The hydrogen is removed by reacting with the oxygen produced from the manganese dioxide to form water. As a result the manganese dioxide is called the **depolariser**.

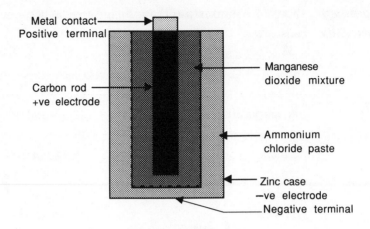

Figure 7.1.4 The zinc-carbon cell

The e.m.f. obtained from this cell is between 1.4 V and 1.6 V with a typical value of 1.5 V and the internal resistance is usually less than 1 Ω. These dry cells are usually obtained in HP16 or AAA, HP7 or AA, HP11 or C and HP2 or D sizes. The D size has a current of up to 150 mA, the smaller sizes have smaller current values. They are used in many small household pieces of equipment, such as bells, torches and a wide range of toys.

Manganese-dioxide alkaline cell

In this cell, shown in figure 7.1.5, the anode consists of powdered zinc and the cathode of manganese dioxide. The electrolyte is some form of alkaline such as potassium hydroxide which gives rise to (OH–) ions. The overall design of the cell leads to a very low internal resistance and high electrolyte conductivity.

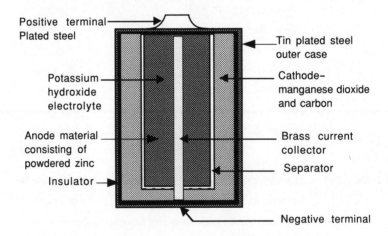

Figure 7.1.5 Construction of an alkaline cell

This cell is available in both primary and secondary batteries and has a typical voltage output of 1.5 V. It is efficient, long-lasting and has a high continuous discharge rate. In addition, it performs very well at low temperatures and has a much better shelf life than that of the Leclanche type cells.

Mercury-oxide cell   This cell consists of a zinc anode and a cathode composed of a mercury compound. The electrolyte is potassium or sodium hydroxide. The e.m.f. of the cell varies between 1.35 V and 1.4 V depending on the make-up of the cathode. The mercury cell has a high current density and discharges at a fairly constant rate. The internal resistance is low and remains fairly constant throughout the life of the cell. They can operate in temperatures of up to 150 °C for short periods of time and continuously at about 55 °C. These cells are usually packaged as miniature button types or flat, round cylindrical types as shown in figure 7.1.6. On the whole they are much more expensive than zinc-carbon cells.

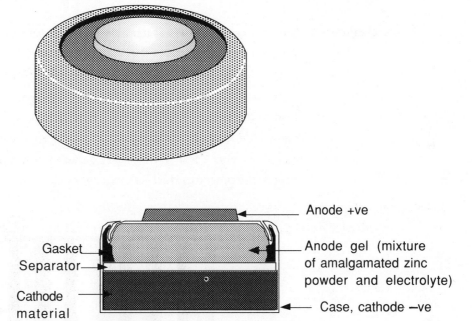

Figure 7.1.6 Button cell of the silver or mercury type

Zinc-chloride cell   The construction of this cell is similar to that of the zinc-carbon, with the difference that the electrolyte is zinc chloride. The chemical reaction within the cell absorbs water and as a result there is no leakage of liquid from the exhausted cell. These cells are able to deliver fairly large currents over much longer periods of time than the zinc-carbon cell and are referred to as heavy-duty cells.

Silver-oxide cell   The anode of this cell is made of zinc and the cathode is made of silver oxide with a little manganese dioxide. The electrolyte is either potassium or sodium hydroxide. The e.m.f. is 1.6 V and 1.5 V when supplying a current to load. It is found mainly as the miniature button type used in watches, calculators and cameras.

Lithium cell   There are two main forms of lithium cells. They are the **lithium-sulphur dioxide** type and **lithium-thionyl chloride** type. These cells may contain additional, fairly toxic, substances. The output voltage from the lithium-sulphur dioxide cell is 2.9 V and that from the lithium-thionyl chloride is 3.7 V. These cells have a number of distinct advantages over many other types of cells. As indicated, their output voltage is fairly high. In addition, they have a very long shelf life of about ten years, a fairly long service life, low weight and small volume. They are small round disc types capable of delivering a small current over a long period of time. Due to safety concerns lithium cells are not widely used. However, they find application in equipment in which frequent changes of battery are not possible, for example satellites and heart pacemakers.

Lead-acid cell   This is an example of a secondary cell, consisting of a number of lead-antimony alloy plates strapped together and immersed in dilute sulphuric acid, which acts as the electrolyte. The plates form a framework in which lead oxide is pasted. When in use, the lead oxide turns to lead peroxide in the positive plate and to lead in the negative plate. Lead-acid cells have a nominal output of 2.1 V and are connected in series of three cells to produce a 6 V battery or six cells to produce a 12 V battery. These batteries are generally used in automobiles in which they supply the power to start the engine.

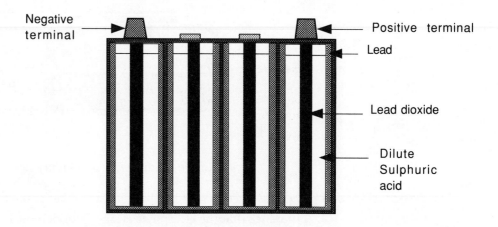

Figure 7.1.7 12 V lead-acid car battery

Lead-acid batteries can be charged and recharged repeatedly. However, excessive currents and high temperatures will shorten the life of the battery.

Nickel-cadmium cell   The two electrodes are nickel (+) and cadmium (−) with potassium hydroxide acting as the electrolyte. It has a nominal output voltage of between 1.2 V and 1.25 V and can be charged and discharged many times whilst delivering fairly high currents. These types of cells are commonly available in the same sizes and shapes as primary cells and are sealed to allow for ease of use. They can be used in all applications in which primary cells are used. However, specific applications would be those in which high current is required such as the operation of portable power tools, and radio and television equipment.

A constant current source is required to recharge the nickel-cadmium cell.

Battery-operated equipment compared with PSUs

Batteries offer a number of advantages:

1 lower voltages mean they are safer to use, although the voltages are limited to fairly low values;

2 batteries are usually small and light, but when large currents and/or voltage is required then the battery can be heavy and bulky;

3 the absence of connecting leads means that the equipment is completely portable.

There are two disadvantages though:

1 batteries do not store well and tend to deteriorate with time; and

2 batteries are exhausted after a period of use and therefore the performance of the equipment must deteriorate with time.

7.2 Power supply units

A power supply unit increases or reduces the mains voltage and then converts it from a.c. to steady d.c. so that it can be used in a range of electronic circuits. PSUs can have additional circuitry to enable them to maintain either a constant current or a constant voltage when supplying a load. The basic PSU consists of a transformer, a full-wave rectifier and a smoothing circuit. It may also contain a stabilised voltage circuit and/or a stabilised current circuit. The block diagram of the arrangement is shown in figure 7.2.1. The transformer was dealt with in section 3.5, and the remaining circuits are covered here.

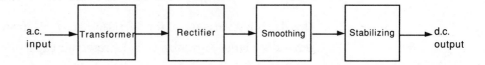

Figure 7.2.1 Block diagram for a power supply unit

Rectification

Rectification is the process of converting alternating current (a.c.) to direct current (d.c.). It is used in PSUs for producing low-power d.c. from the mains 240 V supply. A transformer is used to step down the mains voltage, which is then placed across the diode as shown in the circuit in figure 7.2.2.

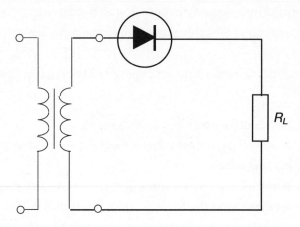

Figure 7.2.2 Half-wave rectifier

As the diode conducts only when its anode is positive, it allows a current to flow only on the positive half-cycles of the a.c. voltage. This current produces a voltage across the load resistor (see figure 7.2.3). This voltage represents only the positive half of the a.c. waveform. It is d.c., in that there are no negative half cycles, but it is unstable, fluctuating at mains frequency (50 Hz).

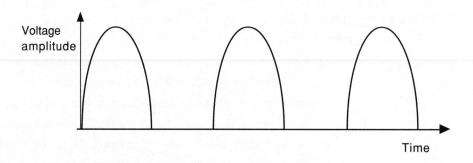

Figure 7.2.3 Voltage waveform from a half-wave rectifier

This d.c. is not very useful for operating most electronic equipment and generally a large capacitor, called a **reservoir capacitor**, is used to smooth out the fluctuations. As only the positive half-cycle of the waveform is being used this process is known as **half-wave rectification**.

Full-wave rectification Two diodes can be arranged as in figure 7.2.4 or as a bridge circuit as in figure 7.2.5. These arrangements produce a positive voltage peak for each half-cycle of the a.c. input voltage. As with the half-wave rectifier, a reservoir capacitor is used to smooth out the the large fluctuations.

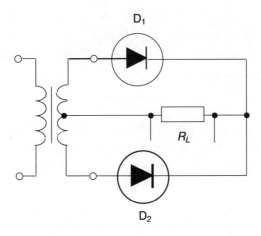

Figure 7.2.4 Full-wave rectifier using a centre-tap transformer

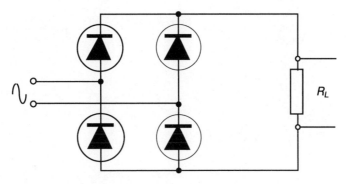

Figure 7.2.5 Bridge rectifier

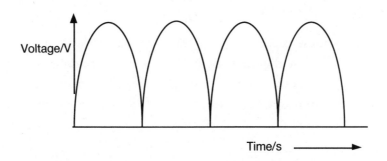

Figure 7.2.6 Output waveform from a bridge rectifier

The variation in voltage obtained after smoothing is much smaller than for half-wave rectification and is called the **ripple voltage**. The ripple frequency is twice that of the a.c. mains supply (see figure 7.2.6). Although the ripple voltage is small when little to no current is drawn by the load, it becomes unacceptably high when there is a significant current flow. The solution is to use a larger smoothing capacitor or additional circuitry to stabilise or regulate the output, as described in the next section.

Voltage regulation

The output voltage from a half-wave rectifier circuit which is not passing a load current is the same as for a full-wave rectifier circuit under the same conditions. When a current is passing, the output voltage from the half-wave rectifier will drop by a greater amount than that of the full-wave rectifier. For very large load currents the fall in the output voltage for the half-wave rectifier is about twice as great as for the full-wave rectifier operating from the same a.c. supply. This fall in the output voltage is referred to as the regulation of the supply, and is illustrated in figure 7.2.7. A perfect power supply would have constant voltage output regardless of the size of the load current .

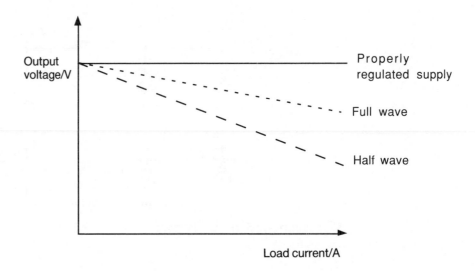

Figure 7.2.7 Voltage regulation

It is important to note the maximum reverse voltage for diodes which are used as rectifiers as they will have to manage safely a voltage equivalent to twice the peak voltage of the supply. In general, a maximum reverse voltage of about four times the root mean square voltage of the transformer secondary should be used.

Smoothing the waveform

This is achieved for both half-wave and full-wave rectification by the use of a fairly large value capacitor called a reservoir capacitor. It is connected to a half-wave rectifier as shown in figure 7.2.8a and to a full-wave rectifier as in figure 7.2.8b.

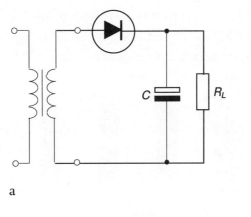

a

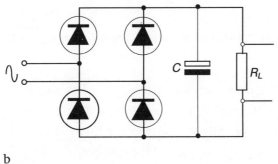

b

Figure 7.2.8 (a) Half-wave rectifier and (b) full-wave rectifier with smoothing capacitor

During the positive half-cycles when the diode is conducting the current flowing charges up the capacitor to a voltage near to that of the a.c. supply. During the negative half-cycles the capacitor discharges in such a direction as to maintain the current flow through the load resistor. This continues until the next pulse of current through the diode recharges the capacitor (see figures 7.2.9 and 7.2.10).

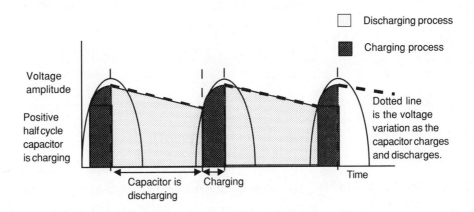

Figure 7.2.9 Output waveform from half-wave rectifier with smoothing capacitor

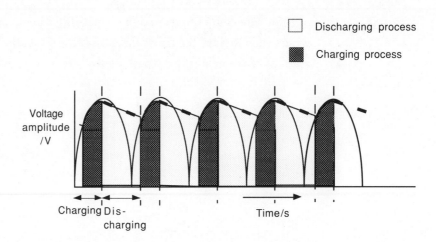

Figure 7.2.10 Output waveform from bridge (full-wave) rectifier with smoothing rectifier

The ripple voltage produced after smoothing is still varying, but this fluctuation is much smaller. The frequency of the ripple voltage is that of the mains in the case of the half-wave rectifier and twice the mains frequency for the full-wave rectifier. This ripple voltage is responsible for causing 'mains hum' in unscreened cables running close by.

The amount of smoothing obtained depends on the size of the capacitor and the size of the load resistance. In fact it depends on the **time constant (CR)**; the larger the time constant the better the smoothing and the smaller the ripple voltage.

Although quite a lot of the smoothing is carried out by the smoothing capacitor, there are filter circuits which, when added, are able to reduce the remaining ripple even further. One such circuit consists of an inductor or choke and a second large capacitor arranged in series as shown in figure 7.2.11.

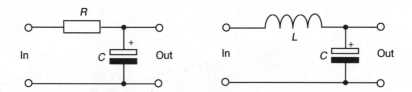

Figure 7.2.11 Additional filter circuits

The varying d.c. voltage can be considered as a d.c. voltage with an a.c. ripple. The inductor offers a greater opposition (impedance) to a.c. than to d.c. and therefore most of the a.c. voltage will appear across the inductor. Similarly the capacitor C offers a greater impedance to d.c. than to the a.c. component of the voltage. This means that all of the d.c. voltage will appear across the capacitor and if the output is taken from across that, this voltage will appear at the output. The components making up the filter are acting as a potential divider which then divides the a.c. voltage from the d.c. voltage and thereby reduces the amount of ripple in the output.

Stabilising circuits   Voltage stabilisation is the process of ensuring that the output remains constant regardless of the loading conditions applied and is commonly achieved through the use of a **Zener diode**. These diodes break down at a specified voltage when they are reverse-biased. The voltage then remains constant over a whole range of reverse currents. If the load is connected across the Zener diode then the voltage is fixed to that of the Zener breakdown voltage and this will remain so regardless of the current it is drawing, as long as the diode remains in the breakdown mode.

A number of discrete voltage regulator circuits are shown in figures 7.2.12–14. In each circuit the input is the smoothed voltage passing from the rectifier and smoothing stages. R_L is the load which draws a current from the supply, the remainder of which flows through the Zener diode. The total current being drawn from the supply is constant and therefore if more current is needed it is at the expense of the current flowing through the Zener diode, i.e. the Zener current is reduced. The Zener diode will continue to operate as long as the current flowing through it does not fall below that required to maintain breakdown and the simplest way of achieving this is to use a higher input voltage than that required at the output.

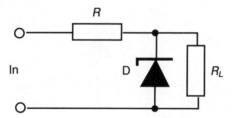

Figure 7.2.12 Zener diode voltage regulator

The first circuit in Figure 7.2.12 is the simple Zener diode shunt regulator, which is only suitable for low-current applications (up to 50 mA) and is capable of producing a regulation of about 10%.

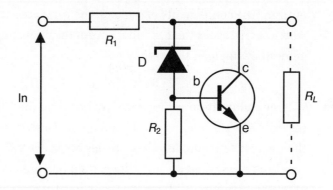

Figure 7.2.13 Amplified Zener diode voltage regulator

If higher currents are required then a modification is to use the arrangement shown in figure 7.2.13. The transistor in this circuit is acting as a shunt allowing the flow of a much greater current than is possible through the Zener diode. The output voltage is 0.7 V greater than the Zener voltage. A major advantage of this circuit is that a collector–emitter short-circuit fault will result in the output voltage falling to zero, whilst in series regulators, a similar fault will result in output voltage rising to the full unregulated output from the rectifier.

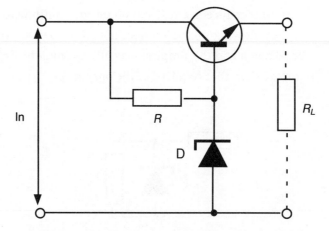

Figure 7.2.14 Transistor series voltage regulator

Due to the increased current-handling capacity, it is important that the series resistors have the correct power rating and perhaps a heat sink to adequately dissipate heat. Figure 7.2.14 shows a basic series regulator circuit. The transistor is connected as an emitter follower and therefore the output voltage will be 0.7 V less than the Zener voltage.

Stabilisation ensures a constant output voltage regardless of the demand of the load and regardless of fluctuations in the mains voltage.

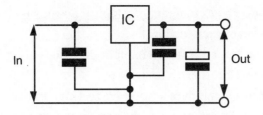

Figure 7.2.15 Integrated voltage regulator

Integrated voltage regulators, as shown in figure 7.2.15, are now available. They come in various different packages and consist of complex circuitry for voltage stabilisation, overload protection and overheating. Integrated circuit regulators are available to cover the range 5 V, 9 V, 15 V, 18 V and 24 V and a range of maximum load current. A common package is the T0220 package and is prefixed with 78 and 79 depending on whether it is a positive input or output type or a negative input or output type.

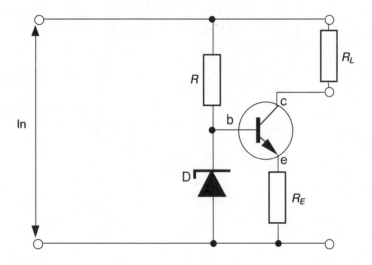

Figure 7.2.16 Constant current regulator

Stabilised current circuits, such as shown in figure 7.2.16, are used to produce a constant current from the PSU. The base of the transistor is held at the Zener voltage and this keeps the voltage across the emitter resistor constant at $V_Z - V_{BE}$. Therefore the collector current, as this depends on V_E/R_E, is constant regardless of the collector–emitter voltage.

1 Draw a block diagram of a typical power supply unit and explain the function of each section.

2 What is rectification? Explain the difference between full-wave and half-wave rectification.

3 Draw a diagram of a full-wave rectifier and give a full explanation with appropriate waveforms of the process involved in the rectification of a.c. to d.c.

4 Explain the function of a reservoir capacitor in a PSU.

5 What is a ripple voltage and what factors determine the size of this voltage?

6 Describe how the output of a properly regulated supply varies with increasing load current. How does this differ from that of a power supply which is poorly regulated?

7 Describe the process of producing a ripple-free output within a PSU.

8 Explain the function of a Zener diode in voltage stabilisation.

9 Draw a circuit which allows a large current to be drawn, whilst still maintaining a stable output.

10 Design a PSU which involves the use of an IC voltage regulator, using a block diagram.

8 Digital electronics

Digital electronics is concerned with **two-state switching circuits**. These circuits are designed to operate on voltage pulses which exist in one of two levels, **'high'** and **'low'**, referred to as logic levels 1 and 0.

Digital circuits are commonly in the form of integrated circuits and range in complexity from simple logic gates to microprocessors. They are used in electronic watches, calculators, domestic appliances, televisions, electronic games, telecommunications equipment and have many industrial applications.

8.1 Logic voltage levels

These are the actual voltage levels used to represent a 'high' or logic 1 and a 'low' or logic 0 level and they differ between **TTL** and **CMOS** logic families. A CMOS (complementary metal-oxide semiconductor) device can operate off supplies ranging from 3 V to 15 V; the logic levels are relative to the supply voltage. A 'high' is therefore greater than $\frac{2}{3}$ of the positive supply rail (V_{DD} for a CMOS circuit) and a 'low' is less than $\frac{1}{3}$ of the supply. Between these two levels there is what is known as an 'intermediate state'.

For TTL (transistor–transistor logic) devices a 'high' logic state is more than 2.0 V, a 'low' is less than 0.8 V and the intermediate state is between 0.8 V and 2.0 V.

Providing logic 1 or logic 0 is simply a matter of connecting the appropriate input(s) to the positive supply rail or to the zero volt rail using one of the methods shown in figures 8.1.1 and 8.1.2.

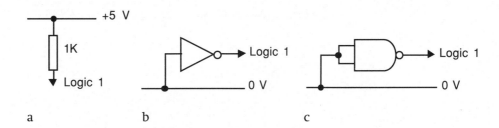

Figure 8.1.1 Ways of providing logic 1

A logic 1 should be obtained by the use of a pull-up resistor (1 kΩ to 10 kΩ) as shown in figure 8.1.1a. This limits the current supplied to the gate and also protects against unpredictable rises in the supply voltage. The alternative arrangement for providing a logic 1 is to invert the 0 V supply, using either the NOT gate as in figure 8.1.1b or a NAND gate connected as an inverter (see figure 8.1.1c). The advantage of this arrangement is to short the input to ground in the case of failure.

Generating logic 0 is by direct connection to the 0 V rail as shown in figure 8.1.2a, or alternatively by the use of a pull-up resistor connected to inverters as shown in figures 8.1.2b and 8.1.2c.

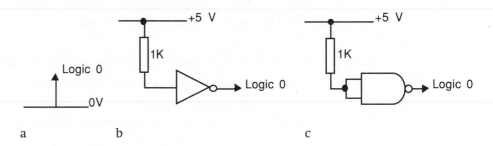

Figure 8.1.2 Ways of providing logic 0

8.2 Logic gates

Logic gates are switching circuits having usually more than one input, but only one output, with the output depending on the combination of signals at the input. The various gates are as follows:

Inverter or NOT
AND
OR
NAND
NOR
EOR
ENOR

These gates are represented by either the **British symbol (BS 3939)** or more commonly the US **American symbol (MIL/ANSI)** and are discussed in more detail below.

Inverter

a

b

Figure 8.2.1 (a) British and (b) American symbol

The inverter is also referred to as a NOT gate. It has only one input and its function is to produce an output which is the complement of the input, i.e. a logic 1 at the input produces a logic 0 at the output and vice versa. The truth table (table 8.2.1) summarises the operation of the circuit.

Table 8.2.1 Inverter truth table

Input X	Output Y
0	1
1	0

AND gate

Figure 8.2.2 Symbols for the AND gate

The AND gate has two or more inputs and one output. It produces a logic 1 only when all of its inputs are at logic 1. If this is not the case then logic 0 is produced.

Table 8.2.2 Truth table for a two-input AND gate

Inputs		Output
A	B	Y
0	0	0
0	1	0
1	0	0
1	1	1

OR gate

Figure 8.2.3 Symbols for the OR gate

This produces a logic 1 output when one or more of its inputs are at logic 1. For a two-input OR gate, this means that the output is at logic 1 if input A or input B or both of these are at logic 1. A logic 0 is produced when all the inputs are at logic 0.

Table 8.2.3 Truth table for a two-input OR gate

	Inputs		Output
A		B	Y
0		0	0
0		1	1
1		0	1
1		1	1

NAND gate

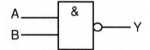 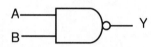

Figure 8.2.4 Symbols for the NAND gate

A NAND gate can be considered as an AND gate followed by an inverter or NOT gate and is symbolised by adding a ∘ to the symbol of the AND gate as shown in figure 8.2.4. It produces a logic 0 output only when all the inputs are simultaneously at logic 1. Logic 1 is produced with any other input combination. For a two-input gate the output is at logic 0 only when both inputs are at logic 1.

Table 8.2.4 Truth table for a two-input NAND gate

	Inputs		Output
A		B	Y
0		0	1
0		1	1
1		0	1
1		1	0

NOR gate

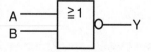 

Figure 8.2.5 Symbols for the NOR gate

A NOR gate can be considered as an OR gate followed by an inverter or a NOT gate. It produces a logic 1 output only when all the inputs are simultaneously at logic 0. Logic 0 is produced with any other combinations of inputs. For a two-input gate the output is logic 1 when both inputs are at logic 0.

Table 8.2.5 Truth table for a two-input NOR gate

Inputs		Output
A	B	Y
0	0	1
0	1	0
1	0	0
1	1	0

Exclusive-OR gate (EOR)

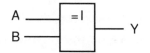 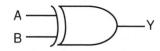

Figure 8.2.6 Symbols for the EOR gate

This gate produces a logic 1 at the output when one or the other but not both inputs have the same logic states. For a two-input gate the output is logic 0 when both inputs are logic 0, or when both inputs are logic 1.

Table 8.2.6 Truth table for the EOR gate

Inputs		Output
A	B	Y
0	0	0
0	1	1
1	0	1
1	1	0

Exclusive-NOR gate (ENOR)

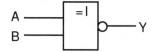 

Figure 8.2.7 Symbols for the ENOR gate

This gate is the NOT-OR the inversion of the EOR gate and gives an output of logic 1 only when all inputs are equal, i.e. all are simultaneously at logic 1 or at logic 0.

Table 8.2.7 Truth table for the ENOR gate

Inputs		Output
A	B	Y
0	0	1
0	1	0
1	0	0
1	1	1

8.3 Combining logic gates

Although there are seven gates described above and indeed for two inputs there could be as many as 15 different truth tables, it is not necessary to manufacture all these different gates. All gates can be created by combining single gates of the same kind. The gate chosen for this is either the NAND gate or the NOR gate.

The NOT gate or the inverter can be obtained from a single-input NAND gate or NOR gate. This is achieved by connecting both the inputs of the gate together as shown in figure 8.3.1.

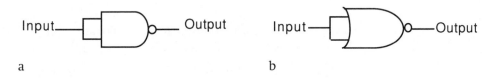

a   b

Figure 8.3.1 (a) NAND gate inverter; (b) NOR gate inverter

An AND gate can be produced from two NAND gates. The first NAND gate is connected to the second, which is configured as an inverter, as shown in figure 8.3.2, the AND gate being a NAND gate followed by an inverter.

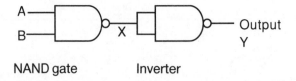

NAND gate   Inverter

Figure 8.3.2 AND gate made from two NAND gates

Table 8.3.1 confirms its behaviour as that of an AND gate.

Table 8.3.1 Truth table for the AND gate built from NAND gates

Inputs			Output
A	B	X	Y
0	0	1	0
0	1	1	0
1	0	1	0
1	1	0	1

Similarly the OR gate is obtained from three NAND gates, two configured as inverters connected to the inputs of the third, as shown in figure 8.3.3, and confirmed in table 8.3.2.

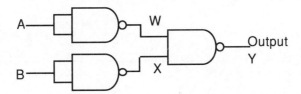

Figure 8.3.3 OR gate made from three NAND gates

Table 8.3.2 Truth table for the OR gate made from three NAND gates

Inputs				Output
A	B	W	X	Y
0	0	1	1	0
0	1	1	0	1
1	0	0	1	1
1	1	0	0	1

Since a NOR gate is an OR gate followed by a NOT gate, the NOR gate can be made from a combination of four NAND gates; two configured as inverters connected to the inputs of the third and the output from the third passing to an inverter. This is shown in figure 8.3.4 and confirmed in table 8.3.3.

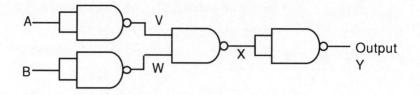

Figure 8.3.4   NOR gate made from four NAND gates

Table 8.3.3 Truth table for the NOR gate made from four NAND gates

Inputs					Output
A	B	V	W	X	Y
0	0	1	1	0	1
0	1	1	0	1	0
1	0	0	1	1	0
1	1	0	0	1	0

The EOR gate is shown in figure 8.3.5. Confirm by drawing up the truth table and comparing it with that for the EOR given in figure 8.2.6. The solution for this is given in table 8.3.4.

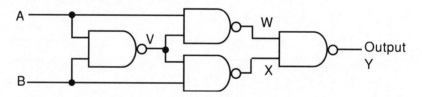

Figure 8.3.5 EOR gate made from four NAND gates

Table 8.3.4 Truth table for the EOR gate made from four NAND gates

Inputs					Output
A	B	V	W	X	Y
0	0	1	1	1	0
0	1	1	1	0	1
1	0	0	0	1	1
1	1	0	1	1	0

8.4 Other combinations of logic gates

A combination of different gates can be used to achieve a specific task. One such task is binary addition, in which two bits (pieces of information) are added together to produce one of four possible outcomes:

$0 + 0 = 0$
$0 + 1 = 1$
$1 + 0 = 1$
$1 + 1 = 10$

This circuit should have two inputs and two outputs with the function summarised in table 8.4.1.

Table 8.4.1 Truth table showing the addition of two bits

Inputs		Outputs	
A	B	X	Y
0	0	0	0
0	1	0	1
1	0	0	1
1	1	1	0

Output X is that of an AND gate, whilst output Y is that of an EOR gate. Therefore by combining these two gates binary addition can be achieved. Output X is called the 'carry' and Y the 'sum'. The circuit for doing this is called a **half adder** and is shown figure 8.4.1.

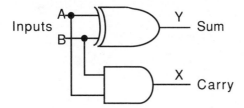

Figure 8.4.1   The half-adder circuit

Since the AND gate can be constructed using two NAND gates (see figure 8.3.2) and the EOR gate can be constructed using four NAND gates (see figure 8.3.5) the half adder could be constructed using six NAND gates. For ease of understanding the single-gate constructions are not used at the design stage.

The full-adder binary circuit

This circuit is required to add numbers consisting of more than one bit. In the simplest case if two-bit numbers are to be added together, for example 3 added to 3, the following sum would be obtained:

$$\begin{array}{r} 11 \\ +11 \\ \hline 110 \end{array}$$

The answer is 110 and this is obtained by first adding the two 1s in the extreme right-hand column

$$1 + 1 = 0 \text{ (sum)} + 1 \text{ (carry)}$$

This results in the next column having three bits to be added together

$$1 + 1 + 1 = 1 \text{ (sum)} + 1 \text{ (carry)}$$

Therefore it is necessary for a full-adder circuit to have three inputs, two for the digits to be added and one for the carry which results from the previous sum. There are two outputs, one for the sum and the other for the carry. The full adder is made by connecting two half adders, one to each of the inputs of an OR gate. Its function is summarised in table 8.4.2.

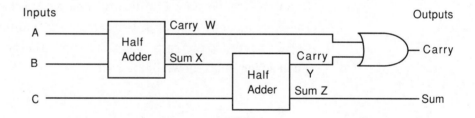

Figure 8.4.2 A full adder

Table 8.4.2 Truth table for the full adder

| Inputs | | | Intermediate | | | Outputs | |
A	B	C	W	X	Y	Sum (Z)	Carry
0	0	0	0	0	0	0	0
0	0	1	0	0	0	1	0
0	1	0	0	1	0	1	0
0	1	1	0	1	1	0	1
1	0	0	0	1	0	1	0
1	0	1	0	1	1	0	1
1	1	0	1	0	0	0	1
1	1	1	1	0	0	1	1

8.5 Monostable and astable logic gates

A monostable has one stable state and when activated will always return to the stable state; it is usually used in timing applications. An astable has no stable state; when activated it 'toggles' repeatedly between the two states, the 'on' state and the 'off' state. Both of these circuits can be made by combining NAND gates as in figure 8.5.1 or NOR gates as in figure 8.5.2.

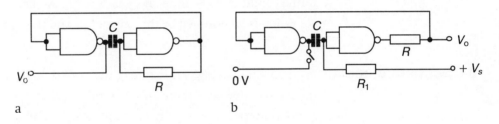

a   b

Figure 8.5.1 (a) NAND gate astable; (b) NAND gate monostable

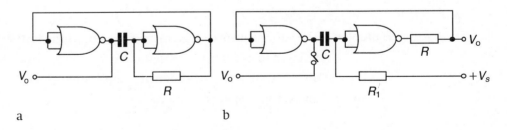

a   b

Figure 8.5.2 (a) NOR gate astable; (b) NOR gate monostable

In the astable circuit shown in figure 8.5.1a the NAND gates are arranged as two inverters in which the output from the second is the input of the first. If the output from the second inverter is 'low' then the input to the first is also 'low' and its output will be 'high'. As the input to the second inverter is 'high' and its output is 'low' the capacitor will begin to discharge through the resistor with the result that the voltage across it will fall. When it is 'low' enough the output of the second inverter will change to 'high'; this will be fed back to the input of the first thus making its output 'low'. The capacitor now begins to charge up through the resistor until the voltage across it is high enough to cause the output of the second inverter to switch once again to 'low'. The process is repeated for as long as power is supplied to the circuit, the frequency of the oscillation between 'high' and 'low' being determined by the values of the resistor and the capacitor in the circuit.

If the monostable started with the output of the second inverter being 'low' (see figure 8.5.1b), then the input of the first will also be 'low' and its output 'high'. This 'high' condition is transmitted through the capacitor to the input of the second inverter thus allowing this initial condition to be maintained. Momentary closure of the switch will cause immediate discharge of the capacitor. This leads to a fall in the voltage across it, with the result that the output of the second inverter, and therefore the output from the circuit, switches to 'high'. This is fed back to the input of the first, which makes its output 'low'. The capacitor now has one of its plates at low voltage and the other at high voltage and therefore it begins to charge through R_1. When the voltage across it is high enough, the output of the second inverter switches once again to 'low' and the output of the first switches to 'high' to re-establish the initial condition. The time taken for the re-establishment of the initial condition is determined by the value of R_1 and the value of the capacitor.

8.6 Sequential logic

In combinational logic, the state of the output depends only on the logic state of the inputs. However, there are other systems in which the output state depends not only on the current state of the inputs but also on the previous inputs. These systems rely on feedback to ensure that the previous input states are 'remembered'. Such circuits are called **sequential logic circuits**.

Bistables

The basic sequential logic circuit element is the **bistable** or **flip-flop**, also referred to as a **latch**. It is defined as having two stable states, an 'on' state and an 'off' state and is used in many applications such as counters, shift registers and various types of memories.

Bistables can also be made from NAND gates or NOR gates; both arrangements are shown in figure 8.6.1. Note that the output from each is fed back to one of the inputs of the other. The two inputs to the bistable are called the **set** (S) and **reset** (R) inputs; consequently the bistable is called a **set/reset** or **SR bistable**. NAND gate bistables are set and reset with logic 0, whilst NOR gate bistables are set and reset with logic 1.

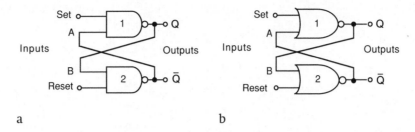

Figure 8.6.1 (a) NAND gate bistable; (b) NOR gate bistable

Looking at the NAND gate bistable, it is set when S = 0 and R = 1 and therefore NAND gate 1 has one of its inputs at logic 0 resulting in its output Q being at logic 1. As this is fed back to the input of NAND gate 2, both of the inputs are at logic 1 and therefore its output $\bar{Q}$ is at logic 0. The bistable is now in its set state, i.e. Q = 1 and $\bar{Q}$ = 0, and will remain so even if the logic level at the set input changes from 0 to 1. In this state the circuit is said to be 'latched'.

The reset state is achieved when S = 1 and R = 0 and the outputs Q = 0 and $\bar{Q}$ = 1. This condition is 'latched' even when R changes from logic 0 to logic 1.

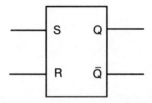

Figure 8.6.2 SR bistable symbol

Bistables made from NAND gates or NOR gates are not very reliable in that they have a third state, known as the **indeterminate state**, in which it is impossible to predict the output when logic 1 is simultaneously applied to the set and reset inputs of the circuit. The only way to avoid this is to ensure that this condition does not occur.

Debounced switches   One application of the SR bistable is that of a debounced switch. Unlike mechanical switching, in which the contacts bounce against each other after the initial contact is made, leading to more than one pulse being produced, the debounced switch produces a single pulse. Therefore it is used in situations where clean switching is required, such as with logic circuits. Debounced switches can be made from NAND gates as in figure 8.6.3, NOR gates as in figure 8.6.4 or from the Schmitt trigger (an inverter with sharp switching action) as in figure 8.6.5.

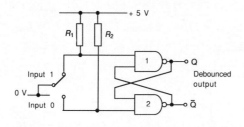

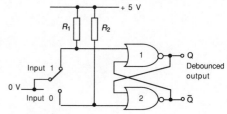

Figure 8.6.3 NAND gate debounced switch

Figure 8.6.4 NOR gate debounced switch

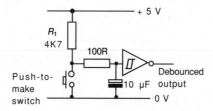

Figure 8.6.5 Schmitt trigger debounced switch

Other types of bistables

Due to the intermediate states, NAND or NOR gate bistables are not generally used as there are a variety of purpose-made integrated bistables that are more predictable. Other types of bistables which are more commonly available in IC form are the **D-type** and the **JK bistable**. The symbols for these are shown in figure 8.6.6.

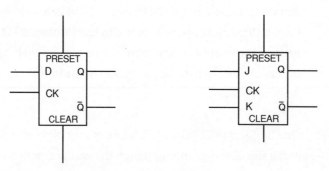

Figure 8.6.6 D-type and JK bistable symbols

The D-type bistable

There are four inputs to this circuit; D (standing for data) and CK (standing for clock) are the two main inputs, whilst the preset and clear inputs are used to set and reset the circuit. The data in the form of logic 0 or logic 1 will only pass through to the outputs (Q or $\bar{Q}$) when a positive-going pulse arrives at the clock input. A negative-going pulse will have no effect on the output. As is the case with all bistables, the data is latched to the output and will remain so until the next rising edge of the clock signal. (The clock signal is a regular repeated transition between the two voltage levels (high and low).) Any change in the data signal between each rising edge of the clock signal will in effect be ignored. In figure 8.6.7 the rising edge is represented by the thicker lines on the clock signal. Look carefully at the data signal and the output signal and see how these are related to the clock pulse.

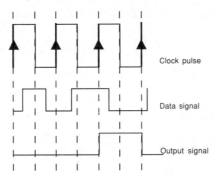

Figure 8.6.7 Timing diagram for D-type bistable

The output of a D-type bistable can be made to switch repeatedly between the high and low logic levels on successive clock pulses by connecting the $\bar{Q}$ output to the data input. As $\bar{Q}$ is low when Q is high, the data signal will consist of a series of logic 1s and 0s. However, the change will be clocked through to the Q output only on a rising edge of the clock pulse. This means that the frequency of the output will be half the frequency of the clock pulses. This way of connecting a D-type bistable so that it 'toggles' on each successive clock pulse converts it into a **T-type bistable**.

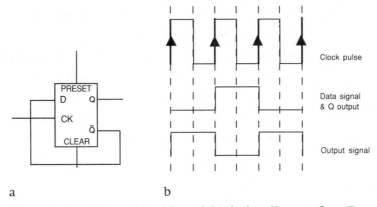

Figure 8.6.8 (a) T-type bistable and (b) timing diagram for a T-type bistable

The JK bistable   This circuit has five inputs and two outputs. The inputs consist of two inputs which are under the control of the clock; these are the J and K inputs. The preset and the clear inputs are used to set and reset the bistable. A logic 0 on the preset input will set the Q output to 1 and a logic 0 on the clear input will set the Q output to 0. The clock input supplies the pulse to clock the J and K inputs. The outputs are the Q and $\bar{Q}$ complementary outputs. Unlike the D-type bistable, the clocking of the J and K inputs is achieved on the falling edge of the clock pulses.

As there are two principal inputs, there are four input conditions and unlike the SR bistable, none of these lead to an indeterminate condition. The result of the four input conditions after the arrival of a clock pulse is summarised in table 8.6.1.

Table 8.6.1 The operation of the JK flip-flop

J and K inputs		Effect on Q output
0	0	Remains either at 1 or 0
0	1	Output resets to 0
1	0	Output sets to 1
1	1	Output logic state changes

The preset and clear inputs will also produce four input conditions, the result of which is summarised in table 8.6.2.

Table 8.6.2 The effect of the preset and clear inputs on the Q output of the JK flip-flop

Preset	Clear	Effect on Q output
0	0	Output indeterminate
0	1	Output sets to 1
1	0	Output resets to 0
1	1	Clock enable condition

8.7 Uses of bistables

As oscillators   The simplest way of making an oscillator is to use a **Schmitt trigger** bistable inverter. The op-amp version of the Schmitt trigger was covered in section 3.6. In this particular instance it is a bistable whose output changes very rapidly from one logic state to another as a result of the change in the input voltage. The oscillator consists of two inverters connected as shown in figure 8.7.1. These are found in the 74LS14 integrated package consisting of six such Schmitt inverters. The frequency of the oscillator is determined by the values of C and R. The variable resistor allows a variable-frequency output.

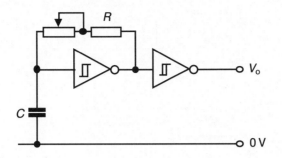

Figure 8.7.1 Schmitt trigger inverter oscillator

As binary counters   A number of bistables can be arranged as a binary ripple counter. The circuit shown below is a four-bit counter binary constructed from 7473 JK bistables. The count is incremented on the arrival of each clock pulse. The least significant bit (l.s.b.) is represented by the Q_0 output and the most significant bit (m.s.b.) by the Q_3 output.

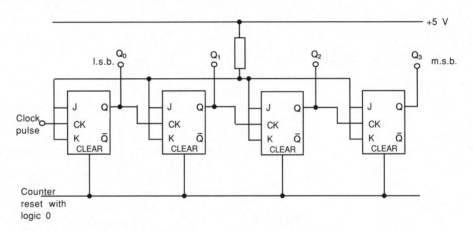

Figure 8.7.2 Four-bit binary counter made from JK bistables

As a decade counter   This is a counter which automatically resets on reaching ten and can be made from 74LS74 D-type bistables. The number 10 in decimal is equivalent to 1010 in base two and as the circuit below counts in binary or base two, with its Q_0 to Q_3 outputs representing the count, 1010 is achieved when $Q_1 = Q_3 = 1$. If the resets of the bistables are connected to the output of an AND gate whose inputs are connected to the Q_1 and Q_3 outputs of the circuit, then the circuit will reset when the count reaches 10 (ten) and the Q_1 and Q_3 outputs are high.

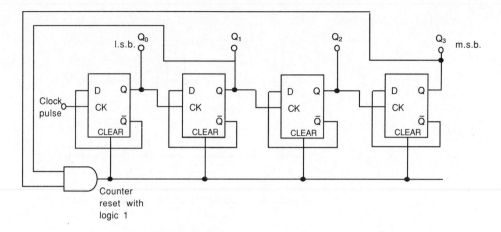

Figure 8.7.3 A decade counter based on the D-type bistable

As parallel registers
A register is a memory which stores a binary number and shifts it out again when required. It consists of a number of bistables grouped together, each bistable being able to store a single bit of the data. Therefore, if the binary number required to be saved consists of eight bits then the register must have eight bistables.

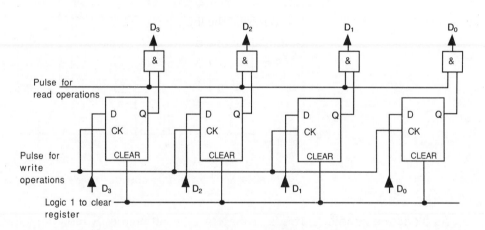

Figure 8.7.4. A read/write four-bit parallel register

In the parallel register shown in figure 8.7.4 data is presented to each bistable on the data lines D_0 to D_3. A write operation consists of a positive-going pulse to each of the clock inputs which transfers the data to the Q outputs. This data is now stored within the bistables and will be unaffected by changes to the data inputs. The read operation sends a pulse to the second input of the AND gates. Thus if Q is 'high' then logic 1 is 'read' out of the register and if Q is 'low' then logic 0 is 'read' out. A read operation does not affect the data stored.

As a shift register   In a shift register (see figure 8.7.5) each bit of data is shifted serially from one bistable to another through the register. The operation enables a serial stream of data to be presented, stored and fed out in parallel form. It is also possible to have parallel registers which can be read serially.

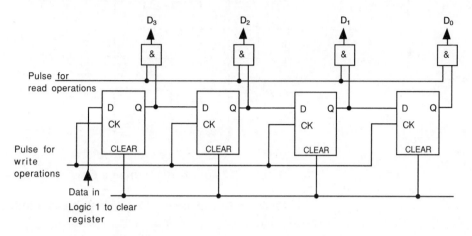

Figure 8.7.5 Serial in parallel-out shift register

Questions

1 What is digital electronics?

2 Describe the logic levels used in both TTL and CMOS logic and show a number of practical ways of achieving logic '0' and logic '1'.

3 Explain the AND gate and the NOR gate, and give the symbol and corresponding truth table for each of these gates.

4 Draw the truth table for the combination of gates shown in figure 8.7.6.

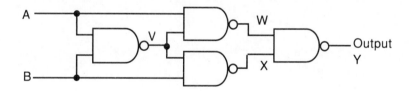

Figure 8.7.6

5 Describe the 'half adder' and explain the use of the gates in this circuit.

6 Explain with diagrams how a number of NAND gates can be connected to produce (a) a monostable and (b) a bistable.

7 What is sequential logic and what type of circuits involve the use of sequential logic?

8 Describe the JK bistable and give an example of one circuit in which it is used.

9 Use the 'timing diagram' shown in figure 8.7.7 to explain how the D-type bistable operates.

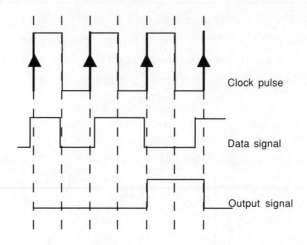

Figure 8.7.7 Timing diagram of a D-type bistable

10 Describe the use of a D-type bistable in a four-bit parallel register.

9 Six projects

The projects in this section are all fully tested working circuits and therefore perseverance will bring success and enjoyment. However, one word of warning, do not experiment on the user port of the computer without knowing what you are doing and never connect an external power supply directly to the user port. Good luck!

9.1 Light-dependent switch

This circuit, in its simplest form as shown in figures 9.1.1 and 9.1.2, uses a light-dependent resistor (LDR) to sense the intensity of light and uses this to switch a transistor on or off.

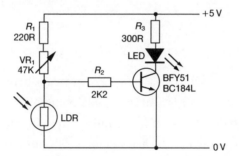

Figure 9.1.1 Dark-operated switch

It can be used in many different situations, e.g. as a car parking light, as a porch light or as part of a burglar alarm. The circuit of figure 9.1.1 is activated by decreasing light levels and the transistor will switch on as darkness approaches. The second circuit, shown in figure 9.1.2, is activated by increasing light levels and the transistor will switch on when light is detected.

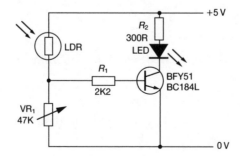

Figure 9.1.2 Light-operated switch

The circuits shown in figures 9.1.1 and 9.1.2 do not remain switched on when the light level returns to the original value and as a result would not serve as an effective light-activated burglar alarm as they stand.

The circuit in figure 9.1.3 has essentially the same function, but on being activated by a change in the light level will remain switched on until the power supply to the circuit is disconnected. In this circuit the transistor is replaced with a device called a silicon control rectifier or thyristor, which was covered in section 3.6.

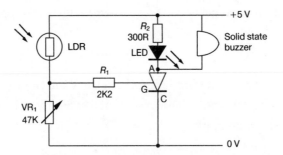

Figure 9.1.3 A thyristor latched light-operated switch

In the circuits of figures 9.1.1 to 9.1.3 an LED is being switched. In figure 9.1.3 a solid state d.c. buzzer is also switched on and off and therefore serves as an audible warning device. If it is required to switch more power then a relay may be used, as is shown in the arrangement of figure 9.1.4.

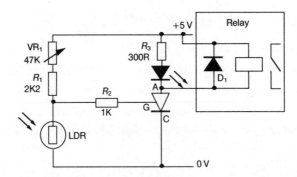

Figure 9.1.4 Dark-operated switch for latching a relay

Exercises

1 Build and test the circuits shown in figures 9.1.1–9.1.3 using a prototype board.
2 Build the circuit of figure 9.1.3 by first producing a printed circuit board according to the diagram in figure 9.1.5.

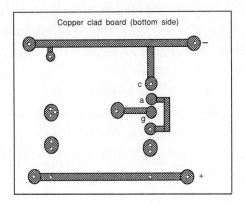

Figure 9.1.5 Printed circuit board layout for the latched light-dependent switch

How the circuits work   The circuit in figure 9.1.6 is similar to the earlier circuits considered and consists of a number of basic parts. The first part comprises three resistors, VR_1, R_1 and the LDR connected in series, between the 5 V and the 0 V lines. Resistors connected like this make up a potential divider network, which splits up the voltage between the resistors according to their value. If the resistors are identical then the voltage is shared equally between them. However, the larger the resistance the higher the share of the voltage across it. Resistor R_1 is there to ensure that when the variable resistor, VR_1, is in its minimum position, the amount of current flowing cannot damage the LDR. It is useful to consider R_1 and VR_1 as a single resistor connected in series with the LDR.

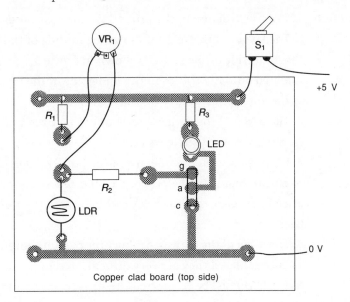

Figure 9.1.6 Printed circuit board layout for the light-dependent switch with components in place

The voltage across the LDR is high when it is in the dark and low when it is in the light. The reason for this is that the LDR has a high resistance in the dark and a low resistance in the light. In fact its resistance changes from about 10 MΩ in the dark to a few hundred ohms in bright sunlight.

In the case of figure 9.1.2, the second part of the circuit comprises the npn silicon transistor switch, which needs a voltage above 0.7 V between its base and emitter for it to be switched on. The base of this transistor is protected against excessive current by the 2.2 kΩ resistor (R_1), and is connected across the VR$_1$ with the consequence that the base-emitter voltage varies as the voltage across the LDR varies. In the dark, this voltage is low, but as more and more light falls onto the LDR the voltage rises. When the voltage reaches 0.7 V, a small current begins to flow into the base of the transistor causing it to switch on, the voltage at its collector falls and a current flows through the LED causing it to light. The resistor in series with the LED (R_2) limits the current flowing through it to a safe level. When in the dark, the voltage across the VR$_1$ falls again and the transistor switches off.

Although figure 9.1.6 uses a thyristor instead of the transistor, the operation of the circuit is very much the same. As the voltage across the LDR rises a small current is driven into the gate of the thyristor causing it to switch on. However, once switched on it remains latched until the power is switched off using switch S$_1$.

Notes on the construction   1 The construction of the printed circuit board is dealt with in section 5.4.
2 The layout of figure 9.1.6 shows the topside of the board, whilst the artwork of the underside of the board is shown in figure 9.1.5. Since the components are soldered onto the tracks on the underside of the board, holes should be drilled at the appropriate places on the board.
3 The LDR and the variable resistor can be fixed to the p.c.b. or connected to the circuit board by flexible wires.
4 If a relay is used then details of the pin arrangement of the relay are needed to ensure that it can be properly connected to the p.c.b. In addition, the diode must be fitted across the relay coil to protect the transistor from damage due to back e.m.f.
5 The leads of the transistor/thyristor must be entered in the correct positions, as once soldered they are very difficult to remove and put right.
6 The LED must be connected the correct way round in the circuit, since it only allows a current to flow when its anode is positive and its cathode is negative.

Testing the circuit and fault finding

Section 5.7 on circuit testing gives details of all the preliminary testing to be carried out. If no obvious fault is detected then the list below should be followed systematically.

1 Ensure that the circuit is correctly connected to the power supply, positive supply line to the positive terminal and negative or zero supply line to the negative or zero terminal.

2 Adjust VR_1 to test: (a) the LDR/resistor network; (b) the transistor/thyristor. Turn it clockwise or anticlockwise until the LED lights. If the LED is already on then adjust VR_1 until it goes off. If the LED is switched on and off when the VR_1 is varied then go to step 7. If nothing happens when VR_1 is varied then there is a fault. Either the LDR and resistor network is faulty or the transistor/thyristor is not switching.

3 Use a voltmeter to check the voltage across the LDR as VR_1 is adjusted. If there is a change in the voltage then go to step 4. If the voltage across the LDR is high all the time, irrespective of the position of VR_1, then the LDR is behaving as an open-circuit or VR_1 is acting as a short-circuit. The LDR should be removed and its resistance, under both light and dark conditions, measured using a multimeter. If there is a difference in its resistance under these conditions, then the fault is not with the LDR. VR_1 should therefore be checked by removing it, connecting it directly across the power supply in its potentiometer mode and measuring the voltage as it is varied. If there is no change in the voltage then it is faulty and should be changed. If all is well then the fault lies with the connection to the board.

If the voltage reading across the LDR is low then this suggests that there is a short-circuit across the LDR. It is possible that the LDR is faulty and it should be removed and checked as above.

4 If the LED is on all the time there may be a short-circuit fault between the collector/anode and emitter/cathode of the transistor/thyristor. Disconnect R_2 from the LDR and connect a positive voltage from the positive supply line to the base of the transistor via R_2. This will make the transistor switch on and the LED will light if it was off. A negative voltage to the base will cause the transistor to switch off and the LED will go off. If there is no effect then either the transistor/thyristor is faulty (go to step 6) or the LED output stage is faulty (go to step 5).

5 Check the connections to the LED. If these are correct then disconnect the negative from the battery and connect the negative terminal of the battery directly to the negative terminal of the LED – it should light showing that all is well. If it does not, then replace it and the series resistor.

6 At this stage all the evidence is pointing to a faulty transistor or thyristor. First, check the connection of the transistor/thyristor. If all is well then remove the transistor/thyristor and measure the resistance between the collector and the emitter. If this is low then the transistor is shorting and is no longer under the control of the base current. It should be replaced with a new transistor/thyristor.

7 If all is well then adjust VR_1 until the LED just lights or just goes out. Now covering the LDR will change the light intensity level and this, in turn, will cause the circuit to latch on. If a d.c. buzzer is connected, then it will continue to sound until the circuit is switched off.

9.2 The buggy drive box

This project involves connecting a buggy to a computer and driving it using appropriate software. The buggy used in this project has two motors, one on the right-hand side and the other on the left, which are switched on and off using relays controlled by transistor switches. The transistors are themselves operated by the signals which are sent out by the computer via the user port.

Exercises

1 Make a list of all the components used in the single transistor circuit shown in figure 9.2.1.

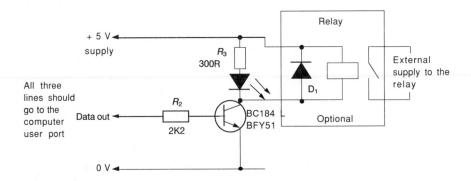

Figure 9.2.1 Single transistor switching circuit

2 Write down the colour code for all the resistors used in this circuit.

3 Obtain all the components needed and construct the circuit on the prototype board, using the arrangement shown in figure 9.2.2.

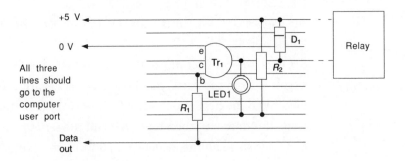

Figure 9.2.2 Basic switching circuit layout diagram

226

4 Test your circuit.

(a) Connect the +5 V supply and the ground (0 V) to the positive and negative of a 5 V power supply unit.

(b) Connect the 'data out' line to the +5 V line. The LED should come on and the sound of the relay switching should be heard. If this does not happen then check your circuit carefully.

(c) Now connect the 'data out' line to the 0 V line. The LED should now be off and again the switching of the relay should be heard.

If everything checks out as in (b) and (c) above then your circuit is working well and you may continue to the next stage. If not, find the fault before you continue.

5 Test the relay.

(a) Connect the lamp and power supply to the relay as shown in figure 9.2.3.

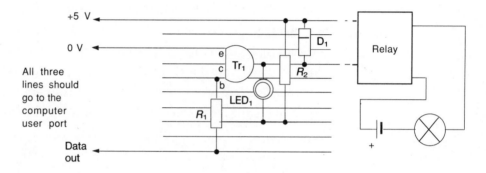

Figure 9.2.3 Basic switching of relay

(b) Now test the circuit by connecting the 'data out' line to the +5 V line and the 0 V line as in steps 4(b) and 4(c) above.

This time when the 'data out' line is connected to the +5 V supply line the relay should switch and the bulb should be on. When it is connected to the 0 V line the relay should switch off causing the bulb to go out. If this does not happen then you should check the connections to the relay.

Driving the buggy   Figure 9.2.4 shows a sketch of the buggy. For the buggy to go forwards, motors 1 and 2 must be on and turning in the same direction. For it to go backwards, motors 1 and 2 must be reversed. To go right, motor 2 must be off and motor 1 forwards. To go left motor 1 must be off and motor 2 forwards.

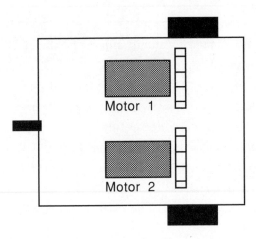

Figure 9.2.4 A simple buggy

The switching of the motors is achieved through the use of three relays, referred to as relays 1, 2 and 3. Relay 1 is a single-pole change-over contact relay, shown in figure 9.2.5a. When its coil is energised it switches the power to motors 1 and 2 causing them to turn in the same direction and the buggy to go forwards. Relays 2 and 3 are double-pole change-over contact relays, as shown in figure 9.2.5b. They are wired so that when their coils are energised they reverse the polarity to the motors and therefore cause them to turn in the reverse direction.

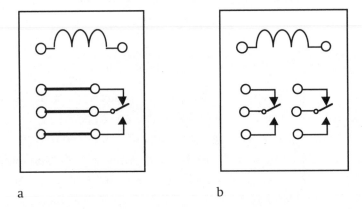

a   b

Figure 9.2.5 (a) Single-pole change-over contact relay; (b) double-pole change-over contact relay

Each relay is driven by a separate transistor switching circuit each of which is controlled by one of three 'data out' lines from the computer. The complete circuit for this is shown in figure 9.2.6, with the corresponding layout diagram in figure 9.2.7, while figure 9.2.8 gives the wiring diagram for the relays.

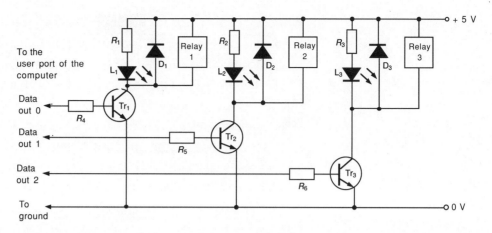

Figure 9.2.6 Full circuit diagram of the buggy drive system: $R_1 = R_2 = R_3 = 270 \,\Omega$; $R_4 = R_5 = R_6 = 2.2 \,k\Omega$; $D_1 = D_2 = D_3 = 1N4148$; $Tr_1 = Tr_2 = Tr_3 = BC184L$.

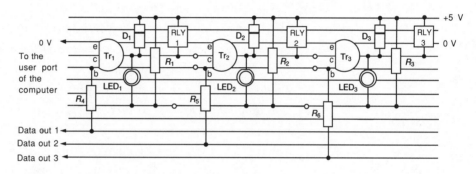

Figure 9.2.7 Circuit layout diagram

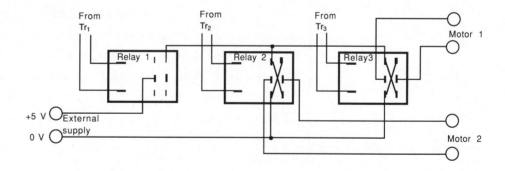

Figure 9.2.8 Relay wiring diagram

Exercises (continued)

6 Build the circuit shown in figure 9.2.6 using the layout diagram of figure 9.2.7. Use prototype board for your construction. Chapter 5 includes details of construction techniques and you should check your circuit with your teacher before actually building it.

7 Design a suitable container to allow your circuit to be easily connected to the user port buffer box using 4-mm plugs. In its simplest form, the buffer box makes the relevant lines of the user port more easily accessible. Opto-isolators can also be used to offer some form of protection against improper connection to the port. If a buffer box is not available, section 9.3 provides information on connecting devices to the computer.

8 Test your circuit and fault finding:

(a) Connect an external power supply to the +5 V and 0 V lines of the circuit.

(b) Connect data out 0 to the positive supply line. LED 1 should come on.

(c) Repeat step (b) for data out 1 and 2. LEDs 2 and 3 should also come on.

(d) Disconnect the data lines. Now all the LEDs should be off.

If any or all of the results outlined above in steps (a) to (d) were not obtained, then carefully carry out the following test procedure:

(i) Use a multimeter to confirm the presence of the +5 V and the 0 V lines. If no voltage is detected, then check the wires bringing the supply to the board and the output of the power supply unit.

(ii) If there is nothing wrong with the supply to the board, then test the LEDs by connecting a wire from the collector to the emitter of each transistor in turn. If all is well they will light. If any fail to light then check that the anode of the LED goes to the positive side of the circuit and also check that the components are the correct value and are connected to the appropriate tracks of the circuit board. If no fault can be identified then replace the LED(s).

(iii) If all the LEDs were lit when the collector and the emitter of the transistor was shorted, then the problem must lie with the transistor itself. Using a 1 kΩ resistor, connect the base of the transistor directly to the +5 V supply line. If the LED does not light then check for a short-circuit between the base and the 0 V line. If there is no short then it is likely that the transistor is faulty and it should be removed and replaced.

(iv) If any of the LEDs are on all the time, then check the particular transistor for a short across the collector and the emitter. If none can be found, then connect the base of the transistor directly to the 0 V line. This should turn off the transistor; if it does not, then the transistor is faulty and should be replaced.

9 Solder the circuit to the 4-mm terminals of your box and securely fix the circuit inside.

10 Connect your box and the buggy as shown in figure 9.2.9.

11 Connect the buffer box to the user port of either a BBC computer or a 480Z computer and then switch on, ready to start testing, but first read the information given on page 231.

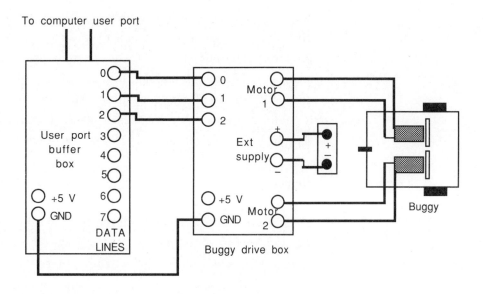

Figure 9.2.9 *Connecting the buggy to the computer*

Program control of the buggy

There are eight lines, numbered 0 to 7, called the 'data out lines', which are used by the computer to transfer a single eight-bit binary number. A bit in this case is simply a high or a low voltage, where a high voltage on a data line means that it is on and a low voltage means it is off. Each of the eight data lines represents a decimal number, as shown in figure 9.2.10, according to its position within the eight-bit binary number.

2^7	2^6	2^5	2^4	2^3	2^2	2^1	2^0	
128	64	32	16	8	4	2	1	
7	6	5	4	3	2	1	0	Data out lines

Figure 9.2.10 *Representation of the data out lines of the user port*

The 480Z has two sets of eight data lines, one reserved for input and the other for output. To switch on any data out line the command is OUT 29, *n*, where *n* is the decimal number representing that data line. To switch on more than one data lines, the decimal number is the sum of the decimal numbers representing all the data lines that are on. Thus OUT 29,3 switches on data lines 0 and 1 together (1 + 2 = 3).

The BBC computer has a single set of eight data lines and each of these can be configured as either input or output. A separate eight-bit register, called the **data direction register**, determines the direction of the data line, and is located at address 65122. To set the direction of the data lines, the command ?65122=*n* is used, where n is a decimal number which when converted into an eight-bit binary number will place a '1' or a '0' on each of the data lines as required. A '1' produces an output whilst a '0' leads to an input. Thus ?65122=255 will place a '1' on all the data lines making them all output lines (since $255_{10} = 11111111_2$) and ?65122=0 will place a '0' on all the data lines and therefore they will all be input lines. For example, ?65122=15 (00001111_2) will set the eight data lines so that the lower four bits are outputs and the upper four bits are inputs.

The BBC computer also has an input/output register, located at 65120, which is used to switch on the data lines. The command ?65120=n places a '1' or '0' onto each data line due to the fact that the decimal number n converts into a binary string consisting of '1s' and '0s'. A '1' switches the line on, so that a 'high' voltage is detected, whilst a '0' switches it off so that a 'low' voltage is detected. Thus, for BBC computers the following line of BASIC is used to switch on data line 0: ?65120=1. To switch it off again the command is: ?65120=0. To control two data lines ?65120=3 has the effect of switching both lines, 0 and 1, simultaneously.

Table 9.2.1 Summary of the output conditions for driving the buggy

Data out 0	Data out 1	Data out 2	Motion
On	Off	Off	Forward
On	On	Off	Right
On	Off	On	Left
On	On	On	Backward

Table 9.2.1 summarises the output conditions of the user port which will cause the buggy to move in four directions: forwards, backwards, right or left. To write any program in BASIC, each line must be accompanied by a line number. Two programs are supplied here as examples. Program 1 causes the buggy to move forwards for five seconds and then stop. What does program 2 do?

Switch on the 480Z computer and press 'N' to boot it (if it is networked) or 'R' to enter BASIC. When the 'READY' prompt appears type in the programs and test them, remembering to enter <RETURN> after each line. If you have a BBC machine, turn on and then type BASIC <RETURN> if the machine is not already in BASIC. Then proceed as for the 480Z.

Program I   For the RM480Z computer:

```
10 OUT 29,0                 (switches off all the data lines)
20 OUT 29,1                 (switches on data line 0)
30 FOR X=1 TO 5000:NEXT     (code is a delay of 5 s)
40 OUT 29,0
50 END
```

For the BBC computer:

```
10 ?65122=255              (sets all lines to output)
20 ?65120=0                (switches off all the data lines)
30 ?65120=1                (switches on data line 0)
40 FOR X=1 TO 5000:NEXT
50 ?65120=0
60 END
```

Program 2   For the 480Z computer:

```
10 OUT 29,0
20 OUT 29,1
30 FOR X=1 TO 5000:NEXT
40 OUT 29,3
50 FOR X=1 TO 1000:NEXT
60 OUT 29,1
70 FOR X=1 TO 5000:NEXT
80 OUT 29,5
90 FOR X=1 TO 1000:NEXT
100 OUT 29,0
110 FOR X=1 TO 1000:NEXT
120 OUT 29,7
130 FOR X=1 TO 5000:NEXT
140 OUT 29,0
150 END
```

For the BBC computer:

```
10 ?65122=255
20 ?65120=0
30 ?65120=1
40 FOR X=1 TO 5000:NEXT
50 ?65120=3
60 FOR X=1 TO 1000:NEXT
70 ?65120=1
80 FOR X=1 TO 5000:NEXT
90 ?65120=5
100 FOR X=1 TO 1000:NEXT
110 ?65120=0
120 FOR X=1 TO 1000:NEXT
130 ?65120=7
140 FOR X=1 TO 5000:NEXT
150 ?65120=0
160 END
```

Exercises (continued)

12 Use the following commands to make the buggy describe a rectangular path, and then explore as much as you can the control of the buggy using the computer.

480Z:		BBC:
OUT 29,0	(STOP)	?65120=0
OUT 29,1	(FORWARDS)	?65120=1
OUT 29,3	(RIGHT)	?65120=3
OUT 29,5	(LEFT)	?65120=5
OUT 29,7	(BACKWARDS)	?65120=7

FOR X=1 TO Y:NEXT or FOR X=1 TO Y:NEXT X (Y is a whole number).
Both forms of this statement will achieve the same thing, which is to make the program wait for a set period of time depending on the value of Y.

GOTO Z   (Z is a line number; and this command sends the program from where it is to that line number.)

9.3 The LED board

In this project six LEDs are arranged as two sets of traffic lights. Each LED can be controlled independently by signals from the computer and therefore, with the aid of a number of simple programs, the board can be used to simulate traffic lights, a pelican crossing or produce a whole range of light displays.

The circuit is shown in figure 9.3.1 and the layout diagram in figure 9.3.2.

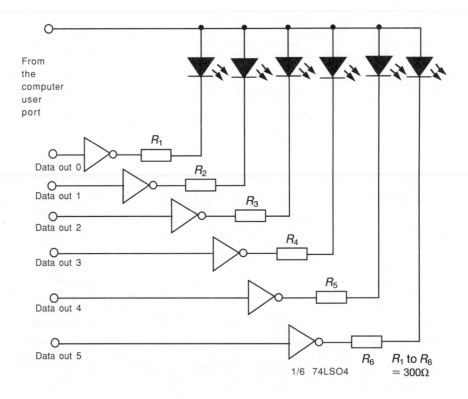

Figure 9.3.1 Circuit diagram of the LED board

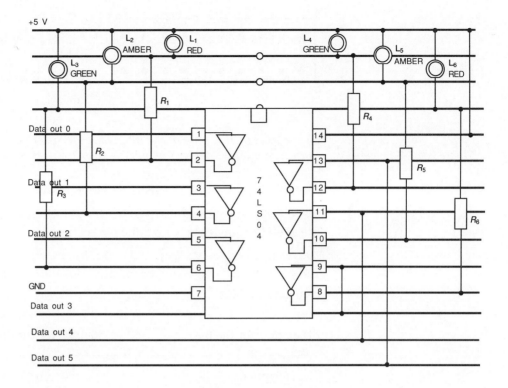

Figure 9.3.2 The LED board layout diagram

Connecting to the computer

1 The data output lines should be connected to a set of eight adjacent terminal blocks and if you are using the 480Z the data input lines should be connected to another set of eight blocks.

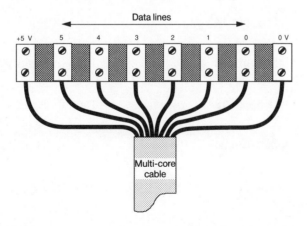

Figure 9.3.3 Using the terminal block connector

2 Using the multicore cable, solder the pins shown in either figure 9.3.4a or figure 9.3.4b depending on whether you are using the BBC or the 480Z computer.

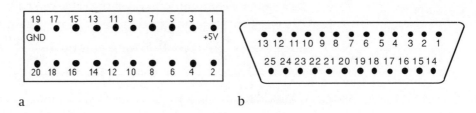

Figure 9.3.4 (a) IDC plug of the BBC computer user port; (b) 25-way 'D' plug of the 480Z user port

Table 9.3.1 gives details of which data line is associated with which pin for both types of connectors. Additional information on the user ports of the BBC and the RM480Z computers is contained in section 9.2.

Table 9.3.1 Details of the pin connections for the IDC (BBC) and the D-type connectors (480Z)

Data pins for the BBC	Data pins for the 480Z	
Data 0=pin 6	Data in 0=pin1	Data out 0=pin 5
Data 1=pin 8	Data in 1=pin14	Data out 1=pin 18
Data 2=pin10	Data in 2=pin2	Data out 2=pin 6
Data 3=pin12	Data in 3=pin 15	Data out 3=pin 19
Data 4=pin 14	Data in 4=pin 3	Data out 4=pin 7
Data 5=pin 16	Data in 5=pin 16	Data out 5=pin 20
Data 6=pin 18	Data in 6=pin 4	Data out 6=pin 8
Data 7=pin 20	Data in 7=pin 17	Data out 7=pin 21
0 V = 5, 7, 9, 11, 13, 15, 17, 19	0 V = pin 23	+5 V = pin 9
+5 V = pins 1 and 3		

3 Connect the +5 V and the ground lines to two further terminal blocks, making a total of 10 (BBC) or 18 (480Z). It is suggested that you make terminal block 1 the +5 V and 10 (BBC) or 18 (480Z) the ground.

4 Carry out a continuity check on the cable you have made to check that you have made no errors in your connections. On a separate sheet describe what you did and draw up a table displaying your results.

Testing for the 480Z computer

1 Push the 'D' plug into the back of the computer and switch on. Press N to boot the 480Z (if it is networked), and type BASIC <RETURN>. If it is not networked then type R for BASIC followed by <RETURN>.

3 When the READY prompt appears, type OUT 29,0 <RETURN>. This command sends a low voltage to all the data output lines.

4 Using the voltmeter, connect its common lead to the ground of the terminal blocks and measure the voltages of the data lines as shown below.

5 Copy table 9.3.2 and fill in the measurements you have made.

Table 9.3.2 Voltage on data output lines when they are all at logic '0'

Data lines	7	6	5	4	3	2	1	0	+5 V
Voltage/V									

6 Now type in: OUT 29,255 <RETURN>. This command sends a high voltage to all the output data lines. Repeat step 4 above and write these new voltages into your copy of table 9.3.3.

Table 9.3.3 Voltage on data output lines when they are all at logic '1'

Data lines	7	6	5	4	3	2	1	0	+5 V
Voltage/V									

7 Type OUT 29,123 <RETURN> and again measure the voltages and fill in your copy of table 9.3.4.

Table 9.3.4 Voltage on data output lines with some at logic '1' and others at logic '0'

Data lines	7	6	5	4	3	2	1	0	+5 V
Voltage/V									

8 Repeat for OUT 29,X (where X is any number between 0 and 255). Fill in the voltage readings and confirm that the 'highs' and 'lows' correspond to that expected for the number you have chosen.

Testing for the BBC computer

1 Push the 'IDC' plug into the I/O socket beneath the computer and switch on.
2 When the 'A>' prompt appears, type ?65122=255 <RETURN>. This command sets the direction of all the data lines for use as outputs.
3 Now type ?65120=0. This command sends a low voltage to all the data output lines.
4 Now repeat steps 4 to 8 above.

Testing your circuit

Connect the +5 V, GND and the data lines of your circuit to the appropriate junctions of the terminal block and depending on which computer you are using type in program 1 below.

Program I

This program flashes all the LEDs on and off at one-second intervals, but if your LEDs are not flashing then check your circuit thoroughly before continuing.

For the 480Z:

10 OUT 29,0	(switches off all the data lines)
20 FOR I=1 TO 1000:NEXT I	(causes the program to delay for one second)
30 OUT 29,255	(switches on all the data lines)
40 FOR I=1 TO 1000:NEXT I	
50 GOTO 10	(returns the program to the start)

For the BBC:

10 ?65122=255	(causes all the data lines to act as output lines)
20 REPEAT	
30 ?65120=255	(switches on all the data output lines)
40 FOR I=1 TO 1000:NEXT I	(causes the program to delay for one second)
50 ?65120=0	(switches off all the data out lines)
60 FOR I=1 TO 1000:NEXT I	
70 UNTIL FALSE	(REPEAT ... UNTIL FALSE will cause execution of the program to continue indefinitely. Use the escape key to break out of the program.)

Traffic light operation   The circuit can now be programmed to operate as traffic lights. The use of the data lines to represent individual lights is shown in table 9.3.5.

Table 9.3.5 Arrangement of data out lines to represent traffic light sequence

Data lines	SET1	Dec no.	Data lines	SET2	Dec no.
D0	Red1	1	D3	Red2	8
D1	Amber1	2	D4	Amber2	16
D2	Green1	4	D5	Green2	32

Traffic light sequence
(SET I)

Lights on	Sum	Dec no
Red1	1	1
Red1 & Amber1	1+2	3
Green1	4	4
Amber1	2	2

For both sets of lights the traffic light sequence (SET1 and SET2) is then

Lights on	Sum	Dec no
Red1 & Green2	1+32	33
Red1 & Amber1 & Amber2	1+2+16	19
Green1 & Red2	4+8	12
Amber1 & Red2 & Amber2	2+8+16	26

Program 2   For the 480Z:

```
10 OUT 29,1              (switches on red LED)
20 FOR I=1 TO 10000:NEXT I    (waits for ten seconds)
30 OUT 29,3              (switches on both red and amber LEDs)
40 FOR I=1 TO 2000:NEXT I     (waits for two seconds)
50 OUT 29,4              (switches on green LED)
60 FOR I=1 TO 10000:NEXT I
70 OUT 29,2              (switches on amber LED)
80 FOR I=1 TO 2000:NEXT I
90 GOTO 10
```

For the BBC:

```
10 ?65122=255           (sets all data lines to output)
20 REPEAT
```

30 ?65120=1	(switches on red LED)
40 FOR I=1 TO 10000:NEXT I	(waits for ten seconds)
50 ?65120=3	(switches on both red and amber)
60 FOR I=1 TO 2000:NEXT I	(waits for two seconds)
70 ?65120=4	(switches on green LED)
80 FOR I=1 TO 10000:NEXT 1	
90 ?65120=2	(switches on amber LED)
100 FOR I=1 TO 2000:NEXT I	
110 UNTIL FALSE	

Type RUN <RETURN> when you have finished. One set of traffic lights should now run through a continuous sequence of change from red to green and back again. To stop this press the control key and the 'Z' key together (480Z) or the 'Escape' if you are using the BBC computer.

Exercises

1 Use the information above and modify program 2 so as to make use of both sets of traffic lights. You want to get one set on red when the other is on green.

The pelican crossing

This program should switch the LEDs to simulate the sequence of changes in a set of pelican lights, including the flashing amber.

Program 3

For the 480Z:

```
10 OUT 29,1
20 FOR I=1 TO 10000:NEXT I
30 GOSUB 100
40 OUT 29,4
50 FOR 1=1 TO 10000:NEXT I
60 GOSUB 100   (flashes the amber)
70 GOTO 10
100 C=0
110 OUT 29,2:C=C+1
120 FOR I=1 TO 1000:NEXT I
130 OUT 29,0
140 FOR I=1 TO 1000:NEXT I
150 IF C=5 THEN 160 ELSE GOTO 110
160 RETURN
```

For the BBC:

```
10 ?65122=255   (set data lines to output)
20 REPEAT
30 ?65120=1
40 FOR I=1 TO 10000:NEXT I
50 GOSUB 110
60 ?65120=4
70 FOR 1=1 TO 10000:NEXT I
80 GOSUB 100   (flashes the amber)
90 UNTIL FALSE
100 END
110 C = 0
120 ?65120=2:C=C+1
130 FOR I=1 TO 1000:NEXT I
140 ?65120=0
150 FOR I=1 TO 1000:NEXT I
160 IF C=5 THEN 160 ELSE GOTO 120
170 RETURN
```

Again type RUN <RETURN> to see the effect of the program.

2 Modify program 3 to make use of both sets of lights.

9.4 The 555 organ

This organ is based on the 555 astable oscillator and is capable of playing single notes whenever any of the switches S_1 to S_8 are pressed and held down. The frequency of the oscillator can be varied using VR_9 to produce a totally different set of notes. The output of this project may be amplified using the LM380 amplifier of section 9.6.

Exercises

1 Make a list of all the components used in the circuit shown in figure 9.4.1.

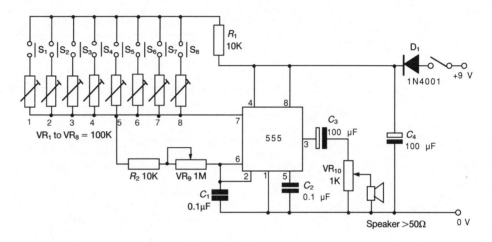

Figure 9.4.1 The 555 organ

2 Write down the colour codes for all the fixed-value resistors used in the circuit.

3 Find all the components and construct the circuit on a prototype board.

How the circuit works

In this circuit, the 555 is connected as an astable oscillator, producing a square wave output at pin 3. A full explanation of the 555 timer in this mode of operation is given in section 6.5. The frequency of the oscillation depends on the total resistance between pins 7 and 8 and between pins 6 and 7. It also depends on the capacitance of C_1. The presets allow a range of frequencies to be set and therefore allows each note to be separately 'tuned'. Pressing any of the push switches will connect that particular preset between 7 and 8, thus changing the frequency of the oscillation accordingly. The set of eight presets is therefore acting as a 'keyboard'.

Diode D_1 protects the circuit from damage if the power supply is incorrectly connected. Capacitor C_3 decouples the circuit from the power supply.

4 Either design a layout diagram or use the layout diagram shown in figure 9.4.2 to construct the circuit on a copper stripboard.

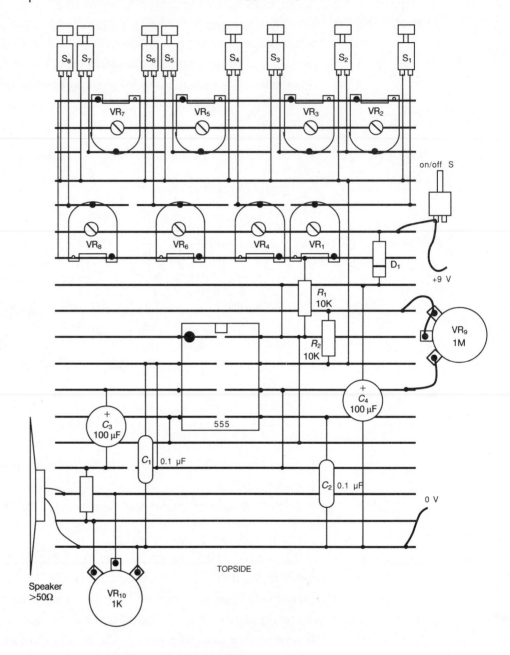

Figure 9.4.2 The 555 organ layout diagram

5 Design a suitable container for the circuit.

Notes on the construction **1** The 555 is an eight-pin DIL package. Therefore it is suggested that an eight-pin socket is used for mounting it.

2 Figure 9.4.2 shows the circuit from the topside of the stripboard. Remember that the components are soldered to the copper strips on the underside of the board.

3 Remember to break the tracks between IC pins and at any positions shown in the diagram.

4 Capacitor C_4 is a decoupling capacitor which is not necessary for prototype board construction but should be used for construction onto stripboard.

5 The presets should be mounted on the circuit board and connected to the push-to-make switch by flexible wires to be mounted on the surface of the container. The on/off switch should be similarly connected. The leg of the preset which is not connected should be bent up under the device or should be snipped off.

6 In addition, VR_9, which adjusts the frequency, and VR_{10}, which controls the volume, should be connected to the board by flexible wires and mounted onto the surface of the container.

Testing the circuit and fault finding

Please read section 5.7 on circuit testing and carry out all the preliminary testing recommended. If no obvious fault is detected then go through the following steps systematically.

1 Make sure that the circuit is correctly connected to the power supply before switching on. On switching on press S_1; a note should be heard.

2 If nothing happens then check each of the other push switches in turn. Note any which are not producing a note and carry out a thorough check of the circuit to find the fault.

3 If nothing happens at all after switching on then the first thing to do is to use a voltmeter to check that power is reaching pin 8 of the chip and also that pin 1 is connected to the 0 V supply line.

4 Use a logic probe, or better still, an oscilloscope, to check the output at pin 3 with each of S_1 to S_8 pressed.

5 Work systematically through the circuit until all faults are located and corrected.

6 When all is well, tune the organ by using a tuning fork or another instrument, adjusting each of the presets until the exact note is produced.

9.5 The visual display timer

This circuit can produce a time delay from 1 second to 99 seconds and the elapsed time is displayed on the seven-segment display. The addition of a d.c. buzzer enables an audible warning at the end of the timing period. The delay time can be adjusted using VR_1 and as a result the circuit can be used in many applications in which small time delays are required, such as a photographic timer, general kitchen timer, quiz game timer, etc.

1 Make a list of all the components used in the circuit shown in figure 9.5.1.

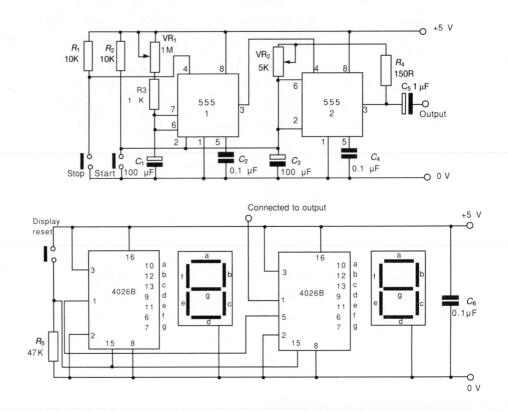

Figure 9.5.1 Circuit diagram of the visual display timer

2 Write down the colour codes for all the fixed-value resistors used in the circuit.

3 Find all the components and make the circuit using the prototype board.

How the circuit works

The circuit consists of two 555 timers, one connected as a monostable and used to set the time delay, and the other connected as an astable and used as a 1 Hz oscillator.

The timing is started by a push switch which momentarily connects pin 2 (the trigger) of 555 1 and 555 2 to 0 V line. The timing period is determined by the resistance between pin 7 and the positive supply line and the capacitance connected between pin 6 and the negative supply line. The output is taken from pin 3 and before timing begins is at 0 V. When the timer is triggered the output goes high (near supply) for the duration of the timing period. Pin 4 of the 555 IC is the 'reset' pin. Reset is achieved by a negative pulse to pin 4 and, on 555 1, this is produced by the 'stop' push switch which when pressed resets the timer to zero. The 'reset' of 555 2 is connected to the output of 555 1 and for the duration of the timing period is at high voltage. This enables 555 2 to operate normally as a square wave oscillator with equal mark–space ratio for this period of time. The frequency is determined by the resistance between pins 3 and 6 and also by the value of the capacitance between pin 6 and the zero supply line. At the end of the timing period the output of 555 1 returns to 'low' voltage and produces a negative pulse to reset 555 2, therefore stopping the oscillation.

The second part of this circuit consists of the display made up from two seven-segment displays and two counter/driver ICs (the 4026). Pin 1 of this chip is the clock input. Its function is to increment the count by one every time a pulse is received. Pin 2 inhibits the clock and needs to be low for the chip to operate normally. Pin 3 enables the display when 'high' and disables it when 'low'. Pin 5 is the 'carry out' pin; it produces a pulse whenever the IC count reaches 10. If the output from this pin is connected to the clock input of another IC, this second IC will then be incremented by one on every ten counts of the first IC. Pin 15 is the 'reset' pin and needs to be 'low' for the IC to reset on reaching a count of 10. A 'high' at any point in its count will make it reset at that point. Therefore, if it is connected to any of the display outputs it can reset on reaching any of the desired numbers between 0 and 9. Pins 6, 7, 9, 10, 11, 12 and 13 should be connected to the anode.

The clock input of the 4026 is connected to the output of the 555 oscillator, which is producing a pulse every second. The counter counts the number of pulses received and sends out signals to light the appropriate segments of the seven-segment display. This will continue until the oscillator is reset, at which time it will display the elapsed time before the reset. The display reset switch is used to reset the counters and the seven-segment displays.

Exercises (continued)

4 Either design a layout diagram or use the layout diagram shown in figure 9.5.2 to construct the circuit on a copper stripboard.

Notes on the construction

1 A 0.3 inch seven-segment display is the common cathode type and will fit into a 14-pin DIL socket. Therefore it is suggested that a 14-pin socket is used for mounting these. It is possible to use the 0.5 inch displays but these will have to be mounted directly onto the board.

2 Figure 9.5.2 shows the circuit from the topside of the stripboard. Remember that the components are soldered to the copper strips on the underside of the board.

3 Remember to break the tracks between IC pins and at any positions shown in the diagram.

4 Capacitor C_6 is a decoupling capacitor which is not necessary for prototype board construction but should be used for construction onto stripboard.

Testing the circuit and fault finding

Please read section 5.7 on circuit testing and carry out all the preliminary testing recommended. If no obvious fault is detected then go through the following steps systematically.

1 Make sure that the circuit is correctly connected to the power supply before switching on. If on switching on nothing happens, then the first thing to do is to check that power is reaching the relevant supply pins of the respective ICs.

2 Your testing should follow a logical pattern, so start with the monostable. Use either a good voltmeter or a logic probe to check to voltage levels at the appropriate pins before and after the 'start' button has been pressed.

3 Work through to the astable and check that it is oscillating properly.

4 Check that the output pulses are actually reaching the clock input of the 4026 IC (use the logic probe to do this).

5 Check that the ICs are counting by looking at the logic states at the output pins and finally check the connections to the anodes of the seven-segment displays.

6 If these checks are conducted systematically then any fault with the construction should come to light.

Calibration

After ensuring that the circuit is working correctly the next thing to do is to calibrate it to ensure that the timing is fairly accurate. The calibration will centre on the monostable and the astable part of the circuit and will involve the use of a stop watch and possibly a d.c. buzzer.

Connect the d.c. between pin 3 of the monostable and the positive supply rail. Press the 'start' button whilst at the same time starting the stopwatch; wait for the buzzer to sound before stopping the watch and recording the time. Adjust VR_1 and repeat after resetting the display; note down the new time. Keep adjusting VR_1 and repeating the timing with the stopwatch until the buzzer sounds exactly after one minute. This setting of VR_1 will give a one-minute timing period.

The astable should give a pulse every second and the simplest way of calibrating this is to use the display. If after one minute the display indicates '60' then all is well. If this is not so then use VR_2 to adjust the frequency of the oscillator so that the display indicates '60' at the same time that the buzzer sounds.

Once calibrated the timer will time and display periods up to a 99-second duration.

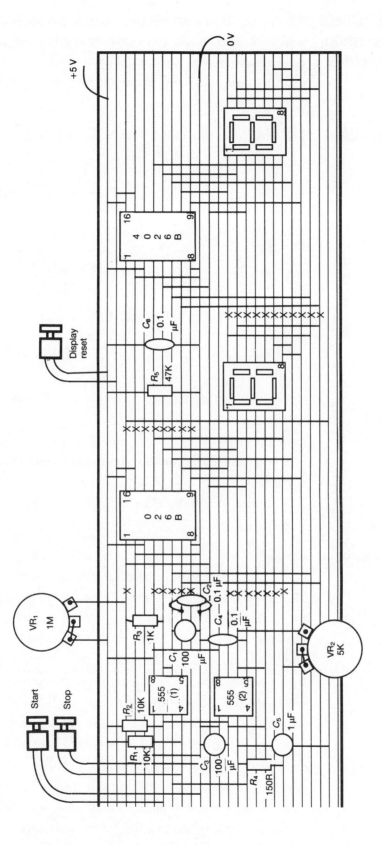

Figure 9.5.2 The visual display timer layout

9.6 The LM380 audiofrequency amplifier

This circuit can operate off a 9–20 V power supply. On a 20 V supply about 3 W can be obtained. It is used to amplify small signals such as those from radio receivers, intercoms, and crystal and ceramic pick-ups, and produces good audiofrequency output of about 500 mW in an 8 Ω speaker.

Exercises

1 Make a list of all the components used in the circuit shown in figure 9.6.1

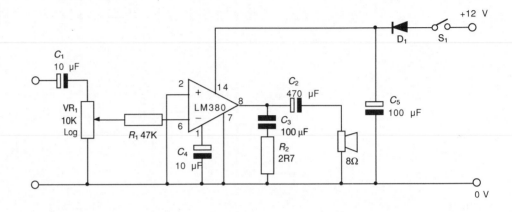

Figure 9.6.1 Circuit diagram of the LM380 audiofrequency amplifier

2 Write down the colour codes for all the fixed-value resistors used in the circuit.

3 Find all the components and make the circuit using the prototype board.

How the circuit works

The signal to be amplified is connected between the signal input and the ground or 0 V line. Capacitor C_1 only allows the a.c. part of the signal to pass through to VR_1. VR_1 is connected as a potentiometer and as a result the power being fed to the IC can vary from zero to full power. It therefore acts as a volume control. The input to the LM380 is via pin 6, and as this is the inverting input the amplifier is an inverting amplifier. The inverted amplified signal is obtained from pin 8 and any d.c. component is removed from the output by capacitor C_4. Pin 14 of the IC goes to the positive supply line and pin 7 to the 0 V supply line. Pins 3, 4, 5, 6, 10, 11 and 12 should also be connected to the 0 V supply. However, as these are joined internally to each other, only one of these needs to be connected externally. C_3 and R_2 are used to prevent instability at high frequencies, particularly with certain reactive loads. Similarly capacitor C_5 is required to prevent instability due to power supply lead inductance. Capacitor C_4, which is connected to pin 1, is used to reduce the effect of ripple or 'hum' on the power supply line, thus improving the signal-to-noise ratio of the amplifier. Diode D_1 protects the circuit from incorrect connection of the power supply leads.

Exercises (continued)

4 Either design a layout diagram or use the layout diagram shown in figure 9.6.2 to construct the circuit on a copper stripboard.

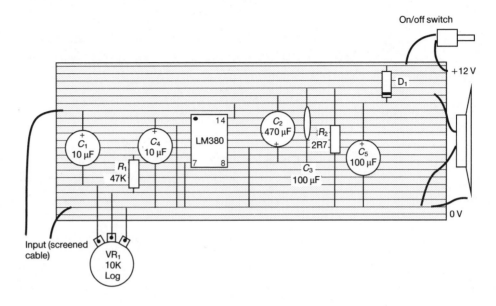

Figure 9.6.2 Copper stripboard layout diagram

Notes on the construction

1 The LM380 is a 14-pin DIL package. Therefore it is suggested that a 14-pin socket is used for mounting it.

2 Figure 9.6.2 shows the circuit from the topside of the stripboard. Remember that the components are soldered to the copperstrips on the underside of the board.

3 Remember to break the tracks between IC pins.

4 Capacitor C_5 is a decoupling capacitor which is not necessary for prototype board construction but should be used for construction onto stripboard. Similarly R_2 and C_3 are not required unless a permanent construction is required.

5 Capacitor C_4 is also optional and can be discarded if battery-operated equipment is used.

6 The circuit is designed for operation with an 8 Ω speaker and although a larger impedance speaker may be used with a corresponding decrease in the volume, a smaller impedance speaker should not be used.

Testing the circuit and fault finding

Please read section 5.7 on circuit testing and carry out all the preliminary testing recommended. If no obvious fault is detected then go through the following steps systematically.

1 Make sure that the circuit is correctly connected to the power supply and that there is a suitable input to the circuit (an audiofrequency generator will do) before switching on. If on switching on nothing happens then try the volume control, turning both clockwise and anticlockwise to see if there is any effect on the output.

2 If still nothing then check that power is reaching pin 14 of the IC. Also check that pin 7 is connected to 0 V.

3 Your testing should follow a logical pattern, so start with the input to the chip. Use either a good voltmeter or an oscilloscope to check the voltage levels before the input capacitor C_1, at VR_1 input and at pin 6 of the IC.

4 Check the output at pin 8 before and after C_2.

5 This sequential testing should throw up any faults with the input stage, the LM380 or the output stage, and appropriate action should be taken accordingly.

Index